MW01253959

Ethnic Conflict in Buddhist Societies

Ethnic Conflict in Buddhist Societies: Sri Lanka, Thailand and Burma

Edited by

K.M. de Silva, Pensri Duke, Ellen S. Goldberg and Nathan Katz

Routledge
Taylor & Francis Group

LONDON AND NEW YORK

First published 1988 by Westview Press

Published 2018 by Routledge
52 Vanderbilt Avenue, New York, NY 10017
2 Park Square, Milton Park, Abingdon, Oxon OX14 4RN

Routledge is an imprint of the Taylor & Francis Group, an informa business

British Library Cataloguing in Publication Data

A CIP catalogue record for this book is available from the British Library

Library of Congress Cataloging in Publication Data

Applied for

Typeset by Associated Typsetters Ltd., Hong Kong.

ISBN 13: 978-0-367-00322-7 (hbk)
ISBN 13: 978-0-367-15309-0 (pbk)

CONTENTS

NOTES ON THE CONTRIBUTORS

K.M. de Silva is Professor of Sri Lanka History at the University of Peradeniya, Sri Lanka, and Executive Director of the International Centre for Ethnic Studies, Kandy, Sri Lanka.

Padmasiri de Silva is Professor and Head of Philosophy at the University of Peradeniya, Sri Lanka.

Chaiwat Satha-Anand is Assistant Professor of Political Science and Associate Director of the Thai Khadi Research Institute at Thammasat University, Bangkok, Thailand.

P.D. Premasiri is Associate Professor of Philosophy at the University of Peradeniya, Sri Lanka.

Ronald D. Renard is Assistant to the President for External Relations at Payap University, Chiang Mai, Thailand.

Likhit Dhiravegin is a member of the Faculty of Political Science, Thammasat University, Bangkok, Thailand.

K.N.O. Dharmadasa is Associate Professor of Sinhala at the University of Peradeniya, Sri Lanka.

Sanit Wongsprasert is a social sciences researcher at the Tribal Research Institute, Chiang Mai, Thailand.

Nathan Katz is Associate Professor of Religious Studies at the University of South Florida, Tampa, and Editor of *USF Monographs in Religion and Public Policy*.

S.W.R. de A. Samarasinghe is Senior Lecturer in Economics at the University of Peradeniya, and Associate Director of the International Centre for Ethnic Studies, Kandy, Sri Lanka.

Trevor O. Ling is Emeritus Professor at Manchester University, England, and is affiliated with the Department of Sociology, National University of Singapore.

Surin Pitsuwan is Professor of Political Science at Thammasat University, Bangkok, Thailand.

PREFACE

This volume contains a selection of the papers presented at a South and South-east Asia regional workshop on 'Minorities in Buddhist Polities: Sri Lanka, Thailand and Burma', organised by the International Centre for Ethnic Studies (ICES), Sri Lanka, and the Thai Studies Programme of Chulalongkorn University, Thailand.

The tenor for 'Minorities in Buddhist Polities' was set by K. M. de Silva, Executive Director of ICES, in his keynote address. While the workshop would focus attention on policy-orientated issues and adopt a practical approach to ethnic conflict in the Buddhist societies examined, he stressed that religion and its impact on society and politics in these nations would be a central concern.

It was decided early in the workshop discussions that a selection of the papers presented should be published in book form. This was the first cross-national workshop in recent times on the theme of ethnic conflict and minority problems in the three main Theravada Buddhist societies in the world. Indeed, the issues involved have great importance at a time when ethnic tensions dominate the political life of many Third World nations, not to mention countries in the First and Second Worlds.

The editors had the unenviable task of making a choice of 15 out of more than 30 papers presented for inclusion in this volume. The choice was eventually determined by the need to prepare a manageable volume which would consider theoretical issues; Buddhism, minorities and public policy; Buddhist institutions and minorities; and case studies of minorities in Buddhist polities. In the preparation of this volume, the editors have had the unstinted co-operation and support of the ICES staff in Kandy. The editors wish to thank Miss Chalani Lokugamage and Miss Sepali Liyanamana for their hard work in preparing the typescript, Miss Nalini Weragama for her secretarial assistance, and Mrs Kanthi Gamage who devoted several hours of her time to checking the proofs.

Finally, the organisers of the seminar would like to express their gratitude to the various organisations which funded the workshop: the Ford Foundation, the Lee Foundation, the United Nations University in Tokyo, and the British Institute in South East Asia.

INTRODUCTION—ETHNIC CONFLICT IN BUDDHIST SOCIETIES: SRI LANKA, THAILAND AND BURMA

K.M.de Silva

The issue of minorities is complex and overdetermined, of necessity raising questions of nationalism, ethnicity, social ethics, minority rights, separatist movements, ecumenism, violence, counter-violence and terrorism. The interdisciplinary nature of the present volume was mandated by the subject-matter itself.

While policy issues are the main focus of this volume, some prior questions about the impact of religion on polities are also addressed, in particular how the Buddhist values of non-violence and a middle path of moderation impinge upon the ethnic crises which seem to dominate our contemporary world. Our specific concern is with ethnic conflict in the Buddhist societies of Sri Lanka, Thailand and Burma. In all three countries Buddhism is the dominant religion, and in all of them relations between the dominant majority—the overwhelming majority in Thailand and Burma—have ranged from unhappy and uncomfortable to decidedly hostile. All three are old societies with a long and troubled history, none longer and none more troubled than Sri Lanka, the smallest of the three.

In the three societies examined, religion and its impact on society and politics is a central concern. To what extent have Buddhist values acted as a restraint on ethnic violence? How does the 'middle path', the emphasis on moderation so crucially important in Buddhist teachings, translate into public policy and practical politics with regard to relations between Buddhists and the minorities in these three polities? Can Buddhism contribute to ethnic unity? These are some of the central issues discussed in this volume.

Texts and theories

This volume explores the attitude of Buddhism towards minorities according to canonical sources. P.D. Premasiri (Chapter 3), while pointing out that there is no specific attitude to minorities that can be

2 K.M. de Silva

discerned from the texts, argues that one can nevertheless seek such implications through the Buddhist attitudes to social groups divided according to caste, language and religion. He draws attention to the condemnation of caste hierarchy as well as the extremely liberal attitude of the Buddha towards religious pluralism. He concludes that minority questions 'should not arise' within the context of Buddhism. Nathan Katz's survey of Sri Lankan monks (Chapter 9) shows that these contemporary exemplars of Buddhist tradition do not always expound the liberal attitudes of the canonical materials. In the discussions that ensued at the workshop on which this volume is based, it was felt that Buddhism as a religious tradition is composed of many layers: the canonical and post-canonical texts; the ascendency of Emperor Asoka in third-century BC India; the 'sacred charter' texts such as the *Mahavamsa*; and popular religion with its syncretic Hindu, animist and folk elements. Understanding the impact of Buddhism upon ethnic crises entailed a view of Buddhism that included all aspects of the tradition.

Two theoretical essays by Chaiwat Satha-Anand (Chapter 2) and Padmasiri de Silva (Chapter 1) are of particular importance in this regard. Satha-Anand, following Michel Foucault's theory, argues that the idea of 'nation' is imaginary. The notion of 'state', though somewhat more concrete, has certain attitudes which in his view are also imaginary. Terrorism is the result of the negative attitudes of the state which sustains an imagined community called 'nation', De Silva's philosophical exploration of the notion of 'collective identity' draws upon the doctrine of *anatta* (non-self) in Buddhism which is a critique of personal identity and, by logical extension, of group identity as well.

A key theme that emerges in the chapters of this volume is the role religions play in both the exacerbation and amelioration of ethnic conflict. Of course, one way in which ethnic groups are defined — and define themselves — is by religious affiliation. But how much do these ready labels tell us about the conflicts themselves? That the conflicts are often between groups which are defined by these affiliations does not entail that the conflicts are religious *per se*. Social, economic and political factors — perhaps not so visible as religious affiliations — often impinge more directly on these tragic situations.

This is not to say that religion plays no role in these conflicts. Once a conflict reaches a certain stage of development, religious legitimation of the conflict becomes a paramount issue. As a tentative paradigm of such conflicts, it seems that the majority groups muster their forces by appealing to a sacralised view of their group's history (e.g., a 'national charter myth'), a historiography often defensive in character. The minority group often appeals to certain values (e.g., liberation, legitimate representation, inalienable rights) whose actualisation is understood as depending upon a sort of 'righteous' struggle.

Thus we begin to understand that while these conflicts are not in essence religious, they nevertheless take on religious overtones, especially when the conflicts become transformed into a cycle of terrorism and counter-terrorism. Participants in the workshop felt that this line of inquiry would be most useful in developing a theoretical understanding of ethnic conflicts, a theme we return to in the third part of this introduction.

Drawing from our theoretical understanding of identity, the symbolic justification of violence is and must be a defence of sacralised identity, which is both a collective and an individual process. Clearly, the process being described deals with the irrational. In ethnic strife, the enlightened self-interest of both contesting groups is often the first casualty. It was felt that only religion is a sufficiently powerful force to trigger such irrational and self-defeating behaviour. In short, as was claimed in the discussion, rational people compromise; fanatics do not.

However, Padmasiri de Silva points towards the Buddhist notion of *anatta* as a crucial insight for the possible resolution or management of these conflicts. This malleability of identity means that it changes with historical currents, so that what it means to 'be a Sinhalese', for example, is something quite different in 1985 than it was in the fifth or fifteenth centuries, and that it will take on an additional nuance and specifically *political* meaning in, say, 1990.

Sri Lanka, Thailand and Burma

Of the three countries examined in this volume, two have had periods of subjection to Western rule; Thailand was spared that experience and humiliation. Burma's experience of Western rule was much shorter than Sri Lanka's. One legacy of that colonial experience common to both Sri Lanka and Burma is the confrontation between Buddhism and the intrusive Christian religion which came with Western rule. Two essays by K. M. de Silva (Chapter 4) and Trevor Ling (Chapter 11) deal with this issue. In Sri Lanka that intrusion and its inevitable tensions with the indigenous religions came with the earliest decades of Portuguese rule in the middle of the sixteenth century. Ling's chapter shows how, in Burma under British rule, Christianity was a minority religion in every sense of the word. In Sri Lanka, on the other hand, Roman Catholicism, Calvinism and Anglicanism each in turn had a special relationship with the ruling power, as well as the prestige and authority of the official religion of the day, while converts to the orthodox version of Christianity—especially under the Portuguese and the Dutch—came to be treated as a privileged group.

Together, the Roman Catholics and the Protestants were never more than a tenth of the population in British times and in the early years of independence. Nine-tenths of the Christians were Roman Catholics. Conversions to Roman Catholicism under the Portuguese had stood the test of persecution under the Dutch and the indifference, if not contempt, of the British. A tenth of the population, however, made them the largest Christian group in all of South Asia in terms of their percentage of the population, and perhaps second only to their counterpart in the Philippines, if one considers South-east Asia as well. There was also the privileged position of the Christian minority. This became one of the most divisive issues in Sri Lanka politics in the years before independence and for over two decades thereafter.

If the strength of Sri Lankan Christianity set Sri Lanka apart from Burma and Thailand, the disestablishment of Buddhism in Sri Lanka and Burma was part of the common colonial experience. Thailand, on the other hand, escaped colonialism during the nineteenth century; the sangha there, far from being disestablished, was brought closer to the government. In Sri Lanka there were attempts from the last quarter of the nineteenth century to re-establish a link between Buddhism and the state. While the British would not go back to the status quo ante 1840 in restoring a formal link between the state and Buddhism, they devised arrangements, and made concessions in the 1870s, that in the long run evolved into a policy whose central feature was a special concern for—if not a special position for—Buddhism within the Sri Lanka polity. Pressure for the restoration of the link between Buddhism and the state increased from the mid-1950s, but Sri Lanka's political leadership has successfully resisted it. The Constitutions of 1972 and 1978, unlike the Constitution of 1946–8, have elevated Buddhism to a special position within the Sri Lankan polity, but one well short of the status of the state religion.

The resistance to making Buddhism the state religion was partly motivated by political considerations, and partly by a commitment to a separation of state and religion. But ironically enough those who agitate for, and welcome, a restoration of the traditional linkage between state and Buddhism, often confronted opposition from surprising sources. In the words of S. J. Tambiah:

> The allied problem faced by Sri Lanka and Burma is that restoration of religion by the state also implies the attempted regulation of the sangha by the state, a proposition that is antithetical to those monastic interests that have come to cherish the decentralized autonomy resulting form [the] British disestablishment of religion.[1]

Chapter 4 points out how, under the leadership of D.S. Senanayake, Sri Lanka's first prime minister, pressure from militant Buddhists urging a clean break from the immediate past for the purpose of creating a new Sri Lanka on 'ideal' traditional Buddhist lines was successfully resisted. S. W. R. D. Bandaranaike's election victory in 1956 was a significant turning point in Sri Lanka's history, for it represented the rejection of the concept of a Sri Lankan nationalism, based on plurality which Senanayake had striven to nurture, and the substitution of a more democratic and populist nationalism, which was at the same time fundamentally divisive in its impact on the country because it was resolutely Sinhalese and Buddhist in content. Ling shows that in this, as in so much else, there was a remarkable similarity in policies between Bandaranaike and Burma's U Nu. The latter made it his aim to achieve national unity through an emphasis on the Burmese culture and the Buddhist religion. On a long-term basis, this programme was not unviable, but the time-span required was decades, not years. Thailand had taken a century or more to work out a similar policy of national unification of the Thai states and its hill peoples within a Thai–Buddhist polity. The system has achieved considerable success; the main — if not the only — resistance has come from Thailand's Malay-Muslim minority. In Burma the resistance was wider and stronger.

The Sri Lankan experience deviates from this in two ways. The intense Buddhist religious fervour of the mid-1950s became the catalyst for a populist nationalism whose explosive effect was derived from its interconnection with language. Language became the basis of nationalism, and this metamorphosis of nationalism affected both the Sinhalese and Tamil populations. Thus the contrast with Burma: U Nu's programme failed to create national unity; in Sri Lanka an existing unity was weakened if not effectively undermined.

The second point is equally significant: the essence of this programme in Burma and Thailand, as several chapters in this volume show, was an assimilationist policy. In Sri Lanka, on the other hand, none of the governments since independence has deliberately or consistently followed assimilationist policies. The attitude to the minorities was embodied in a mixture of policies, sometimes emphasising national integration, and sometimes recognising the advantages of a pluralist approach. So long as the territorial integrity of the country is not threatened in any way — and indeed even in the face of separatist pressure — there has been no attempt to assimilate the diverse minority groups in the country to the dominant Sinhalese-Buddhist culture. Thus not only is there genuine religious tolerance — as in Thailand — but a greater acceptance of cultural pluralism than in Thailand where cultural pluralism, perceived as having strong political undertones, is deemed unacceptable.

Chapters focusing on the situation in Sri Lanka include studies by K. N. O. Dharmadasa (Chapter 7) and S. W. R. de A. Samarasinghe (Chapter 10). Dharmadasa surveys the Buddhist agitation for the rectification of Christian privilege enjoyed under colonial rule. A focal point of the discussion was the part played by the sangha and the Buddhist intelligentsia in the struggle against the privileged position of the Christian minority, especially in the schools system, during the period 1940–65. The growth of Buddhist influence in the Sri Lanka polity was a major concern. Specific studies of the 'Indian' Tamils by Samarasinghe and of Sri Lanka's Muslims by K. M. de Silva (Chapter 13) provide further insights into the minority issues in Sri Lanka.

Although the coverage on Burma was not extensive, unlike on Sri Lanka and Thailand, the two chapters published here (Chapters 5 and 11) use new conceptual tools to analyse the issue of minorities. Ronald D. Renard (Chapter 5), who traces the notion of 'a minority' through Burmese history, examines new ways of defining minorities during the pre-British period. He points out that in historical times ethnic and political boundaries did not coincide and that there was a constant intermingling of ethnic groups. Minorities were those who did not have access to power and lived beyond the pail of the Hindu-Buddhist cultural group. It was purely coincidental that some of these minorities belonged to certain ethnic groups, and the current demarcation of ethnic minorities was brought about by colonial attitudes, and an understanding of this fact is necessary to deal effectively with the present problem of minorities in Burma. Ling (Chapter 11) discusses the complexities of the problem of religious minorities in

Burma, evident in the relationship between the majority Burman Buddhists and the Chins, the Kachins, the Mons, the Shans and the Muslims since Ne Win's government assumed power in 1962. Except for Arakan, where there is a Muslim majority, the differences between the Burmese state and the minorities are shown as reflecting a dichotomy between 'Burman Buddhist' and 'Shan Buddhist' or 'Karen Buddhist' as the case may be. The part played by Christianity in the entire scheme of minority attitudes is not entirely overlooked.

As the workshop was held in Bangkok, the opportunity for close study of the minorities' situation in Thailand was not lost. Likhit Dhiravegin (Chapter 6) provides an empirical study of nationalism and ethnocentrism in Thailand. Thai nationalism, it is explained, is bound up with the notion of a Thai identity based on loyalty to the monarchy, adherence to Buddhism and a sense of a common history. The policy towards non-Thai groups has been one of assimilation and integration. That Thai nationalism had yet to mature and take a more rational form were Dhiravegin's concluding thoughts.

The controversial issue of the Muslims of southern Thailand is examined by Surin Pitsuwan (Chapter 12). Criticising the ethno-centrism of the Thai state, a plea is made for cultural pluralism, so necessary in a multi-ethnic society, where each ethnic community is permitted to retain and develop its own identity without negative interference by the state. Pitsuwan analyses the reasons for communal and religious tensions and conflicts in southern Thailand, and holds that the attempts of the Thai government at national integration were and are counter-productive, as they help to harden the attitudes of the Muslims. The policy towards the south is interpreted as an attempt to make Islamic culture compromise with a Buddhist state, a policy which has met with resistance. It is concluded that the crescent should be left alone without trying to integrate it with the lotus, the author drawing his symbolism from a mosque built by the state in southern Thailand, shaped like a lotus bud (a Buddhist symbol) on which has been placed the Islamic crescent.

Official Thai policy coincides with the attitude of the Thai majority that assimilation is the answer to the minorities issue in Thailand. Sanit Wongsprasert's analysis (Chapter 8) of the work of the Dhammacarik bhikkhus among the hill tribes illustrates this. The main objective of these monks is to win the tribal people to the Buddhist way of life, and through Buddhism to the mainstream of Thai society.

Separatist movements today

Grievances or demands of a political nature often constitute the
essence of ethnic conflict in plural societies. All three countries
confront the most unmanageable of such demands: a separatist
movement. Burma's separatism is *sui qeneris*, and indeed separatism
there has been described as a way of life. In Thailand's southern
regions, separatism has existed for decades. In Sri Lanka, separatism,
advocated by the principal Tamil political party, is a recent
phenomenon but poses a grave threat to the stability of the Sri
Lankan political system, if not to the integrity of the Sri Lankan state.

There is always a potential base for secessionist movements where
an ethnic minority is concentrated in a particular region of a country,
and constitutes the overwhelming majority of the population in that
region — which is the case with the Malay Muslims of the southern
border regions of Thailand, and the Tamils of the five component
districts of the Sri Lankan northern province.

The important ingredients in the emergence of separatism are ethnic
cohesion and a sense of ethnic identity. These will help generate a
separatist movement once other factors emerge: for example, as in the
case of the Sri Lanka Tamils, a perceived threat to ethnic identity
from political, economic and cultural policies; perceived grievances of
a political or economic nature or both; and a sense of relative
deprivation at the loss of, or imminent loss of, an advantageous or
privileged position. These separatist movements have the advantage of
extra-territorial elements of support at present: the attractions of the
Malay world in the case of the Malay Muslims of Thailand, and the
active support of the Tamils of Tamilnadu in southern India in the
case of the Sri Lankan Tamils.

These factors, operating in combination, have helped generate
Tamil separatism in Sri Lanka. The threat it poses to the Sri Lanka
polity is all the greater because of the operation of another factor,
once more a potent combination of geography and demography — the
existence of a great reservoir of Tamil separatist sentiment and a
powerful sense of Tamil ethnic identity just across the narrow seas
that separate Jaffna from Tamilnadu on the Indian subcontinent.
Once a separatist movement emerged among the Tamils of Sri Lanka,
it was fostered, nurtured and protected in Tamilnadu, as a surrogate
for the Tamil state which the Tamils of Tamilnadu had been
compelled by law — as the first line of the Indian central government's
armoury of attack — to abjure in their own country.

Separatism is a recent phenomenon in Sri Lanka. Earlier the demand was for a federal constitution. But Sinhalese opinion generally viewed the Tamils' demand for a federal state as nothing less than the thin end of the wedge of a separatist movement. Those in the forefront of the agitation for a federal state were vague, deliberately or unconsciously, in the terminology used in their arguments, and the distinction between provincial autonomy, states' rights in a federal union, and a separate state was blurred by a fog of verbiage. In their political demands there was, almost inevitably, an element of ambiguity. Partly as a result of this ambiguity, the response to this agitation on the part of the island's successive governments has been an unwillingness to concede legitimacy to the political activity involved in the agitation for a federal state. The hostility to separatism has naturally been even stronger.

The politics of the Islamic communities in Thailand is complicated by the duality represented by the two principal segments — of the Thai-Muslims and the Malay-Muslims — and their duality of approach to political issues, between the separatism of the latter and the integrationist desires of the former. The Malay-Muslims are all too conscious of their majority status in border regions of south Thailand, and conscious, too, of their strong dissimilarity to the core Thai nationality in almost every aspect of their lives: in culture, religion, values, historical memory and tradition. They are well aware that their incorporation into the Thai polity is in the nature of a historical accident. Their response has been one of opposition to their incorporation, and a desire for a separate existence which would either leave them apart from the Thai polity or would help them merge with the Malay world in some political form. Their commitment to separatism has disturbed the peace of southern Thailand for over four decades, and constitutes a serious political threat to the Thai polity.

The problem of separatism is often complicated by its links with terrorist movements. Separatist agitation, whether in Sri Lanka or in the Basque country in Spain, in Corsica, or briefly in Quebec, leads to a radicalisation of the political process in the affected region or regions. Inevitably this radicalisation leads to terrorism at the fringes of such movements or, as in the case of Sri Lanka, from the beginning, at their core. Some of the issues relating to terrorism are discussed by Chaiwat Satha-Anand (Chapter 2). In Sri Lanka this terrorist movement raises other issues, such as the legitimacy of terrorist violence by non-elected groups for achieving their political ends in liberal democracies. There is a consensus emerging among political scientists that such violence is an 'illegitimate and unjustifiable use of force'. Thus Conor Cruise O'Brien argues that 'the force used by a democratic state is legitimate while the *violence* of a terrorist is not legitimate',[2] and the claims of terrorist groups to be 'liberation movements or groups engaged in "guerrilla" warfare are attempts to inject terrorist groups with a legitimacy that most contemporary terrorist groups lack'.[3] Or, again, there is James Q. Wilson, at the more conservative end of the academic spectrum, arguing that 'if terror is practised in a society with free elections, open courts, and a legitimate opposition it is more despicable than when terrorism... occurs in a society where no alternative means of change exists'.[4] He goes on to show that there are

> essentially two ways of thinking about terrorism. One is to assume that terrorists are but an extreme expression of underlying social injustices and political tensions and that this symptom cannot be treated without first treating the underlying causes...
>
> This is an error because it overlooks the second way of thinking about terrorism...that, whatever the root causes of terrorism and the under-ground political culture that gives it nurture, the terrorists quickly and inevitably develop a stake in opposing solutions to the problems. They will do whatever they can, make whatever alliances are necessary (including alliances with common criminals and homicidal maniacs) to prevent any 'political solution' short of the destruction of the state itself. They will thus direct their attacks chiefly against groups desirous of constructive change.[5]

One must necessarily conclude this introduction on a pessimistic note. Buddhist polities have been no more successful than others in translating their central values into policies that generate unity and harmony in society. One sometimes thinks, as does Ling in Chapter 11, of Lord Acton's dictum: 'All power tends to corrupt and absolute power tends to corrupt absolutely.' I would suggest a deviation on this theme: the corruption begins as it did in Sri Lanka and Burma from a consciousness of a *lack* of power in colonial times and through a purposeful bid to redress historic grievances.

Notes

1. S. J. Tambiah, *World Conqueror and World Renouncer* (Cambridge: Cambridge University Press, 1976), p. 527.
2. Conor Cruise O'Brien, *Herod: Reflections on Political Violence* (London: Hutchinson, 1978), p. 33.

3. Ibid., p.72.
4. James Q. Wilson, 'Thinking About Terrorism', *Commentary*, July 1981, p.38.
5. Ibid.

PART I: THEORETICAL ISSUES

1 THE LOGIC OF IDENTITY PROFILES AND THE ETHIC OF COMMUNAL VIOLENCE: A BUDDHIST PERSPECTIVE

Padmasiri de Silva

Introduction

For those who are beset with the sense of incongruity, disharmony, suffering and tribulation embedded in the human predicament, the Buddha has a message with a perennial cast. For those who make a temporary pact with the social order, attempting to find the Buddha's distinctive contribution to the development of social relationships, the ideals of righteous government and inter-group harmony, there is a message of sorts. Some have found his insights on society and polity revealing and useful. Others have even constructed socio-political orientations for guiding and enhancing political and social activity.

However, there appears to be a kind of interim, provisional — even transient — quality in the norms we use to deal with questions pertaining to society and polity. There is a great deal of taxing our imagination and reason. Situations and contexts demand special attention. The spirit of what we do emerges as more important than the letter of ethical rules, and conflicting alternatives agonise our consciences. The Buddha's own teachings about morality, society and polity have no fundamentalism or any absolutism; they have a restrained pragmatic outlook, but one which would not embrace complete value relativism. This is a significant point in the context of our times, as the world in which the Buddha lived was somewhat or even greatly different to ours. The complexities of our time were not present in their intensity and extent in the world in which the Buddha preached. In formulating a lay ethic, he was not disturbed by issues such as nuclear war, genetic engineering, artificially manipulated sex changes, biomedical and population ethics and, more crucial, sporadic brands of insurgency and terrorism as found today. The ethics of intervening and managing questions of this sort are born and bred within crisis situations. It is true that the Buddha has a very rational, analytical critique of caste and its application to race and other group concepts,[1] including a very frank, compassionate, considerate and tolerant view of other religions.[2] But even minority issues of the kind that plague us today did not exist at that time. This is an important point for reflection.

Discussing minorities in Buddhist polities, we can present some very rational, analytic inquiries the Buddha made regarding irrational group concepts such as caste and race. We can also cite the *Discourse on the Parable of the Water Snake,*[3] which brings in the parable of the raft: the Dhamma is like a raft meant for crossing the river, not for carrying on one's shoulders after crossing the river; it is not meant to be converted into a label, an ornament, a bone of intellectual contention, a moribund institution and an object of infatuation and conceit. In spite of great doctrinal contributions, socio-historical data clearly illustrate the tremendous distortions, reversals and contradictions found in actual practice. A number of articles in this volume will perhaps betray this duality. But this article will examine a third dimension — the tension points, the conflict, the dilemmas which emerge as doctrinal resources encounter problematic social realities. Conceptualisation of these issues is in relation to two problem areas. The first deals with the logic of identity profiles, which is even more than a set of emerging dilemmas because it is a veritable tangle. The second problem area is more specifically called the 'dilemmatic' because it has reference to the norms of managing inter-group conflicts and violence.

Identity profiles and inter-group conflicts

This analysis is rooted in the Sri Lankan experience of group conflicts, where over the years people have had to cope with religious, linguistic and ethnic differentiations of varied types. Sri Lanka is a multi-religious, multi-ethnic and multi-linguistic community with conflicting profiles of collective identities. Within the major religious orientations of Buddhism, Christianity, Hinduism and Islam — as well as the ethnic groups, Sinhala, Tamil and Muslim — the concept of Sinhala-Buddhist identity has been the subject of prolonged discussion, especially so in the context of Sinhala–Tamil conflict. The practice of religion often results in the formation of communities and collectivities. The relationship between such a community and another religious community can generate tension and conflict. In general, during recent years conflict between religious groups has been minimal, but ethnic conflicts have figured in a very prominent way. In understanding inter-group ethnic conflicts between Sinhalese and Tamils, perception of group identities is the crucial point: 'The real dilemma concerning the relation between the two communities lies in the mutually conflicting historical perceptions they have of their own and each other's identity.'[4]

In general, the teachings of the Buddha present a critique of *personal identity*, which is one of the deepest and richest facets of the doctrine, though its logical implications for what may be called *collective identities* at the doctrinal level has not been probed extensively. There are interesting logical strands in the Buddhist concept of personal identity which throw their own shadows on understanding collective identities, both in the context of the doctrine as well as certain historical realities.

This concept of personal identity within Buddhism as religion is even more basic than its counterpart expression of collective identity in socio-political contexts. As Bardwell Smith observes:

> At the heart of identity always is what it means to be a person, a community, which is a religious more than it is a social or political or ethnic issue. In fact, it is significantly religious to the very degree that it not only takes seriously these other aspects of personhood (i.e., one's communal, national and cultural roots) *but does not bestow ultimate status upon them.*[5]

He adds that this authentic quest involves continuous self-criticism: 'While religious traditions may or may not address themselves to these sorts of issues, the problem at its deepest is inescapably religious, for the identity of persons is corporate as well as individual.'[6]

Historically, in the development of many nation states, there were stages of re-examining the roots of culture, and thus occurred the uneasy drift from cultural diversity to ethnocentricism. This ambivalence is built into our perception of history. The movement towards modernity by the revitalisation of tradition raises the danger that healthy pride in one's heritage is converted into fanaticism. The semantic bridge between healthy national pride and fanaticism has become hazy and clouded and has to be penetrated by the process of continuous self-criticism. The discussion which follows attempts to unravel some points of tension, both at the doctrinal level and at the challenges of real situations.

Two conflicting strands in our identity profiles

According to the Buddhist diagnosis of human suffering, the deepest roots of suffering emerge from the futile attempt at preserving a false conception of self, with its attendant diverse forms of selfidentification. The fivefold identification emerging from corporeality, feeling, perception, dispositions and consciousness manifests in four different ways, thus generating twenty kinds of personality belief. The ideologies which feed forms of group identifications and feelings, and the desires which feed ideologies (*ditthi*), have a central place in the Buddhist analysis of conflict. The emergence of fear, anxiety and aggression in terms of certain defence mechanisms has been discussed in recent works on the psychology of Buddhism. [7]

In spite of all these complex forms of identification, these identity manifestations are seen as part of a grand illusion. Yet the problem arises: Are we a kind of protoplasm with no sense of direction, purpose and goal?

On the one hand, the doctrine of egolessness focuses attention on the basic indeterminacy, ambiguity and formlessness in human existence:

> the basic indeterminacy of the human creature, the ambiguity and formlessness at the center of their lives, and with their tendency to try to fix their identity upon some cluster of transient identifications with which they become involved in learning to live in a particular time and place. [8]

On the other hand, within the ruins and the debris of the illusion, we have to generate a lifestyle without falling into the traps of these transient identifications. For the dissolution of the ego does not imply a dimunition of one's co-ordinating and cognitive powers. Somewhere within the narrow ridge between the paths of chaos and nihilism and the traps of identity illusions, one has to penetrate through a razor's edge, [9] a realm of interim and critical unities, dissolving them as we cross them, transcending them as we cut across their inner dialectic. The reality of personal and group identities all flounder on this narrow ridge, and to steer clear of the traps is the greatest challenge. The fact that the so-called ego is a bundle of five factors does not mean that man is a psychological protoplasm without directionality, self-criticism and patterning. Perhaps the metaphor of an arrow, conveying the idea of 'directionality without fixation', is useful. But as Clifford Geertz remarks:

The power of a metaphor derives precisely from the interplay between discordant meanings it symbolically coerces into a unitary conceptual framework and from the degree to which that coercion is successful in overcoming the psychic resistance such semantic tension inevitably generates.[10]

These are the paradoxes which emerge in the study of identity profiles. The notion of involvement without fixation has been discussed in an analysis of 'The Scarcity of Identity' by Joseph Tamney.[11] He raises the question whether a strong religious identity prevents a person from developing an identity with a non-religious nation state.

This duality can be seen in more technical contexts such as the contemporary encounter between psychotherapy and Buddhism. While psychotherapy considers the 'lack of a self' as inherently problematic, the Buddhist psychologists find the presence of a self a crucial problem. While the therapeutic issue in psychotherapy is how to regrow a basic sense of self, the therapeutic issue in Buddhism is how to see through the illusion of self. The conflict between the *illusionist* and the *integrative* notions of identity formation runs through both issues of personal identity and corporate identity.

In the Western clinical scene today, the inability to feel a real or cohesive being represents a disorder of the self. In the Buddhist context, heightened, overdone and bolstered identities generate many forms of fixation, anxiety, fear and aggression. Perhaps this is only an apparent duality, and the tension between the two ways of looking at personal identity would dissolve at a deeper level. The two goals need not be mutually exclusive. To present the situation in a simple way, the acceptance of the doctrine of egolessness does not imply that people should not struggle with the notion of 'Who am I?'. The case has been well-presented in this manner:

If, as Buddhism teaches, I do not have a self and am not a self, and if I should abandon all identifications based on any sense of the self, this is often misrepresented to mean I do not need to struggle with the task of identity formation or with finding out who I am, what my capacities are, what my needs are, what my responsibilities are, how I am related to other selves.[12]

There should be no premature abandonment of essential psychosocial tasks.

This point provides a logical extension to understanding collective identities in the context of Buddhism in Sri Lanka, where Buddhism considers forms of group conceits as extensions of the personal ego. To examine the inroads of self-pathology as manifestations of group identity, we can work out a tentative typology: (i) bolstered identity profiles emerging on conceits and narcissistic self images; (ii) strands of thinking presenting the illusionist profile of collective identities; (iii) the ever-recurring struggle to maintain critical and interim unities; (iv) nihilistic identity profiles (like terrorism and certain forms of insurgency) heading towards chaos and anomie. The inevitable tension between (ii) and (iii) present the most fascinating terrain for the study of collective identity profiles in the context of Buddhism. It may be limited to elitist kinds of doctrinal analysis, but it is a central concern of the norms about identity formation, norms which have to guide us in the encounter between doctrinal Buddhism and problematic social realities.

The forms of collective identifications in the Sri Lankan context which deeply concern us in this chapter are group identifications in terms of *religion*; group identifications in terms of *ethnic links*; and group identifications in terms of *language*. Cultural symbols and activities may be linked to both religion and ethnicity or may run through both of them, bringing them together; territorial concentration of people or the sense of physical space, as in Sri Lanka, adds intensity to ethnic cleavages; the sense of history is a strong ingredient in group identity profiles which operates through the forms of myth, literature, stereotypes, etc.; sense of power, or more specifically political power; and finally economic competition for jobs — these are all ingredients in the trends which generate group conflict, religious or ethnic. Unlike in the case of blacks in the U.S.A., physical appearance is not a crucial generator of ethnic prejudices, though language provides an equally powerful obstacle towards healthy relations. A psychology of mutual suspicion, fear, anxiety and the ever-recurrent cycle of defence mechanisms generate the conflicting identity profiles between Sinhala and Tamil people in Sri Lanka.

On the one hand, ethnic identities such as Sinhala and Tamil have no rationality, no scientific basis, and are illusory labels. But, on the other hand, policies must be articulated which realistically intervene in competing group claims about human rights, regional autonomy, admissions to university, employment ratios, etc. On the one hand, we reject these identity profiles as illusory, and, on the other hand, we hear the voices of communal grievance, mutual debate, justification and condemnation, physical threat, sporadic expressions of terrorism, claims for separation — not to mention the requirements for the defence of the country. This is a dilemma of our times. We try to dissolve these identity profiles and yet we recognise them and mediate in terms of these concepts.

This essay is not a horizontal, historical sketch of the birth and development of 'national identity', but rather the logical and analogical extensions of personal identity into corporate identity. In this study the sense of history is merely a background.

The ethic of managing violence and terrorism

In 1959 Sidney Hook, the American philosopher, wrote a disturbing essay called 'Pragmatism and the Tragic Sense of Life'. It was disturbing not for what he said about pragmatism but for what he said about Buddhism. Hook argued that the Buddha renounced the world because of three factors — sickness, old age and death — but that these conditions are merely pitiful, not realities fundamental to the tragic sense of life.[13] Hook maintained that an authentic sense of the tragic refers to 'a genuine experience of moral doubt and perplexity' which issues out of a conflict of moral ideals. Thus there are conflicts between the good and the good, the good and the right and between the right and the right.[14] He also refers to three approaches of dealing with such tragic conflicts: the approach of history typified by Hegel; the approach of love; and the method of creative intelligence (pragmatic method). He rejects the first as unsatisfactory, rejects the second as incomplete and ambiguous, and supports the third method. In the light of his own method, he rejects the way of Buddhism, because the Buddhist saint who out of compassion refuses to use force or kill, when they are the only methods, leaves room for greater evil. He refuses to accept what he refers to as the 'Christian and especially the Buddhist ethics of purity'.

In an article entitled 'Buddhism and the Tragic Sense of Life',[15] I presented a critique of Hook's analysis of Buddhism on a number of grounds. Space does not permit me to spell out all the arguments, but it should be mentioned the concept of *dukkha* is not limited to sickness, old age and death, but it deals with the basic sense of incongruity, disharmony and what the Buddha refers to as the state of unsatisfactoriness. The Buddha does not limit human suffering to moral perplexity alone. He attempted to diagnose the nature of both moral perplexity and intellectual puzzlement. Hook exaggerated the dilemmatic in life situations and he tried to build moral values on extreme situations. The Buddha was not interested merely in the moral dilemmas of exceptional people under extraordinary circumstances, but also probed the moral debility of the common run of humanity:

> What parades heroically as a conflict is often a clash of interests in which the voice of ethical imperative is clear but unpleasant, or it is a command imperfectly understood.... Their seeming importance is doubtless related to our fascination by tragedy, which features ethical conflicts to a degree unusual in life.[16]

Ethics is not the ultimate realm of human realisation. It is a step on the way. The very conflicting options for actions and their moral evaluation was also a part of the complexities of life, maybe a facet of *dukkha*. Buddhism offers a long-range therapeutic stance. 'Why do people get into problematic situations?' is even more crucial than 'How do we solve this particular problematic situation?'.

Sidney Hook responded privately to this criticism, agreeing to a wider definition of different definitions of the tragic, but was quite firm on his comments on Buddhist pacifism.[17] This problem haunts us again, not merely as a specific problem but a whole dimension which has crept into the contemporary world.[18] Questions of nuclear warfare, terrorism and global conflict have placed great strains on our traditional value systems, and during the 26 years since Hook wrote this essay, his sense of the tragic in life has gradually come more and more to the fore. Today the great question is the feasibility of the morally required policy options, the tension between the desirable and the possible.

In the more academic study of ethics, too, we discern some interesting shifts. The traditional ethics of the Greeks as well as the ethics found in religious systems may be described as 'normative ethics' which dealt with the recommendations of life ideals, prescriptions for happiness, codes of conduct, etc. During more recent times there emerged an ethics called 'meta-ethics', which has been neutral on normative matters but dissects and analyses the meaning of ethical concepts like 'good' and 'bad' and the role of moral language. A more recent trend focusing on the complexity of situations and their relative uniqueness has generated a need for 'situational ethics'. The interest in dilemmas, too, is a facet of the focus on situations, but it is more concerned with the conflict of existing rules or ethical concepts generated by the complexities of modern society.

A recent work dealing with the dilemmas of professional ethics and centred on the *Ethical Dilemmas of Development in Asia*[19] is concerned with the 'ethical dilemmas that face policy-makers and governments of developing countries in their effort to manage the process of development'.[20] The work presents some refreshing insights on the question of 'Values and Development'.[21] It is a study of ethical dilemmas in relation to the developmental setting of a number of Asian countries, and the chapter on Sri Lanka deals with "Violence and Development." Ethical dilemmas arise out of the inescapable choices we have to make, and whatever alternative we opt for, there is a loss of values. But choices have to be made, alternative strategies devised and sense of empowerment and commitment to the detailed execution of the projects made. But dilemmas worry us: 'The management of a crisis in law and order will entail some denial of democratic freedom; the rediscovery of cultural identity can heighten ethnic antagonisms in the pluralistic society',[22] and so on. According to the authors, development dilemmas have an intrinsic ethical content, a component of human values that demands specific responses in the management of the development process. Such choices are not value-neutral and cannot be 'based exclusively on techno-economic criteria'.[23]

Buddhist ethics leaves no place for the use of violence or revolution for changing the social system. Serious ethical issues emerge for the government when it has to deal with forms of collective violence and terrorism. Human lives may be lost in these operations. Sidney Hook says:

> But I cannot understand how anyone can reasonably deny that if X is confronted by a situation in which his refusal to take the life of a hate-crazed maniac would result in the horrible destruction of thousands of innocent creatures…then X is co-responsible for the death of these creatures, providing of course that this is the only way this death can be prevented.[24]

Matters of course become more complicated when we have to deal with forms of collective action and, more so, forms of sporadic terrorism. This is why we find the philosophy of non-violence put to the greatest strain today. The world is *not* arranged in such a way that non-violence will automatically triumph because it is the 'right way'.[25] It is true that non-violence always has a moral superiority as a means which the way of violence lacks, and it is true that 'it retains this superiority even when it fails to achieve the political or social goal to which it is directed'.[26] In fact someone like Socrates or Gandhi would say that material loss or physical harm consequent on upholding high moral principles is not a loss in the real sense of the word, but a gain indeed. Yet such a strain of idealism, inspiring though it may be, places us against a wall, for people who are immersed in the worst forms of violence cannot respond with such magnanimity.

Having viewed the dilemmatic context of collective forms of violence, and the duty of the state to handle this situation, we may consider some alternative paths for reflection and action:

1. There is the way of Socrates and Gandhi, where material loss consequent on holding high moral principles is not considered a loss at all.
2. Non-violence may be considered as a way of life rather than a strategy for intervention in a crisis situation. It cannot always and at all times be a moral principle, a strategy for action *and* a way of life. This technique may not settle the immediate problem, but emphasises its long-term diagnostic function.
3. We can change the paradigms of confrontation or bring about institutional changes.[27]
4. We can make a case for confronting violence, even the destruction of human lives, in the name of effective action. This is the case for the exceptional instance.

If the logic of circumstances forces a Buddhist to have recourse to the destruction of some life (as in the example of Hook), what he could say in his own defence is that he selected the lesser evil. We may work out analogies with euthanasia and related factors, but such arguments are not very convincing.

The case for killing or destroying human life in an exceptional situation finds an interesting and almost a dramatic expression in the *Bhagavad Gita*. If one looks clearly into the conceptual framework of the ethics of the *Bhagavad Gita* and the ethics of Buddhism, they present two paradigms for moral issues in the human setting today.

The *Bhagavad Gita* has been discussed by many philosophers and there have been a number of interpretations: Some feel that the *Gita* does not advocate the waging of war as the concept of the battlefield is only a metaphor, while others feel that the *Gita* literally preaches war. A third point of view is that the *Gita* prescribes war in the exceptional situation as a matter of *sacred duty*.[28] The third view point is upheld to show that the ethics of the *Gita* fall in line with the ideal of "Duty for Duty's sake", similar to the ethics of Immanual Kant. An ethical theory of this sort is described as "deontological ethics" in contrast to "teleological ethics" which emphasise the importance of beneficial consequence to society and to the individual. If we use these categories, the ethics of the *Gita* may be described as "deontological ethics" and the ethics of Buddhism as "teleological ethics". Though these descriptions may be useful in the context of the waging of war, they do not completely cover the texture of Buddhist ethics because Buddhism has its own definition of beneficial consequences. In general these two ethical stances are used to analyse modern moral dilemmas and often there could be a tension between these two ethical stances.

The *Bhagavad Gita* uses the concept of a warrior to provide doctrinal resources for a military solution to terrorism. The Buddhist ethic faces the strains of a dilemma in this context. Perhaps Sidney Hook is correct at least on one point, that the dilemmatic in ethics today forms a central facet of the Buddhist concept of *dukkha*.

Concluding thoughts

In face of the dilemmatic, Western diplomacy has moved from what is called 'idealism' to realism. From traditional ethics, they have imbibed the notion of *prudence* as a cardinal virtue:

> prudence as an operative political principle was not the rigid formulation or precise definition of what was right or wrong but a method of practical reason in the search for righteousness and justice under a given set of circumstances. Practical morality involves the reconciliation of what is morally desirable and politically possible.[29]

In our folk traditions there is the notion of 'wisdom that is relevant to the occasion'. In the Buddhist tradition there is the idea of 'skill in means.' Along these lines, an ethics structured for contextual skills is yet to be born, and the dilemmatic in life will go on.[30]

Notes

1. See Padmasiri de Silva, 'The Concept of Equality in the Theravada Buddhist Tradition' in R. Siriwardene, ed., *Equality and the Religious Traditions of Asia* (London: Frances Pinter Publishers, 1987), pp. 74–97.
2. See Padmasiri de Silva, 'Religious Pluralism in Sri Lanka: A Buddhist

Perspective' in John Hick and Hasan Askari, eds, *The Experience of Religious Diversity* (London: Avebury, in press).

3. *Middle Length Sayings*, Sutta 22.
4. Godfrey Gunatilleke, Neelan Tiruchelvam, and Radhika Coomaraswamy, eds., *Ethical Dilemmas of Development in Asia* (Toronto: Lexington Books, 1983), p.149.
5. Bardwell L. Smith, *Religion and Social Conflict in South Asia* (Leiden: Brill, 1976), p.4 (emphasis in original).
6. Ibid.
7. See Padmasiri de Silva, *An Introduction to Buddhist Psychology* (London: Macmillan, 1979), pp.94–7; Rune Johanson, 'Defense Mechanisms According to Psychoanalysis and the Pali Nikayas' in Nathan Katz, ed., *Buddhist and Western Psychology* (Boulder, Co: Prajna Press, 1983), pp. 11–24.
8. Nolan Pliny Jacobson, *Buddhism, The Religion of Analysis* (Carbondale, Illinois: Southern Illinois University Press, 1970), p.61.
9. For the use of the notion of the 'razor's edge' in relation to the analysis of the concept of persons in Buddhism, see Padmasiri de Silva, *Persons and Phantoms*, Gunapala Malalasekera Memorial Lecture (Kandy, Sri Lanka: Sithumina Printers, 1976).
10. Clifford Geertz, *The Interpretation of Cultures* (New York: Basic Books, 1973), p.211.
11. Joseph B. Tamney, 'The Scarcity of Identity: The Relation Between Religioius Identity and National Identity', in Hans-Dierer Evers (ed.) *Modernization in South-East Asia*, Oxford University Press, London, 1973, pp.175–98.
12. See John H. Engler, 'Vicissitudes of the Self according to Psychoanalysis and Buddhism: A Spectrum Model of Object Relations Development', unpublished paper, June 1981.
13. Sidney Hook, 'Pragmatism and the Tragic Sense of Life'. *Proceedings and Addresses of the American Philosophical Association, 33*, 1959–60, pp.5–26.
14. Ibid., pp.16–17.
15. Padmasiri de Silva, 'Buddhism and the Tragic Sense of Life', *University of Ceylon Review*, April–October 1967; reprinted with a few modifications in Padmasiri de Silva, *Tangles and Webs* (Colombo: Lake House Investments, 1976).
16. Henry Margensu, *Ethics and Language*; quoted in de Silva, 'Buddhism and the Tragic Sense of Life', pp.76–7.
17. Personal correspondence during late 1971.
18. For the dilemmas of professionals, see Sissela Bok, *Lying: Moral Choice in Public Life* (New York: Vintage Books, 1979). The book, however, deals only with one core value in morality, the question of 'truthfulness'. or, in the context of Buddhist ethics, the precept regarding uttering falsehood.
19. Gunatilleke *et al.*, op. cit.
20. Ibid., p.1.
21. Ibid., ch. 1.
22. Ibid., p.1.
23. Ibid., p.2.

24. Sidney Hook, personal correspondence.
25. See John E. Smith, 'The Inescapable Ambiguity of Non-violence', *Philosophy East and West*, April 1969, p. 158.
26. Ibid.
27. This point is discussed in Padmasiri de Silva, 'The Ethic of Care and the Ethic of Rights: Conflicting Models of Human Relationships' in P. de Silva, ed., *Two Concepts of Peace* (Colombo: Lake House Investments, 1985).
28. The same kind of tension is found in the discussion on the 'ethics of nuclear warfare'.
29. Kenneth Thompson, 'Ethical Dimensions of Diplomacy'. *The Review of Politics*, July 1984, pp. 386–7.
30. As a supplement to the present paper, see the following study on moral emotions: Padmasiri de Silva. 'Ethics of Moral Indignation and the Logic of Violence', V.F. Gunaratne Memorial Lecture, December 1984. This paper discusses the notions of justice, righteous indignation, revenge, etc., in relation to anger and violence.

2 OF IMAGINATION AND THE STATE

Chaiwat Satha-Anand

Today's world is seriously plagued by the spread of violence. Terrorist violence has been and is being widely used to attain several objectives, as a cursory glance at current newspapers would reveal. In general, terrorists expect to receive recognition while educating society about their goals. A government counter-terrorist campaign can be seen by terrorists as a major victory in that they have been recognised officially as a credible political force. As a result, they can broaden their power base while undermining the morale and prestige of the government. Any overreaction by the government will simply legitimise the terrorists' cause in the eyes of the public. A recent cross-national survey of political assassinations in 123 nations from 1968 to 1980 points to the startling fact that over 20 per cent of all assassinations in the survey could be directly attributed to a political separatist group.[1]

Separatism is one of the major socio-political problems in the contemporary world. Almost daily, the media report some separatist struggle around the world, such as the Basques in Spain, the Armenians in Turkey, the Eritreans in Ethiopia, the Kurds in Iran, the IRA in the United Kingdom or the Nagas and Mizos in India and the Tamils in Sri Lanka. Attempts have been made to explain the phenomenon of separatist-inspired violence. From the government's perspective, it is convenient to explain away such phenomena as minority problems.[2] Basically, students of a given society pay too much attention to the inner structure of any minority group. They fail to see that to comprehend adequately the minority problem, an analysis of the majority must also be included.[3] This point is significant because the existence of a minority group is defined by the majority group and vice versa. As a matter of fact, it can be argued that the minority problem is constituted, among other things, by the majority's problems. The majority's lack of self-understanding in relation to other groups of people with whom a modern nation state is constituted contributes to the rift that is already in existence. In addition, the majority's lack of trust produces a similar attitude from the minority. Policies that have been formulated with neither adequate understanding of the problem nor trust are doomed to fail.[4]

When analysing such minority problems as Malay Muslim separatism in Thailand, serious scholars probe deeper into the inner dimensions of the problem. For example, Uthai Dulyakasem attempts in a recent study to present aspects of the socio-economic and politico-cultural background and underpinnings of the Malay Muslim society in southern Thailand. He argues that these factors have contributed to, sustained and legitimised the separatists' continuing political revolt.[5] Omar Farouk adds an interesting touch to the study of the Malay Muslims in southern Thailand by examining the historical development of the separatist movement while highlighting the structural as well as the ideological orientations of these movements.[6]

This chapter attempts to move beyond those treatments of the minority problem outlined above. Ruth McVey points out that 'Separatism is a figment of the imagination of the nation-state'.[7] But what usually has been missing in most analyses concerning minorities is the nature of the nation and the state themselves. This work is a modest attempt to contribute to such an academic endeavour.

The nation as imagination

Why is it so easy for people to die for, let us say, Germany or the Philippines or Libya or Afghanistan, but much more difficult for liberalism or capitalism? In *Trinity: A Novel of Ireland*, Leon Uris has one of his characters say: 'there is a mystery that defies all attempts to explain it. There is no mystery more intense than a man's love for his country. It is the most terrible beauty of all.'[8] In a few short sentences, Uris novelist has captured the paradox of human social existence better than most social scientists. The beauty and the terror coexist side by side. A person's love for his nation is beautiful. But violence inflicted on human beings defined as 'the others' often arises out of this beautiful love.

The notion of nation goes back to the idea of a group of people who were born in a certain place, or refers to the idea of a group of people who all have a 'common place of natural origin'.[9] But whatever changes take place with the concept, the magic never seems to leave it. Ben Anderson suggests that the nation 'is an imagined political community—and imagined as both inherently limited and sovereign'.[10] He argues that it is imagined because the members of even the smallest nation will never know most of their fellow members, meet them or even hear them. Nevertheless, the relationship between and among members of a given nation exists in the minds of each in the form of the image of their communion.

What Anderson suggests is, in effect, a specific idea of reality which is defined basically by immediate sense perception. Three common factors constitute the core around which the nation is imagined. First, it is imagined as limited because even the largest of them, encompassing over a billion people (the People's Republic of China), has finite — though elastic — boundaries, beyond which lie other nations. Second, it is sovereign in imagination because the concept was born in an age in which enlightenment and revolution were destroying the legitimacy of the divinely ordained, hierarchical dynastic realm. When faith in religions was called into question, the nation as imagination seemed to rise to assume the pride of place in the public mind. Third, it is imagined as a community because, regardless of the actual equality and exploitation that may prevail in each, the nation is always conceived as a horizontal relationship. Anderson concludes: 'Ultimately it is this fraternity that makes it possible, over the past two centuries, for so many millions of people, not so much to kill, as willingly to die for such limited imaginings.'[11]

Before the rise of nations, men were bound together by three basic factors. First, men believed that there was such a thing as transcontinental solidarity nurtured by a particular sacred language which had access to ontological truth. Second, they believed that society was organized hierachically. Such hierarchy was natural and existed under a high centre, such as the divine monarch. Third, there was a conception of temporality in which cosmology and history were indistinguishable, the origin of the world and of men essentially identical. The age of reason demythologised these three factors. Thus, the bondage of man which gave meaning to their life and death had been severely shaken. The impact of economic change, together with the development of increasingly rapid communications, added unimaginable blows to the former root of men. The concept of 'nation' seems to be a new way of linking fraternity, power and time meaningfully together.[12]

Anderson's account of the rise of the nation is not without serious problems. The three factors that he argues were fading away, seem to be alive and well in Asia and Africa. Recent events concerning the revival of Islam all over the globe suggest that the traditional fraternity which transcends continental boundaries still exists, though somewhat tarnished by 'internal' wars among Muslims. The existence of authoritarian states in developing countries indicates that the notion of classical hierarchy has not disappeared. Lastly, for Asians the temporal dimension has not changed drastically. With the notion of 'karma', a Buddhist can transcend the present and explain his happiness or tragedy by past lives. A Hindu in Bali still worships his many gods with offerings. The offerings may have changed, but the fact that people continue to do it suggests a remarkable continuity. As for a Muslim, the idea of an *Umma* or transnational community of Muslims, goes back to the time of the Prophet. Anderson's notion of 'nation' as imagination thus still deserves serious consideration.

Long before him, another scholar, Rudolf Rocker, provided a vivid discussion of this imagination through a discussion of two different concepts, 'people' and 'nation', in which he distinguished between the two.

> A people is always a community with narrow boundaries. But a nation, as a rule, encompasses a whole array of different peoples and groups of peoples who have by more or less violent means been pressed into the frame of a common state.

He concludes that:

> National states are political church organizations...All nationalism is reactionary in nature, for it strives to enforce on the separate parts of the great human family a definite character according to a preconceived idea... Nationalism creates artificial separation and partitions within that organic unity which finds its expression in the genus Man.[13]

Rocker's linkage of 'nation' with the artificial struggle for political power is open to the criticism that, if this is truly the case, it is possible to ask whether political power is itself real. If the answer is 'no' then another question follows: when will political power be real and not artificial? Does it mean that all political communities tied together with political power also become artificial? Rocker's point is not dissimilar to Anderson's notion of nation as an imagined entity. Rocker suggested that a people is not artificial because it is 'the natural result of social union'. This, too, is open to criticism especially when he groups language, climate and geographic environment together as external conditions of living and considers them all as natural. Because it can be argued that language itself is a form of social construction, and the key creator of the social worlds people experience, language cannot be understood usefully as a tool for describing objective reality.

Nevertheless, Rocker's analysis seems to be quite prophetic when he points out that nationalism creates artificial separations and partitions within the organic unity of man. Ten years after his analysis was published, an incident which best illustrated it occurred which the world calls the 'partition of India'.

What happened on 15 August 1947 was the emergence of two imagined communities. The way in which both India and Pakistan were 'created' exemplifies what Anderson, and Rocker before him, characterise as 'imagined' and 'artificial' respectively.

After a long struggle for independence, the British yielded to the emergence of the new Indian spirit. Yet inside India there was a deep-rooted conflict. M.A. Jinnah, the leader of the Muslim League, intended to have created a separate country constituted mainly of Muslims — 'Pakistan'. Instinctively, Jawaharlal Nehru, one of the leaders of the Congress Party, abhorred partition; yet his rationalist spirit informed him it was the only answer. Mohandas K. Gandhi, the gentle apostle of non-violence, opposed the partition of India vehemently because his years in the villages had given him an intuitive feeling for the soul of Mother India. Deep in his heart, he knew that partition would not be peaceful and orderly. He knew that it would bring the dreadful slaughter of thousands in those villages. Blood would flow simply to achieve an imaginary end which would entail the division of the subcontinent into two antagonistic parts. The prospect of peace would then disappear forever.[14] In the end, Gandhi's intuition lost to the Hindu rationale and the Muslim iron will.

The burden of implementing the partition of the subcontinent fell on the shoulders of a brilliant British lawyer, Sir Cyril Radcliffe. The problem, however, was that, despite his encyclopedic knowledge of a vast array of subjects,

> Radcliffe knew virtually nothing about India. He had never written about it or become involved in any of its complex legal problems. Indeed, Radcliffe had never even set foot on the subcontinent. Paradoxically, it was for that very reason that Radcliffe was summoned from his chambers to the office of the Lord Chancellor of England on the afternoon of June 27, 1947.[15]

That a person who knew absolutely nothing about India should take on such an onus is in itself closer to fantasy than reality. Lord Mountbatten informed him that he alone would have to shoulder the responsibility for passing all judgements. Radcliffe was to draw his boundary lines 'ascertaining the contiguous majority areas of

Moslems and non-Moslems'. In so doing he would 'take into account other factors' which were spelled out by no one for fear of creating unending arguments between Nehru and Jinnah.

The unrealistic nature of a nation is best crystallised by the process by which Radcliffe worked to realise his objectives. Collins and Lapierre captured the imagining quality of the birth of two nations best with their vivid description of Sir Cyril at work.[16]

Every line that Radcliffe drew not only left its mark on the Indian rice paper he was working on, but also cut through the land and the lives of a multitude of people. Lines on paper transformed a massive land into two geographically distinct nations. The effects of Radcliffe's pen-marks were to be felt in the blood and tears of people whose houses were split, whose families were torn apart, whose exodus had to be endured and whose lives were forever changed towards a destiny they did not partake in the process of forming. Radcliffe's line sliced into two parts the lands and peoples of India's most closely knit, militant community, the Sikhs. The effect of Radcliffe's lines can be felt even today.

The example of the partition of India helps elucidate the fact that a multitude of people often suffers the consequences of the power of imagination of a ruling few. Another case in point is the question of Palestine and the creation of Israel.

At the time when Theodor Herzl laboured hard towards the establishment of the Jewish state, he thought of Palestine. When he turned to Sultan Abdul Hamid, the Turkish overlord said: 'I cannot agree to vivisection...[M]y people fought for this land and fertilized it with their blood...[L]et the Jews keep their millions'.[17] When Herzl turned to the British, Colonial Secretary Joseph Chamberlain offered him present-day Kenya. But this proposal was dropped because most political Zionists could not envision a Jewish state anywhere but in biblical Zion. It is important to acknowledge a significant — but usually ignored — fact, that Herzl had only the most meagre knowledge of what Palestine was actually like. He had to be told by one of his close associates during one of his few visits to the country that there were Arabs living there.

Both incidents again attest to the imagining quality of the emergence of a nation with a specified territory. There is, besides, a remarkable similarity between Radcliffe in the Indian example and Herzl in the Israeli example in both men's ignorance of the lives and lands their decisions were to affect in the future.

But if a 'nation' is but an imagination, why is it so powerful? Why do people die for it? The nation — as a sense of self and community based on an amalgam of language, territory, religion and custom, which 'today appears to be the natural mode of the state', and a principle for which people can properly be expected to die — is in fact, everywhere a new thing.[18] What makes these imagined communities so omnipotent? Here again, Rocker's admonition should be heeded. He writes: 'It is the state which creates the nation'.[19] Perhaps a clue to the existence and perpetuation of the nation as imagination can be comprehended once the relationship between the nation and the state is examined.

The State as abstraction

The word 'state' came into its modern usage in Europe at the time of the Renaissance. The concept of 'state' is closely related to that of 'estate'. Tivey argues that the factor of land or territory is common to both terms, and both descend from a feudal system in which forms of land-holding were fundamental to the political structure.[20] Skinner, however, argues that the uniquely modern idea of the state is that it is a form of public power separate from both the ruler and the ruled. The crucial element is that of an 'independent political apparatus' distinct from the ruler, and which the ruler had a duty to maintain.[21]

In *States and Social Revolutions*, a currently popular academic text, Theda Skocpol considers Ted Gurr's *Why Men Rebel* and Chalmers Johnson's *Revolutionary Change*, and suggests that for them the state is an aspect of either utilitarian consensus (Gurr) or value consensus (Johnson) in society. In contrast to Marxist theorists who see the state basically as a form of organised coercion, they think that the state utilises force in the name of popular consensus and legitimacy.[22] Instead of adopting the Marxists' or the non-Marxists' notions, Skocpol argues: 'The state properly conceived is no mere arena in which socioeconomic struggles are fought out. It is, rather, a set of administrative, policing and military organizations headed, and more or less well coordinated by, an executive authority.'[23] She refuses to treat states as if they were mere analytic aspects of abstractly conceived modes of production, or even political aspects of concrete class relations and struggles. Rather, she insists that states are actual organisations controlling territories and people.

The attempt to advance the idea of the possible autonomy of the state is not new. From the early 1950s, Ernest Barker pointed out that the 'state' is a particular and special association, existing for the special purpose of maintaining a compulsory scheme of legal order, and acting therefore through laws enforced by prescribed and definite sanctions. He argued that totalitarian state theorists gave a simple answer by denying the distinction between state and society and shelved the question which it raised.[24]

But both Skocpol and Barker are, in effect, looking at the state from a limited functionalist approach. Admittedly, in functioning as an administrative entity, the state produces various positive effects. Nevertheless, as an organisation with 'an executive authority', 'police' and 'the military', it implements certain policies. The process whereby priorities are set and agenda formed is a political process. It also implies decision-making. The question then becomes: who are these decision-makers? Is it realistic to consider them as value-free social agents? Perhaps the best critique of the functionalist approach to the 'state' comes from Lenin. In *State and Revolution* Lenin argues:

> The state is the product and the manifestation of the *irreconcilability* of class antagonisms. The state arises when, where, and to the extent that the class antagonisms *cannot* be objectively reconciled. And, *conversely*, the existence of the state proves that the class antagonisms *are* irreconcilable...
>
> According to Marx, the state is an organ of class *domination*, an organ of *oppression* of one class by another; its aim is the creation of 'order' which legalises and perpetuates this oppression by moderating the collisions between the classes.[25]

What is important to understand at this point is that the analysis may be far from complete if the state is perceived only as a neutral arbiter or an engine of domination. Like Janus, the two-faced god, the state exists as both the order-keeper and protector of the interests of the state power holders. Duverger points out that:

> Power is never used exclusively in the service of the social order and the general interest...It depends primarily on the people in power. When the state is in the hands of the privileged classes they use it basically in their own interests and only secondarily in the general interest.... When the state falls into the hands of those who have till then been dominated and exploited, in their efforts to suppress domination and exploitation they act in the general interest by acting in their own interest.[26]

It is one thing to understand the functions of the state; it is quite another to comprehend how it performs such functions. Compared to 'nation', the 'state' is much more concrete. Basically, a people — or an individual — encounter the state not in abstraction but through its apparatus. A non-Muslim policeman who enters a Muslim's house while its owners are praying (in southern Thailand) means more than just a social interaction. In the eyes of the villagers whose abstraction of the state may be shadowy, that policeman is the closest approximation of the state. Therefore, if that policeman has not been trained to be sensitive to Islamic customs, he might have perceived their silence at prayer time as an act of defiance against his authority. As a result of his own inadequate understanding, he might have done things that would be perceived negatively by the Muslims. For them, his action as an individual can hardly be separated from that which is sanctioned by the state. Without these apparatuses, the state would be less real.

Perhaps the nature of the state has been best explained by a British classical political philosopher, Thomas Hobbes, in *Leviathan*, published in 1651. In it he distinguishes between 'nature', which is the art whereby God has made and governs the world, and 'art', which is man's power attempting to imitate nature. By trying to imitate the most excellent work of nature which is man itself, Leviathan is created. Hobbes writes: 'For by art is created that great LEVIATHAN called a COMMONWEALTH, or STATE, (in Latin CIVITAS) which is but an Artificial Man; though of great stature and strength than the natural, for whose protection and defence it was intended.[27] Hobbes pointed out that from the very beginning the state (his Leviathan) is artificial. In other words, it is a creation of man. It does not exist in nature. What logically follows from this analysis is that since it is not natural, and if nature is considered perpetual, the state may not exist forever.

Nevertheless, this very fact seems to be quite difficult to live with. Even Lenin, having written that 'The state in general, i.e. most complete democracy, can only wither away',[28] found this position untenable. For he wrote, later in the same volume, that with human nature as it is, the state is necessary and cannot wither away. The question, then, is whether human nature can be changed or not. If the answer is 'no', then the state will not 'wither away' as Marx wanted it to. If the answer is 'yes', then the question is how can human nature be changed. In addition, the notion of human nature as generally conceived may have to be redefined. At this point, the question then is: how can a social entity that is artificial be so powerful? Is it only because of its machinery or its coercive force?

An answer may be that the state is more than an abstraction. In a recent review article,[29] the state has been conceptualised as: government, by which is meant that collective set of personnel in positions of decisional authority in the polity; public bureaucracy or administrative apparatus as a coherent totality and as an institutionalised legal order; ruling class; and normative order, as in Clifford Geertz's *Negara*. But others argue that the state is a complex political organisation consisting of the following components: territory, population, continuity, government, functions (security, order, justice, welfare), resources, finances, bureaucracy, sovereignty, and existence as part of a society of states. The significance of each component differs.[30] Of all these ten components, it is interesting to note that at least six are concrete attributes. Territory and population are physical attributes, while the strength of the state depends on three factors: resources, finances and bureaucracy. Government itself is a collective set of personnel formulating policies. But functions are relatively less static than the six components mentioned above. The notion of security or justice is more difficult to define and, thus, more elusive. The existence of the state within the present international system depends on its strength and how it interacts with other states. Therefore, it can be quite uncertain.

By far the most interesting attributes of the state in relation to imagination are 'continuity' and 'sovereignty'. Continuity is a characteristic which is provided by ideas embodied in tradition and vision. It links people living today with those who have died and with future generations. Sovereignty is considered an exclusive jurisdiction over their respective territories. The point is that continuity and sovereignty are closely linked. Continuity as an abstract linkage needs its boundary. Sovereignty provides the much needed component to transform abstraction into subjective understanding. History plays an important role in this connection because its power does not lie with scholarly works of history nor chronological events. Instead it lies with the subjective meaning that a group of people gives to history as they strive to maintain their imagined community which helps define their way of life.

Where the qualitative abstract attributes of the state shade into imagined community, a common social experience is formed. Such social experiences normally expressed symbolically, fulfil a specific task: the task of objectification.[31]

Myth is an objectification of man's social experience, not his individual experience; when received by the public its 'mythical' origin is usually forgotten. As Cassirer explains, genuine myth is not conducive to the use of intellect. In fact, the images in which myth lives are not known as images. They are not regarded as symbols but as realities that cannot be rejected or criticised but are accepted in a passive way.[32] This analysis can explain the public fury whenever national symbols (such as the national flag) are defamed. It is also important to note that imagination and abstraction do not transform themselves into myth. Instead, they have been made to become one. As mentioned above, some of the components of the state are concrete and, thus, are far from mere abstractions. The state, through the government, can utilise its basic strength factors, namely resources, finances and bureaucracy, to create conditions conducive to the existence and perpetuation of the myth it puts forth. For example, in a complex modern society the economy, education, culture, art, scientific progress, town and country planning, and relationships with other states are for a large part determined by the government. In fact, governmental organisation of society extends to the whole range of collective activity.[33] These plans and policies are implemented by apparatuses of the state. The bureaucracy certainly plays a significant role in maintaining those myths because it is but a neutral tool of the state. As a result, imagination and an artificial entity assume their respective realistic forms in the pages of history textbooks, in news broadcasts via nation-wide radio networks, in the daily press, in the supposedly 'entertaining' television programmes which may be produced from popular novels and even in postage stamps.[34] This very process is what some authors called 'social reproduction'.[35]

Bourdieu and Passeron describe how an education system functions to realise the process of social reproduction.

> The educational system succeeds so perfectly in fulfilling its ideological function of legitimating the established order only because this masterpiece of social mechanics succeeds in concealing, as if by the interlocking of false bottomed boxes, the relations which, in a class-divided society, unite the function of inculcation, that is, the function of intellectual and moral integration with the function of conserving the structure of class relations characteristic of that society.[36]

Through the process of social reproduction, the educational system serves to realise imaginations of the state by socialising its people; allocating its members to each appropriate place in a stratified society;

and, lastly, by legitimising the existing established order.

At this point, a question can be raised about the power of the state. If social reproduction as a process produced by the state is so omnipotent, how can dissent within the state be explained? This question leads to the final part of this chapter, where consequences of the nation and the state as imagination nurtured by artificial social entities in the form of myth will be discussed.

Conclusion: duality of violence

[M]odern political myths proceeded in quite a different manner. They did not begin with demanding or prohibiting certain actions. They undertook to change the men, in order to be able to regulate and control their deeds. The political myths acted in the same way as a serpent that tries to paralyze its victims before attacking them. Men fell victims to them without any serious resistance.[37]

By its varying nature, the state embodies a double form of violence. First, the government as a necessary component of the state has several tasks. But a basic task of the government is to govern the lives of others which is, in effect, to direct their immediate potentials towards a goal that might not be shared by the followers themselves. In this sense, their potentials have necessarily been confined. It is important to understand that structural violence occurs when there is an increase in the distance between the potential and the actual, and that which impedes the decrease of this distance. Therefore, it is possible to conclude that the existence of the government, and hence the state, seems to embody structural violence by its very nature.

Second, in the process of social reproduction, another kind of violence occurs. It is what Bourdieu calls 'symbolic violence' which manifests itself in the exercise of symbolic practices. It is a 'gentle, invisible form of violence'.[38] It is, in fact, a form of domination. This kind of violence assumes different forms in various types of society where relations of domination are sustained by objectified institutions, especially the state.[39] Symbolic violence occurs when a dominant culture is reproduced. By virtue of being dominant, the relationship between the state-sponsored culture and other types of culture becomes asymmetric. In other words, the dominant culture dominates other cultures which differ significantly from it. Dissent, therefore, frequently results from such pressured domination. For example, symbolic violence manifests itself in the hierarchy of language used in that particular polity. When one specific language is considered official, other languages become more or less unofficial. If the process of social reproduction is more powerful, those who use 'unofficial languages' may be made to feel embarrassed in using them. But if symbolic violence occurs alongside structural violence (i.e. poverty or other forms of social injustice), then the people who belong to the oppressed cultures will try to find a way out. Behavioural violence such as terrorism is one form of response these people can summon to counteract the state.

At present, the nation state still stands as 'the norm of modern political organization'.[40] True, it can be argued that the state serves human beings well as integrator, regulating the common good and creating order and justice. But these positive contributions of the state should not blind concerned individuals to its negative nature. At the core of the imagined community, which is usually sustained by the state, lies an extended concept of self. With such a concept, a certain rationality emerges to provide its support. Self-interest, which is considered a truism for all living beings, is an integral part of that rationality. To protect the 'self', identity must be formed. Once it comes into being, identity serves as an imagined wall to define and protect those who are 'in'. But as a 'wall' it also curtails the potentialities of those inside to reach out and relate to those outside as equal human beings.

The tragic side of rationality, based upon imagination perpetuated by both concrete and abstract attributes of the state, is that violence is considered normal if used against people who are not 'one of us'. In an age when humanity is facing the threat of total annihilation by modern weapons, such imagination and the myth which accompanies it should be critically demythologised.

Notes

1. Thomas H. Snitch, 'Terrorism and Political Assassinations: A Transnational Assessment, 1968–1980', *Annals* (AAPSS), *463*, September 1982, pp. 54–68.
2. Supatra Duangpatra *et al.*, 'Minority in Thailand: A Case Study of the Thai Muslims in the Four Southern Provinces' in Likhit Dhiravegin, ed., *Minorities in Thailand* (Bangkok: Praepittaya, 1978), pp. 157–274 (in Thai).
3. Arong Suthasat, 'An Analysis of the Concept of Minority', *Journal of*

Social Science (Chulalongkorn University) *15* (1), January–March 1978, pp. 104–66 (in Thai).

4. Chaiwat Satha-Anand, *Islam and Violence: A Case Study of Violent Events in the Four Southern Provinces, Thailand, 1976–1981* (Tampa, Florida: University of South Florida, 1987). No. 2 in their series of monographs in Religion and Public Policy.

5. Uthai Dulyakasem, 'Muslim Malay Separatism in Southern Thailand: Factors Underlying the Political Revolt' in Lim Joo-Jock and S. Vani, eds. *Armed Separatism in Southeast Asia* (Singapore: Institute of Southeast Asian Studies, 1984), pp. 217–33.

6. Omar Farouk, 'The Historical and Transnational Dimensions of Malay Muslim Separatism in Southern Thailand' in Lim Joo Jock and S. Vani, eds, *Armed Separatism in Southeast Asia*, pp. 237–57.

7. Ruth McVey, 'Separatism and the Paradoxes of the Nation-State in Perspective' in Lim and Vani, *Armed Separatism in Southeast Asia*, pp. 3–29.

8. Quoted in Bryant Wedge, 'Self and Nation, War and Peace', *The Philosophy Forum, 16* (112), 1979, pp. 29–41.

9. Jay Weinroth, 'Nation and Race: Two Destructive Concepts', *The Philosophy Forum, 16* (112), p. 71.

10. Benedict Anderson, *Imagined Communities: Reflections on the Origin and Spread of Nationalism* (London: Verso, 1983), p. 15.

11. Ibid., p. 16.

12. Ibid., pp. 17–40.

13. Rudolph Rocker, *Nationalism and Culture* (1937) quoted in G. Ostergaard, 'Resisting the Nation-State: The Pacifist and Anarchist Traditions' in L. Tivey, ed., *The Nation-State: The Formation of Modern Politics* (Oxford: Martin Robertson, 1981), p. 187.

14. Larry Collins and Dominique LaPierre, *Freedom at Midnight* (New York: Avon, 1975), pp. 140–1.

15. Ibid., p. 211.

16. Ibid., p. 247.

17. Alfred M. Lilienthal, *The Zionist Connection* (New York: Dodd, Mead & Company, 1978), p. 11.

18. Mc Vey, 'Separatism' p. 4.

19. Rocker, quoted in Ostergaard, '*Resisting the Nation-State*', p. 187.

20. Tivey, *The Nation-State*, p. 3.

21. Quentin Skinner, *The Foundations of Modern Political Thought*, vol. 2 (Cambridge: Cambridge University Press, 1979), p. 353.

22. Theda Skocpol, *States and Social Revolutions* (New York: Cambridge University Press, 1980), pp. 22–33.

23. Ibid., p. 29.

24. Sir Ernest Barker, *Principles of Social and Political Theory* (London: Oxford University Press, 1961), p. 5.

25. V.I. Lenin, *State and Revolution* (New York: International Publishers, 1974 [1917]), pp. 8–9.

26. Maurice Duverger, *The Idea of Politics: The Uses of Power in Society*, transl. R. North and R. Murphy (Chicago: A Gateway, 1970), pp. 194–5.

27. Thomas Hobbes, *Leviathan*, ed. C.B. MacPherson, (Harmondsworth:

Penguin, 1972 [1651]), p.81.
28. Lenin, *State and Revolution*, p.17.
29. Stephen D. Krasner, 'Approaches to the State: Alternative Conceptions and Historical Dynamics', *Comparative Politics, 16* (2), January 1984, pp. 223–46.
30. Howard H. Lentner, 'The Concept of the State: A Response to Stephen Krasner', *Comparative Politics, 16* (3), April 1984, pp.367–377.
31. Ernst Cassirer, *The Myth of the State* (New Haven, CT, and London: Yale University Press, 1975 [1948]), p.45.
32. Ibid., p.47.
33. Duverger, *The Idea of Politics*, p.81.
34. S. Chantornvong, *Stamp Kap Sangkom* (Stamp and Society) (Bangkok, 1983). (in Thai).
35. John B. Thompson, *Studies in the Theory of Ideology* (Cambridge: Polity Press, 1984), p.54.
36. Pierre Bourdieu, and Jean-Claude Passeron, Reproduction in *Education, Society and Culture*, transl. R. Nice, (London and Beverly Hills, CA: Sage, 1977), pp.199–200.
37. Cassirer, *The Myth of the State*, p.286.
38. Thompson, *Studies in the Theory of Ideology*, p.43.
39. Ibid., p.56.
40. Ostergaard, 'Resisting the Nation-State', p.192.

3 MINORITIES IN BUDDHIST DOCTRINE

P.D. Premasiri

Introduction

The concept of minority, as it applies to a cultural group, is of very recent origin. It could therefore be considered an anachronism to discuss the treatment of minorities in orthodox Buddhist doctrine. One might say it is relevant if we talk about the way minorities are actually treated in modern polities where the dominant group professes to be Buddhist. But this type of inquiry is moot in the context of the period and social order in which Buddhism arose, when there was no problem of minorities. It is true that contemporary society is confronted with new problems due not only to certain changes in our moral attitudes and ideological standpoints, but also complexities resultant of the vast changes that have taken place with the passage of history and the growth of science and technology. However, it is an undeniable fact that religious ideologies continue to have a dominant influence on contemporary societies. Where religion is the prevailing ideology that moulds people's attitudes and guides human behaviour, it is not inappropriate for those who profess a particular religious ideology to wonder what is explicitly or implicitly the theoretical position of that religion regarding issues that have an immediate relevance to their lives. This article explores a possible answer to questions pertaining to minorities in terms of what can be identified as the original message of the Buddha. Indeed, as the title of this article suggests, the present inquiry will be confined mainly to an analysis of the textual material which serves as the primary source of information about the tenets of the original Buddhist doctrine.

If we look at the context in which Buddhism arose, it is clear that social groups which could be described as minorities did exist during that period. The Buddha himself was born into a group which during that time was considered to be the politically dominant group, the *ksatriya* (warrior) caste. There is evidence that the society in which Buddhism arose was a pluralistic one, in that there existed different religious and linguistic groups and ethnically-based caste groups. Discriminatory attitudes on ethnic and religious lines were not uncommon. Formulating its teachings in such a social context, Buddhism took an ideological standpoint having a universal appeal, preaching an ideal which transcended parochial attitudes. The notion of a common humanity and the essentials of a common law of righteousness (Dhamma) for the welfare of humanity is predominant in the teaching of the Buddha, a feature which should have significant implications on minority problems.

In so far as tensions between social groups are determined by certain attitudes nourished by deep-rooted delusions about the nature of man and the human predicament, the teaching of the Buddha can be very conducive to the reduction of such tensions through the education of attitudes and emotions. We shall therefore deal with some of the basic tenets of the doctrine which can be said to have a bearing on attitudinal aspects that determine human behaviour and draw from such discussion the implications on minority problems.

Buddhism and ethnic minorities

One of the principal criteria proposed to classify minorities is that of race or ethnicity. Racial or ethnic minority problems stem from discriminatory treatment by one dominant ethnic group against a weaker one, thereby violating the right of the non-dominant group to live as equals. Such discrimination is often the result of beliefs or assumptions by the dominant group about its superiority. Occasionally there have been attempts to give scientific credibility to the view that humans can be classified into superior and inferior groups on biological grounds as in the case of animals.[1] Apart from doubtful scientific attempts at such classification, one's notion of racial superiority may depend on primitive racial myths and legends of the community or on inherent psychological desires to exalt oneself and disparage another.

In the 1978 Declaration on Race and Racial Prejudice, the first to be adopted by the General Conference of UNESCO, racism is defined as:

> any theory which involves the claim that racial or ethnic groups are inherently superior or inferior, thus implying that some would be entitled to dominate or eliminate others presumed to be inferior, or which bases value judgments on racial differentiation.

Buddhism has attempted quite explicitly to remove the myth of racial hierarchies in its critique of the then current view of the nature of society. The same moral ideology is reflected by UNESCO today.

It is believed that caste prejudice in ancient India had racial or ethnic origins. There is also a close analogy between prejudice and discrimination as operative in a society recognising rigid caste distinctions. Therefore, most of the Buddha's observations on caste discrimination are relevent and applicable to discrimination on ethnic grounds as well. On the authority of the Veda,[2] the then tradition upheld a static conception of a fourfold social order created by Brahma. It was believed that Brahma created the fourfold caste order, with specific aptitudes and functions pertaining to each caste, and people born into different castes had these aptitudes as biologically inherited features of their personalities. The brahmins felt themselves to be superior to other castes by viture of what they perceived as certain hereditary features they possessed; they referred to such physical characteristics in support of their claim to superiority and preferential treatment. The Buddhist texts refer to the brahmins' claim that they were 'handsome (*abhirupo*), fair (*dassaniya*) and endowed with an excellent complexion (*paramaya vanna pokkharataya samannagato*)'.[3] Also noted was that: 'Brahmins alone are the highest *vanna* and others are inferior, Brahmins alone are capable of spiritual purification, and are the only legitimate progeny of Brahma himself.'[4] It was believed that persons of low caste were physically ugly, loathsome and deformed. Their deficiencies were not believed to be confined to physical appearance only. In the opinion of the high castes, the *sudras* were thought to be intellectually and morally deficient as well.[5]

As a result of this conception of human beings' worth and dignity, discrimination and exploitation of the lower castes became legalised. There is evidence that the lower castes were subjected to discriminatory treatment — the denial of equal opportunity in the political, economic and social spheres as well as denial of religious freedom and equality before the law.[6]

In Buddhism the current myth of a divinely ordained society of hierarchical castes was replaced by the *Aggannasutta* account on genesis which gives an evolutionary account of society. The *Aggannasutta* is a critique of the creation theory and a rejection of the static conception of the nature of society. Social groups' aptitudes and interests are explained in the *Aggannasutta* as contingent social phenomena appearing in the natural evolutionary process of society. The theory of hereditary differences in human aptitudes, due to their originally belonging to distinguishable species created by Brahma, is rejected in Buddhism. According to the Buddha, human beings were originally born equal and belonged to a common species.[7] According to the *Madhurasutta*, the brahmin claim is merely a cry, an invalid assumption which does not accord with actual facts about society (*qhoso yeva kho eso lokasmin...brahmanava settho vanno...*).[8] People who belong to all four castes are equal (*ime cattaro vanna samasama*). The Buddha also points out the sociological fact that in some societies a caste system did not exist at all. Instead, they had a flexible class system comprising nobles and slaves.[9]

The theory that human beings cannot be distinguished and separated into a hierarchy of species differing in aptitudes is consistently held in the social philosophy of Buddhism. Buddhism emphasises the unity of mankind as a single species, and supports this view with biological arguments. In the *Vasetthasutta*, we find the most convincing expression of this Buddhist position:

> Know ye that among the worms and the moths, and the different sorts of ants...among the four footed animals small and large...among the serpents and the long backed snakes...among the fish that range in the water...among the birds there are different species and they possess marks that constitute different species.[10]
>
> But such characteristic differences which warrant the division of human beings into species [are] not found among human beings.[11]

Classifications, when made of human beings, are not absolute ones; they are merely conventional (*voharam ca manussesu samannaya pavuccati*).

Conforming to the Buddha's teaching on the biological equality of man, the Buddhist philosopher Ashvaghosa says in the *Vajrasuci*:

> Brahmins and ksatriyas and the rest are alike in flesh and skin, and blood and bones and figure and excrements and mode of birth. It is surely then clear that they are of one species of race. Again, tell me, is a brahmin's sense of pleasure and pain different from that of a ksatriya? Does not the one sustain life in the same way, and find death from the same causes as the other? Do they differ in their intellectual faculties, in their actions or the objects of those actions; in the manner of their birth or in their subjection to fear and hope? Not a whit. It is therefore clear that they are essentially the same.[12]

The Buddha also insists that the moral law of karma operates irrespective of caste distinction.[13]

Rejecting birth as a criterion for greatness, the Buddha adopts a strictly moral principle for assessing the worth of man. It is not by birth that one becomes a brahmana ('brahmana' understood here to mean a noble or dignified person)or an outcast (*vasala*), but by action.[14] One becomes inferior or superior by one's behaviour, one's purity of character, the particular level of spiritual and intellectual development one has achieved, but not in terms of one's colour, caste or race. Buddhism not only attempts to change radically the criteria for assessing the worth of human beings, but also warns that those who are bound by racial and tribal prejudices (*jativadanvinibandha, gottavadavinibandha*) are far from the goal of perfection in knowledge and conduct (*araka anuttaraya vijjacaranasampadaya*).[15]

As opposed to the claim that only brahmins are capable of spiritual purification, Buddhism maintained that the highest fruits of the religious life can be attained by a person belonging to any caste.[16] The term *ariyan* was sometimes used in pre-Buddhist India to indicate a racial sense of superiority. Buddhism has completely divested this term of its racial meaning, and adopted it to indicate the nobility of persons who are either on the path of spiritual perfection or those who have already perfected themselves. Angulimala, a brahmin by birth, was a cruel murderer. After turning to the Dhamma, the moral transformation of his personality entitled him to call himself one who was reborn with a noble birth (*ariyaya jatiya jato*).[17] Sunita was born to a low caste, and served in a menial job as road-sweeper and scavenger. According to the Buddhist texts, after attaining arahatship he is said to have been venerated by great gods like Indra and Brahma. He was called *Purisuttama* (noblest man) by these divine beings who came to worship him.[18]

The Buddha's view is that among mankind what is of supreme value is righteousness (*dhammo settho jane tasmim*). As opposed to those who think in terms of their tribal identity (*ye gottapatisarino*), the Buddha says a person endowed with knowledge and righteous behaviour is the highest among gods and men (*Vijacaranasampanno so settho devamanuse*).[19]

The term 'Dhamma' was never used in Buddhism to stand for the particular caste duty of a person (*svadharma*). A person's moral duty or righteousness is far superior to mere conformity to contingent caste duties, violation of which the pre-Buddhist tradition considered as a heinous crime against morality.

With the spiritual community which the Buddha established, no recognition at all was given to caste, race or colour. All those who joined the Buddhist order of monks were expected to drop their respective caste identities.[20] In fact, the Buddha himself set an example within the spiritual community over which he exercised authority. He disregarded caste or color, recognising only a person's merit in elevating him or her to a high position within the community. It is perhaps noteworthy that, according to Buddhist tradition, of the two chief male disciples of the Buddha, Sariputta was fair in complexion and Moggallana was dark; of the two chief female disciples, Khema was fair and Uppalavanna dark. According to the *Vinaya*, which was the accepted legal code as well as the constitution governing the affairs of the sangha, responsible positions in the sangha should be held by persons who have the required qualifications. In keeping with the theoretical position of Buddhism regarding racial or caste identities, Buddhism clearly ignores racial superiority as a qualification for holding responsible positions. The possession of moral virtue (*asekkhena silakkhandena samannagato hoti*) and other spiritual attainments, such as mental culture and wisdom (*asekkhena samadhikkhandena...asekkhena pannakkhandhena*), are among the foremost qualifications.

Second, a person must have the ability to carry out the function assigned to him in a competent and efficient manner (*patibalo hoti*).[21] Any person holding responsible office must be free from the four bases on which one is liable to commit an unjust act, namely committing injustice through favour, malice, ignorance and fear (*chanda, dosa, bhaya* and *moha*).[22] How early in its history Buddhism adhered to this principle, of recognising a person's merit rather than caste, is evidenced in the high position assigned to Upali who, having joined the sangha from a barber's family, later became the custodian of the Buddhist *Vinaya*.[23] The Buddha declared Khujjuttara, a slave woman, foremost among lay women because of her extensive knowledge (*bahussutanam*).[24]

Buddhism and religious minorities

The other significant criterion proposed to classify a minority is that of religion. In this respect, too, the Buddhist doctrinal position attempts to promote an attitude of nondogmatism and tolerance conducive to the minimisation of conflict.

Sometimes religious fanaticism and a lack of open-mindedness hinder people from appreciating the inner affinity between one's own and other religions. Instances are quite common, if we look at global events today, of religion being the source of social conflict and misery rather than the source of goodwill and harmony. Religious fanaticism generates precisely those evils that the founders of such religions exhorted their followers to eliminate. Religious pluralism is not a new phenomenon to Buddhism; it is one which Buddhism had to cope with from its very inception. In the Buddha's teaching there is direct guidance for a Buddhist life in a multi-religious social context. The Buddha himself has set guidelines on the issue of attitudes toward other religious groups.

There are certain intrinsic features of the Buddhist doctrine which promote attitudes of tolerance toward other faiths. Buddhism advocates a critical, non-dogmatic attitude towards all views. Critical scrutiny and testing in the light of one's own experience is recommended even with regard to the word of the Buddha. Buddhism advocates free inquiry unhindered by prejudice and emotional involvement in dogmatic views. Facing criticisms of one's own religion by others, the Buddha warns it would be dangerous to get unduly excited.

> Bhikkhus, if others should speak ill of me or of the doctrine, or of the order, you should not on that account either bear malice or suffer dejection or become unhappy. If you on that account, would be angry, and hurt it will be a danger to yourselves. Bhikkhus, if when others should speak ill of me, or of the doctrine, or of the order, you feel angry and hurt, would you know whether what they say is appropriate or not?[25]

The Buddha did not demand uncritical faith in himself or his doctrine. Nor was he interested in the mere conversion of people from other faiths to expand his following. He attempted to appeal only to a person's reasonable judgement. In the *Upalisutta* of the *Majjhimanikaya*, there is mention of the Buddha setting a grand example to his followers. Upali, a follower of another religious sect who was well versed in polemics and debate, confronted the Buddha on a doctrinal issue. At the end of the discussion, he was convinced of the Buddha's position, and expressed his desire to become a disciple. The Buddha advised Upali not to rush to a conclusion, but instead investigate further (*anuviccakaro hohi*) before he finally made a decision. In this instance, Upali expresses amazement as well as confidence in the Buddha:

I, revered Sir, am even exceedingly pleased and satisfied with that which the Lord has said to me: 'Now, householder, make a proper investigation. Proper investigation is right in the case of well-known men like yourself.' For if, revered Sir, members of other sects had secured me as a disciple, they would have paraded a banner all round Nalanda, saying: 'The householder Upali has joined our disciplehood.'[26]

Upali patronised the religious order in which he reposed faith prior to his conversion to Buddhism. The Buddha, who was aware of this, advised Upali immediately after his conversion to continue his patronage of them as well.

A Buddhist who strictly follows the example of the Buddha should not worry about the sectarian identity of a person. One does not become a noble person merely because one calls oneself a Buddhist. Indeed, a non-Buddhist may lead a life which is more in keeping with the noble principles of the *Buddhadhamma* than one who calls oneself a Buddhist. Identifying oneself by sectarian labels tends to create an attachment, an extension of the ego which results in conflict. The Buddha shows how one avoids such conflict without compromising the noble ideals for which one stands. The Buddha once preached the Dhamma to a wandering ascetic called Nigrodha, leader of a religious group, and assured him that the primary motive of the teaching was to guide others in the path of well-being, not to make converts.

Maybe Nigrodha you will think: 'Samana Gotama has said this from a desire to get pupils'; but you are not thus to explain my words. Let him who is your teacher be your teacher still. Maybe Nigrodha, you think: 'The samana Gotama has said this from a desire to make us secede from our rule'; but you are not thus to explain my words. Let that which is your rule be your rule still...Maybe Nigrodha you will think, 'The samana Gotama has said this from a desire to detach us from such points in the doctrines as are good, reckoned good by those in our community'; but you are not thus to explain my words. Let those points in your doctrines which are good, reckoned to be good, by those in your community remain so still. But O Nigrodha, there are bad things not put away, corrupting, resulting in ill... And it is for the putting away of these that I teach the Norm, according to which if you do walk, the things that corrupt shall be put away, the things that make for purity shall grow and flourish and ye shall attain to and abide in each one for himself even here and now, the understanding and the realization of full and abounding insight.[27]

In the *Alagaddupamasutta* (Discourse on the Simile of the Snake), the Buddha speaks of some people who learn the Dhamma either with the intent of attacking others' theses (*uparambhanisamsam*) or defending their own (*itivada pamokkhanisamsam*). The Buddha views such uses of the Dhamma as grasping the snake by its tail.[28] The Dhamma, according to his advice, is to be used like a raft to cross over to the safety of *nibbana* but not to carry as one's burden, identifying oneself with it and becoming emotionally involved in one's sectarian identity. The Dhamma is to serve no other purpose than spiritual upliftment and transformation of a person's dispositions and attitudes. When it is grasped as a dogma and when one identifies oneself with it, that itself becomes a source of conflict (*kalaha, viggaha, vivada*). The main theme of the Buddha's teaching contained in the *Atthakavagga* of the *Suttanipata* is the futility of hostile debates and conflicts among believers in different doctrines. The Buddha repeatedly emphasises the need to destroy those unwholesome motivational roots which impel people to participate in such hostilities. In the *Culaviyuhasutta* of the *Atthakavagga*, the Buddha says:

> If one who does not agree with another's doctrine becomes a fool, a brute, an idiot merely because of such disagreement, then all [those who disagree with others] must be idiots. For all of them cling passionately to their own respective views.[29]

A tolerant and non-fanatical approach can be said to be an intrinsic quality of the Buddhist doctrine, which ought to be emphasised especially in a multi-religious social context.

The Buddha views the Dhamma as universal; it cannot be the monopoly of any sect. Wherever the Dhamma is found, there one can find salvation and peace. The Dhamma leads to the resolution of conflict both within the individual and outside in society. The attempt to give a sectarian bias to the universal Dhamma only results in unnecessary conflict. The Buddhist view was that saints can be found wherever the practice of the noble eightfold path is found.[30] There is nothing in the eightfold path that could be objectionable from the point of view of any religion which desires the spiritual elevation of man. According to Buddhism, religious life becomes fruitful not by virtue of the sectarian label but by the universality of the Dhamma which is practised.

When the Buddha speaks of spiritual guides, he does not specify that they must be of the Buddhist order. He speaks generally of *samanabrahmana*, the religious community. Their fitness to give spiritual guidance is not considered to be dependant on any sectarian label attached to them, but on the virtues they possess. In the *Cakkavattisihanadasutta* of the *Dighanikaya*, a ruler is advised to seek the moral guidance of samanas and brahmanas in his kingdom. There is no reference here to a particular religious sect, but only a general description of the virtues of such spiritual guides. They must be free from sensuous intoxication and negligent behaviour; established in patience and gentle demeanour; restrain themselves from evil; cultivate peace within themselves and make themselves totally tranquil.[31]

Similarly, in the *Sigalovadasutta*, the Buddha advises Sigala to venerate samanas and brahmanas. They should be treated with friendliness in body, word and mind, and should be supported with their material requirements. The spiritual community, according to Buddhism, is an essential ingredient in society. For they turn men away from evil, establish them in virtue, show sympathy towards men with compassionate mind, give them new instructions on spiritual matters and clarify whatever spiritual instructions they have already received, and show them the path to heaven.[32] A Buddhist cannot disparage, nor discriminate against, a follower of another religion without violating the fundamental principles of the Buddhist doctrine.

The general framework of Buddhist ideology and its implications for minority problems

The foregoing account has focused attention on aspects of the Buddhist doctrine which have special bearing on racial and religious discrimination. There are also significant implications for minority problems which could be derived from the general theory of reality and the ethical doctrine of Buddhism. Discriminatory attitudes, ethnocentricity, hostility towards and insensitivity to the interests of persons who do not belong to one's own group can, according to Buddhism, be explained as the manifestations of *lobha* (greed), *dosa* (hatred) and *moha* (delusion), the three basic roots of all evil (*akusalamula*). Evil or unethical behaviour proceeds from these psychological roots. All forms of violence — whether they are based on ethnic, religious or any other type of division — are nothing more than the product of mental defilements (*kilesa*). Buddhism traces most conflicts in society to their psychological roots. Various external factors which tend to cause sudden eruptions of violence are only the symptoms of a more deep-rooted disease.

The pivotal point on which greedy and malicious acts revolve, creating suffering both for the individual and society, and resulting in tangles within (*anto jata*) and tangles without (*bahijata*), is ignorance (*avijja*). The manifestation of this ignorance takes the form of passionate grasping or clinging to the factors of one's own personality. Here begins the process of bifurcating the objects of experience into what belongs to oneself and what does not belong to oneself. Thoughts of 'I' (*aham*) and 'mine' (*mama*) are involved in all acts that proceed from ignorance. Buddhism teaches that, at a deeper level of insight and intuitive realisation, there is nothing that can be grasped as 'I' and 'mine'. All elements of experience, when understood in their real nature (*yathabhutam*), are merely passing and evanescent phenomena. The psychology of discrimination may be explained as rooted in the notion of ego and its ramifications. This is a mental state characterised by fear, mutual distrust and feelings of insecurity. The result is conflict even with one's own kith and kin.[33]

To lessen those destructive impulses of the mind, Buddhism recommends the cultivation of certain wholesome attitudes such as the four *brahmaviharas*, namely, *metta* (loving kindness), *karuna* (sympathy), *mudita* (sympathetic joy) and *upekkha* (equanimity). These are foremost among the meditations in Buddhism. The cultivation of the values, such as *caga* (charity), *metta*, and *panna* (wisdom), help in the growth of qualities which are opposites of three roots of evil. Unless the roots of evil are toned down by more positive and wholesome qualities of mind, no just society can be founded. In the *Mettasutta*, the attitude recommended for Buddhists is to cultivate thoughts of loving kindness towards all sentient beings in the way that a mother loves her only child (*mata yatha niyam puttam ayusa ekaputtam anurakkha evam pi sabbabhutesu manasam bhavaye aparimanam*).[34] Such an ethic should, by implication, not only be opposed to the attempt to deprive any human being of his basic rights, but also encourage people to contribute positively to safeguarding human rights.

It is in accordance with this doctrine of universal compassion that Buddhism emphasised the necessity to have at heart the well-being of all, whether it is spiritual or material. Buddhism may be considered the earliest missionary religion which worked with zeal to bring the message of peace, truth and love to all mankind. Unrealistic distinctions to divide mankind were completely overlooked. The Buddha said to his disciples:

Go ye forth and wander for the gain of the many, for the welfare of the many, out of compassion for the world, for the good, for the gain and for the welfare of gods and men. Let not two of you go the same way.[35]

Instructing his disciples, the Buddha insisted that their training in the practice of compassion be such that they would contravene his instructions were they to express the slightest irritation or anger even if wily robbers were to get hold of them and cut them limb from limb with a double-handled saw. The compassion of the Buddha's early disciples was so great that, heeding their master's advice, the thought of any risks or hazards of going into communities of strange, even rough and dangerous peoples did not deter them from carrying out their noble mission.

There is testimony in the early Buddhist literature that there were disciples of the Buddha who adhered to the letter and spirit of this teaching of love and compassion. One of the finest examples is found in the *Punnovadasutta* of the *Majjhimanikaya*. After being instructed by the Buddha, Punna wished to reside in a remote district known as Sunaparanta, notorious for its inhabitants' cruelty and roughness. The Buddha tested Punna's moral strength, courage, forbearance and ability to endure any atrocities he might have to face by living in the midst of an unfriendly people. When asked how he would respond were he reviled, abused, assaulted, struck with clods of earth, stabbed or even dealt fatal injuries by these inhabitants, Punna answered that he would not show anger and ill-will toward them. Punna set out on his mission with such determination, and instructed a large number of people of that region in the principles of the Dhamma.[36]

The doctrinal postion in early Buddhism does not advocate violence under any circumstances as a means of solving social conflicts. Love in return for hatred, forbearance and truth are the only weapons Buddhism permits for the resolution of such problems. 'Hatred should be conquered by non-hatred. Unrighteousness should be conquered by righteousness. Miserliness should be conquered by generosity. A person who speaks untruth should be conquered by truth.'[37] Even in the case of aggression, Buddhism advocates kindness, and espouses the belief that in the long run it is more conducive to stability than violence. The *Jataka* notes two alternative policies, followed respectively by two kings, for ruling a country: either he meets force with force, mildness with mildness, wins over good with good and conquers evil with evil; or he conquers wrath with kindness, evil with good, greed with charity and falsehood with truth.[38] Buddhism considers the second policy to be superior. The Buddha's teaching recommended the resolution of conflicts between groups through peaceful reconciliation, not through violence, for violence only breeds hatred. Victory through violence is no permanent resolution of a conflict. 'Victory arouses enmity and the defeated live in sorrow.'[39] Reconciliatory methods of conflict resolution are therefore far more useful than the coercive. According to the *Dhammapada*, 'Hatred is never appeased by hatred in this world'.[40]

Buddhism attempts to remind people of the fact of the transient nature of life itself. Everyone is destined to die one day, leaving aside all the accidental identities to which one so tenaciously clings. According to Buddhism, reflection of this fact alone should help resolve many conflicts that occur in society. The *Dhammapada* says: 'Many people do not realize that death is inevitable for all of us here. Those who realize this have their disputes settled as a result.'[41]

Buddhism views an individual's position in a single life span on the background of the unlimited process of *samsara*, a point of view which, if reflected upon, should awaken a person to the folly of attaching great significance to petty divisions between men. According to the *Samyuttanikaya*, in this vast expanse of samsaric existence, it is not easy to find another being who has not been one's own mother, father, brother or sister at some time in the cycle of births.[42] In fact, as an aid to develop *metta* and get rid of feelings of maliciousness, Buddhism recommends this as a matter upon which one should meditate.

The Buddha and his early disciples set examples by exerting themselves primarily for the spiritual well-being of all men, paying no heed to petty conventional divisions. The Buddha is said to have been born for the welfare and happiness of mankind (*manussaloke hitasukhataya jato*).[43] The Buddhist doctrine insists that it is the duty of the temporal ruler, as well, to have a similar broadness of vision and purpose in working primarily towards the material well-being of society. In Buddhism there is a concept of a world ruler who, like the Buddha, is said to be born 'for the welfare and happiness of mankind, for the weal, welfare and happiness of gods and men'.[44]

Early Buddhist suttas speak of the possibility of setting up a universal political order, which encompasses all peoples and races based on just and righteous principles of government. Such a ruler is said to conquer the world not by the might of armaments but by the might of the Dhamma (*adandena asatthena dhammene abhivijiya*).[45] He is supposed to be guided purely by the principles of justice and righteousness, and he should provide watch, ward and protection to all sections of the society with no discrimination. His benevolence should extend not only to man, but also to beasts and birds.[46] For rulers and their officials as well as ordinary men, Buddhism recommends the four bases of social welfare (*cattari sangahavatthuni*), namely, charitability (*dana*), affability (*piyavacana*), service (*attha-cariya*), and a sense of equal respect for all (*samanattata*). These comprise and are considered to be the linchpin on which the wheel of society moves.[47] They are virtues that have social consequences of tremendous value conducive to the building and maintenance of a harmonious social order.

Precept and practice

A question that might be reasonably asked by those who take a critical look at societies in which Buddhism is acknowledged to be the dominant religion is: should these principles remain at the level of doctrine only? The gap between the ideals cognitively acknowledged and how individuals and groups professing these ideals behave in actual life situations has, however, been the eternal malady that has affected the grand ideals of all known prophets in history. In the case of Buddhism, instances are cited when attempts were made to practise these ideals with all sincerity of purpose. The finest historical example would be the Indian Emperor Asoka of the third century BC. As a Buddhist ruler, Asoka attempted to put into practice the Buddhist principles of Dhamma throughout his empire. He also tried to disseminate them outside his empire. Asoka's Rock Edict XII bears testimony to the fact that the ideal of Buddhist tolerance in the religious sphere was propagated by the emperor within his empire:

> King Priyadarsin, beloved of the Gods, honours [men of] all sects, ascetics and householders and honours [them] with gift and manifold honour. But the beloved of the 'gods' does not think so much of gift and honour as... what?... as that there should be a growth of the essential among [men of] all sects. The growth of the essential, however, is of various kinds. But the root of it is restraint of speech...how?...namely, there should not be honour to one's own sect or condemnation of another sect without any occasion; or it may be little on this and that occasion. On the contrary other sects should be honoured on this and that occasion. By so doing one promotes one's own sect, and benefits another's sect. For one who honours one's own sect and condemns another's sect all through

attachment to one's own sect...why?...in order that one may illuminate one's own sect in reality by so doing injures, more assuredly, one's own sect. Concourse is therefore commendable...why?...in order that they may hear and desire to hear [further] one another's dhamma.[48]

In Rock Edict VII, Asoka says: 'King Priyadarsin, beloved of the Gods, wishes that all sects may dwell at all places because they all desire self-restraint and purification of heart.'[49]

In Asoka's Rock Edicts we discover his attempt to emulate the character of the 'world ruler' (*cakkavatti raja*) described in the Buddhist suttas. In Rock Edict VI, Asoka says: 'There is no duty [other] than the welfare of the whole world.'[50] In the Kalinga Edicts, Asoka says: 'All men are my offspring. Just as for [my] offspring I desire that they be united with all welfare and happiness of this world and the next, precisely do I desire it for all men.'[51] Asoka expresses his desire to become sovereign over all countries so that he can ensure the welfare and happiness of all men. He has evidently drawn inspiration from the political ideals of Buddhism, specifically from the Buddhist concept of the world ruler who conquers by Dhamma, not by war.

Within a polity governed by Buddhist principles, the problem of minority rights should not exist at all. Discrimination against social groups on grounds of ethnicity, caste and religion does not accord with a social and political doctrine that preaches the equality of man and advocates the fair treatment of all men. Yet instances are not uncommon when so called Buddhist polities have fallen short of this ideal. This, however, is inevitable, and has happened to all known ideals of mankind. It is from imperfect men that we expect the implementation of ideals. Buddhism, at so early a historical age, represented the most enlightened moral positions regarding human rights — positions which do not differ significantly from those held with the consensus of all enlightened men and nations today. Yet however noble these ideals may be, if the Dhamma is grasped (as the Buddha himself feared it could be) as the snake by its tail, it can be dangerous. The need today is to return to the noble ideals, which inspired the founders of great religions to recognise the holistic approach to life which each religion promotes, and to take into account the insights they provide regarding the inner springs of human action. This is all the more important since changes and adjustments in institutional structures alone have proved to be ineffective. At the same time, the paradox of religion, as we amply witness in the contemporary world, is its divisive influence. It is unfortunate if , under such circumstances, we decide to throw out the baby with the bathwater. Religious ideals ought to be cherished, but not by way of fanaticism based on false identities. Ideals we need to have, for sure, and we should be constantly reminded of them. Although we may fail at times to comply fully with them, it is no untruth that mankind has been spared a large proportion of suffering in its civilised existence due to professing high moral ideals and striving towards the realisation of them.

Notes

1. For a critical examination of such attempts see, *Racism, Science and Pseudo Science* (Paris: Unesco, 1981).
2. *Rg Veda*, 10:90.
3. *Dighanikaya*, (London; Pali Text Society, 1949), 1.119 (hereafter: *D*).
4. *D*, 3.81, 1947.
5. *Satapatha Brahmana* (transl. Eggeling), V, p. 446; *Aitareya Brahmana*, VII: 29; G.S. Ghurye, *Caste and Race in India* (London: Kegan Paul, 1932), p. 84; K.N. Jayatillake and G.P. Malalasekera, *Buddhism and the Race Question* (U, 1958), p.26.
6. Jayatillake and Malalasekera, *Buddhism and Race*, pp.26–8.
7. *D*, 3.95, 1947.
8. *Majjhimanikaya* (London: Pali Text Society, 1951), 2.84 (hereafter: *M*).
9. *M*, 2.149, 1951.
10. *Suttanipata* (London; Pali Text Society, 1965), pp.117–118 (hereafter: *Sn*).
11. *Yatha etasu jatisu linqam hatimayam puthu Evam natthi manussesu linqam jatimayam puthu*, (*Sn*, v. 607, 1965).
12. H.H. Wilson, *Indian Caste* (London: 1977), pp. 302–3.
13. *M*, 2.86, 149, 1951; *D*, 3.82.
14. *Sn*, v. 142, 1965.
15. *D*, 1.99, 1949.
16. *M*, 2.151, 1951.
17. *M*, 2.103, 1951.
18. *Theraqatha*, 1966, vv. 620–31.
19. *D*, 3.97, 1947.
20. *Udana* (London: Pali Text Society, 1885), p.55.
21. *Vinaya*, 1.62, 1929.
22. *Anquttaranikaya* (London: Pali Text Society, 1958), 3.274. (hereinafter: *A*).
23. G.P. Malalasekera, *Dictionary of Pali Proper Names* (London: Pali Text Society, 1960), vol. 1, p.408; *A*, 1.25, 1961.
24. Malalasekera, *Dictionary*, 1960 vol. 1, p. 719; *A*, 1.26.
25. *D*, 1.2–3, 1949.
26. *Middle Length Sayings* (London: Pali Text Society, 1957), 2.44.
27. *Sacred Books of the Buddhists*, ed. T.W. Rhys Davids, 1957, vol. IV, *Dialogues of the Buddha*, 3.51–52.
28. *M*, 1.133f, 1948.

58   *P.D. Premasiri*

29. *Sn*, v. 880, 1965.
30. *D*, 2.151, 1966.
31. *D*, 2.61.
32. *D*, 3.191, 1947.
33. *M*, 1.86, 1948.
34. *Sn*, v. 149, 1965.
35. *Vinaya*, 1.21, 1929.
36. *M*, 1.129, 1948.
37. *Dhammapada* (London: Pali Text Society, 1914), v. 223 (hereinafter: *Dhp*).
38. *Jataka* (London: Pali Text Society, 1963), 2.314.
39. *Samyuttanikaya* (London; Pali Text Society, 1960), 1.83 (hereinafter: *S*).
40. *Dhp*, 5, 1914.
41. *Dhp*, 6, 1914.
42. *S*, 2.189, 1960.
43. *Sn*, 683, 1965.
44. *A*, 1.76, 1961.
45. *D*, 3.59, 1947.
46. *D*, 3.61, 1947.
47. *A*, 2.32, 1955.
48. D.R. Bhandarkar, *Asoka* (Calcutta: Sibendranath Kanjilal, Calcutta University Press, 1955), p.288.
49. Ibid., p.281.
50. Ibid., p.277.
51. Ibid., p.323.

PART II: BUDDHISM, MINORITIES AND PUBLIC POLICY

4 NATIONALISM AND THE STATE IN SRI LANKA

K.M. de Silva

Religion, nationalism and the colonial state

Sri Lanka provides one of the most striking illustrations of the truth of Anthony Low's comment that 'Empire was as much a religious as a political or economic or ideological problem'. Christianity in its Roman Catholic and various Protestant forms came to the island with the three Western powers, Portugal, Holland and Great Britain, which had control over either parts of Sri Lanka (Portugal and Holland) or the whole of it (Great Britain) from the mid-sixteenth century. Portuguese colonialism was very much the child of the Counter-Reformation, just as Calvinism, introduced to the island by the Dutch, was a child of the Reformation. If the colonial state under Portuguese rule in Sri Lanka was a Roman Catholic one, the role of religion in the state system was no less significant under the Dutch, although the maritime regions conquered by them from the Portuguese were administered by a commercial company. Severe restrictions, if not penalties, were imposed on the practice of the traditional religions, Buddhism, Hinduism and Islam. These were most severe under the Portuguese; the Dutch widened the scope of these restrictions to include Roman Catholicism as well. Forced conversions increased the number of adherents of the official religion. Once again, these were more frequent and the pressure most persistent under the Portuguese. However, at the time of the conquest of the Dutch possessions in the island by the British in 1795–6, the majority of the citizens of these territories were classified as Protestant Christians. With the more relaxed outlook of the British, the superficiality of conversions to the Dutch Reformed Church was amply demonstrated when a great majority of people returned to their traditional faiths. And once the legal restrictions on Roman Catholics were removed between 1806 and 1829, they emerged as the largest of the Christian groups in the island, a position they retained until the end of British rule and still retain today.

While the link between state and Christianity continued in the early years of British rule in the maritime regions of Sri Lanka, the attitude to the Anglican church — theoretically the established church — was ambiguous at best. By the 1840s it was evident that neither the metropolitan government nor the British administration on the island was committed to giving the Anglicans the same support that the parent church had in Britain. All Christian missions in the island — save the Roman Catholics — were treated as equals.

The problem of Church–state relations became infinitely more complicated once the British gained control over the whole island with the absorption in 1815–18 of the Kandyan kingdom — the last of the independent Sinhalese kingdoms of Sri Lanka — within the Crown colony of Sri Lanka. The British confronted one of the most perplexing and intricate problems they were called upon to handle in Sri Lanka, the definition of the state's relations with Buddhism. At the cession of the Kandyan kingdom in 1815, the British had given an undertaking to protect and maintain Buddhism. Nevertheless, from the beginning the attitude to Buddhism was one of reluctant neutrality rather than open support. And in the 1840s, under evangelical pressure, the decision was taken to sever the connection between the government and Buddhism.[1] It marked the severance of the traditional bond between Buddhism and the rulers of Sri Lanka which had lasted almost without interruption from the earliest days of the ancient Sinhalese kingdom. Kandyan opinion viewed this as a gross betrayal of the solemn undertaking given on the occasion of the signing of the Kandyan Convention in March 1815. The withdrawal of the traditional patronage accorded to Buddhism, and the consequent loss of precedence and prestige, was deeply resented by the Buddhists in general, not merely by the Kandyans. The British would not go back to the status quo ante 1840 in restoring the formal link between the state and Buddhism.

The insistence on the separation of Church and state was a double-edged weapon. If it was designed to be used against the association of the state with Buddhism, it could also be used against a similar connection with other religious organisations as well.[2] The state's neutrality in religious affairs, asserted often in the mid-1850s and thereafter, was demonstrated in a manner at once open and vigorous by the disestablishment of the Anglican Church in 1881. With that, the separation of Church and state was very nearly complete.

The Buddhist revival of the last quarter of the nineteenth century posed awkward difficulties for the colonial government. Because the Buddhist movement did not present demands for constitutional or administrative reform — the two main points of interest in the incipient formal political activity of the day — men like Governors Sir William Gregory (1872–7) and Sir Arthur Gordon (1883–90) were more sympathetic than they may otherwise have been and sought to accommodate them in regard to some of their principal demands. First, the crucial principle of the state's neutrality in religion was established, with studied deliberation and moving from one precedent to another. There was no mistaking the general trend: the new policy was advantageous to the Buddhists. Gordon went beyond this to the principle that the state had a special obligation towards Buddhism, a judicious patronage of Buddhism which could easily be transformed into a special responsibility towards that religion. With this the breakthrough was consolidated.

Reviving an initiative attempted by Gregory, Gordon broke through a barrier of bureaucratic inertia and missionary opposition to give the Buddhists some satisfaction over their long-standing demand for some measure of state assistance in the maintenance and supervision of Buddhist temporalities. However, his ordinance of 1889 proved to be too complicated and cumbersome in its working and neither eliminated, nor for that matter even significantly reduced, corruption and peculation among the trustees of these temporalities. Thus Buddhist activists continued their agitation for stronger measures to eradicate these and the colonial government responded to this, in the early years of the twentieth century, with fresh and more effective legislation. By this time the Buddhist movement was pitching its demands higher. It wanted the state to assume direct responsibility for the administration of Buddhist temporalities and renewed the pressure for a more positive, in the sense of a formal, link between the state and Buddhism.

The Buddhist revival and the colonial state

By the early years of the twentieth century, the expansion of evangelical activity gave way to consolidation and contraction. As late as the turn of the century, there had been little co-operation among the Christian groups working in the island. This changed, gradually, as a result of the proceedings of the World Missionary Conference which met in Edinburgh in 1910. It led to the establishment of the first permanent instrument of Christian co-operation outside the Roman Catholic Church; its impact began to be felt in Sri Lanka in the 1920s and after, and its influence fitted in neatly with the practical necessity of closing ranks in the face of a resurgent Buddhism. Nevertheless, this co-ordination of activity did not encompass the Roman Catholics, who stood aloof from the other Christian groups.

In the early 1920s, Christian groups on the island began, at last, to confront the implications of the changes brought about by the rise of nationalism and the renewed opposition to the prominence of Sri Lanka's powerful Christian minority in the island's public life.[3] In response to this new challenge they sought to transform the missions and churches into genuinely indigenous institutions, less conspicuously under Euopean (or American) leadership and direction, a change that was fundamentally at variance with misssionary thinking and practice on the island in the nineteenth century. Up to that time no attempt had been made to adapt the forms of worship to a national, that is to say Sinhalese and Tamil, mode or to blend with the local culture. As a result, the Christians, especially the Protestants, were not only a privileged group, but one whose emulation of the lifestyle and patterns of worship of the British middle class set them apart from the rest of the population which remained Buddhist, Hindu or Muslim. And, more serious still, soul-searching about the relationship between Christianity and national identity, which appeared in many parts of Asia and Africa at the end of the nineteenth century, either did not emerge at all or did so a full generation later and on a more modest and diffident note.[4]

Moreover, most of the Protestant missionaries in British times shared some of the basic assumptions of the secular advocates of the Empire — faith in the permanence of British rule being one of them — and identified themselves with the processes of colonial rule to the point where they appeared, to the indigenous population, as the spiritual arm of the ruling power. Not that there was a total identity of interests between Christianity and the state, or that the missionaries were uncritical of the government; but their association, a blend of collaboration and critical appraisal of each other's work, was close enough for the missionary movement to suffer when colonial rule came under attack just as it benefited enormously from its association with the Empire.[5]

The pressures on the missionaries eased somewhat in the inter-war years because Buddhist activists failed to convert the religious enthusiasm they generated into a program of political action. Buddhist militancy receded to the background after the outbreak of the First World War for more than a generation. The reasons for this lay in the field of politics where a new mood of restraint and excessive caution, coupled with a distrust of enthusiasm, its most notable characteristics, spilled over into religious activity as well. More importantly, the elite leadership in politics, 'the constitutionalists', took over the lead in the Buddhist movement as well. F.R. Senanayake (1882–1925) and D.B. Jayatilaka (1868–1944), the most prominent of these leaders, kept a tight rein on religious enthusiasm. They set the tone from about 1918 until Jayatilaka's retirement from active politics in 1943.

However, the political changes which followed upon the introduction of the Donoughmore constitution in Sri Lanka were soon to have their repercussions on the standing of religious bodies, in a perceptible diminution of the influence of missionary organisations on the island. With the introduction of universal suffrage after 1931, politicians of the first (1931–5) and second (1939–47) State Councils — as the national legislature of this period was called — unlike their predecessors in the Legislative Council, were subject to the pressure of a popular electorate. Buddhist pressure groups could now work through the electoral process to influence the election of supporters to the national legislature. Significantly, the issue of Buddhist temporalities was settled very early, and Ordinance 19 of 1931 conceded the demand which Buddhist opinion had been making for several decades for state intervention in and supervision of the administration of Buddhist temporalities. While the government still emphasised its neutrality in religious affairs, it had become politic to underline the sense of a special obligation towards Buddhism, evidence of the continuing validity of the formula which had been evolved in the days of Governors William Gregory and Arthur Gordon.

In retrospect it would seem that the inter-war period was the most decisive phase in the reconciliation of the Christian minority to a diminished role in the affairs of the country — if not yet a ready acceptance of Buddhist dominance in the Sri Lanka polity. That is not to say there were no differences of attitude in this policy of accommodation among the various Christian groups. Most of these centred on education and the schools. Conflicts on these issues determined the pattern of relations between the Buddhist majority and Christian minority both in the later years of British rule and in the years after independence — especially the rivalries, if not conflicts, between the Roman Catholics, who emerged as the most outspoken and committed defenders of

Christian interests in education, and the Buddhists. For too long education had been feared as a means of religious conversion, and demands for fundamental reform in education were thus inevitable.

With the Donoughmore reforms of 1931 and the increasing devolution of political power and responsibility to Sri Lankans, the educational system dominated by Christian missions was challenged more consistently, citing the wasteful competition and unhealthy rivalry it engendered as its principal flaws, apart of course from the more fundamental objection to its use of the educational process as a means of conversion to Christianity. In the 1940s, Buddhist pressure to make the island's educational system more responsive to the local environment and to enlarge the role of the state in education at the expense of the missions was one of the key features of political activity. Resistance to these reforms succeeded in delaying their implementation and in eliminating some of the more far-reaching aspects which were regarded as being especially inimical to the existing system.

Indeed the political leadership of the day successfully postponed the inevitable confrontation between a militant Buddhist movement, urging a clean break from the immediate past for the purpose of creating a new state on 'ideal' traditional Buddhist lines, and those others who were committed to the maintenance of the liberal ideal of a secular state in which the lines between state power and religion were carefully demarcated.

The moderating influence of D.B. Jayatilaka, the most prominent Buddhist leader of this period, is very significant in this context. Even more important was the work of D.S. Senanayake, whose opposition to education reforms introduced in the 1940s was unconcealed and who, as Prime Minister (1947–52), contrived to soften their impact considerably. He also succeeded in diverting attention away from the wider issue of a closer association of the new state with the Buddhist religion and the restoration of traditional patronage for it, with the precedence and prestige that accompanied such patronage, and also in thwarting all efforts to abandon the concept of a secular state and the principle of the state's religious neutrality. The success he achieved was such that in 1947–8, at the time of the transfer of power, there seemed little or no evidence of the religious turmoil and linguistic conflicts which were to burst to the surface in 1956.

Nationalism and the post-independence state

For nearly a decade after 1947, the issues which the Buddhist activists of the 1940s had raised lay dormant but were not extinct. The confrontation between the advocates of a secular state and those others who sought to underline the primacy of Buddhism and the Sinhalese in Sri Lanka was renewed in the mid-1950s.

In the years after independence, one of the major preoccupations of the government was with the need to establish a sense of Sri Lankan nationalism on territorial lines; under D.S. Senanayake's leadership, political leaders aimed at subordinating communal differences to the common goal of strengthening the foundations of nationhood. The primary aim was the establishment of a stable equilibrium of ethnic forces within a poly-ethnic polity.

Their vision of the goal of political endeavour was of a territorial nationalism without any special, much less exclusive, association with any ethnic group or any section of an ethnic group. In this as well as in the emphasis on the concept of a poly-ethnic polity, they were at one with their Marxist critics. Indeed the Marxist version was much more comprehensive because it encompassed the Indian plantation workers as well, a group which not even the most liberal of mainstream politicians were willing to regard as an integral element of a Sri Lankan polity. Sri Lanka was to be a secular state. In this, too, they and their Marxist critics saw eye to eye. For many years it seemed as though these policies had succeeded, but beneath the surface powerful forces were at work to upset the equilibrium; policies of reconciliation and harmony were undermined by the powerful divisive forces of language and religion. The Sinhalese-Buddhist majority, long dormant, began to assert its national dominance. S.W.R.D. Bandaranaike's (1899–1959) landmark election victory of 1956 represented the rejection of the concept of a Sri Lankan nationalism, based on a commitment to pluralism which Senanayake had striven to nurture, and the substitution for it of a more democratic and populist nationalism which was at the same time dangerously divisive in its impact on the country because it was resolutely Sinhalese and Buddhist in content. Against the background of the *Buddha Jayanti*, the world-wide commemoration in 1956 marking the 2,500th anniversary of the death of the Buddha, an intense religious fervour became the catalyst of a populist nationalism whose explosive effect was derived from its interconnection with language. Language became the basis of nationalism, and this metamorphosis of nationalism affected both the Sinhalese and Tamil populations.[6]

All the major Sri Lankan political parties of the day were baffled by this novel political phenomenon of linguistic nationalism. Yet the imperatives of their calling compelled each in turn to define their attitude to it. Most of them eventually succumbed to the blandishments of linguistic nationalism. None understood the perils involved.

This phenomenon of linguistic nationalism had a profoundly disturbing impact on the politics of South Asia. It compelled a reluctant and sceptical Jawaharlal Nehru to yield to its pressures by appointing a Boundaries Commission on whose recommendations the Indian states and provinces were reorganised to accommodate the principle of linguistic, provincial or regional entities, in short a system of linguistic states; it eventually proved to be a stronger force than religion in its disruptive effects on the old Pakistan of two distinct wings. And in Sri Lanka it helped destroy the civil peace for a decade or more.

Linguistic nationalism and Buddhism

Thus the mid-1950s mark a watershed in the recent history of the island.[7] The emotional content in the religious fervour associated with the *Buddha Jayanti* increased exponentially from its connection with language — Buddhism and Sinhalese were so closely inter-twined that it became impossible to treat either in isolation in the mid-1950s and early 1960s. Buddhist activism, which had been directed so far against the privileged position enjoyed by Christianity and Christians in Sri Lanka , shifted its attention to the Tamil minority as well. Buddhist activists and the Sinhalese-educated intelligentsia had, in the recent past, seldom exerted influence on a national scale; they felt that they had been unjustly excluded by the English-educated elite from a share of power commensurate with their numbers, and that rewarding careers were closed to them by the pervasive dominance of English as the language of administration. Concentrating their attention on the superior educational advantages enjoyed by the Tamil minority, they set their sights on the demolition of the language settlement arrived at in 1944–5 — that Sinhalese and Tamil should eventually replace English as the national languages — and insisted instead on 'Sinhala only', the slogan which became the main plank of the coalition of parties set up by Bandaranaike in anticipation of the general election of 1956. (Bandaranaike himself had strongly endorsed the language-settlement of 1944–5). The 'Sinhala-only' campaign brought together a formidable array of forces united in support of a common program: Sinhalese schoolteachers, Ayurvedic physicians (practitioners of traditional medicine), Sinhalese writers, bhikkhus (members of the Buddhist order, the sangha) and the rural elite, claiming to speak on behalf of the peasants.

For Tamils the implications of a change in language policy were starkly clear. It meant that in the future they would be at a great disadvantage in employment, in the administration of the country and, eventually, in the professions as well. Moreover, with language as the prime determinant of national consciousness, there were fears that the Tamils' identity as a distinct ethnic group would be eroded. This transformation of nationalism affected them as well — language became the focal point of a new ethnic consciousness, of two rival nationalisms.

Buddhism and Buddhist interests had suffered, and in the perception of Buddhist activists continued to suffer from the decline in status and prestige that had occurred under colonial rule. The drive by the Buddhist leadership to redress historical grievances had as its fundamental principle the granting of compensatory concessions to Buddhists. Through the efforts of organisations such as the Buddhist Theosophical Society, Buddhists had made substantial progress in regaining some of their influence in the country and in fact in compelling the hitherto resurgent forces of Christianity to adopt policies of retrenchment and consolidation. Nevertheless, at independence and in the first decade after independence, the advances they had made so far only served to make them all the more impatient to reduce the narrowing gap between aspirations and achievement, and to do that as speedily as possible.

The crux of the problem was that, while the political system had accommodated itself since 1931 to the fact of Buddhist-Sinhalese predominance, other areas of public life lagged far behind in adjusting to that same demographic reality. What happened in the mid-1950s was that a concern for the enhancement of the status of Buddhism and the sense of outrage and indignation of the Buddhists at what they regarded as the historic injustices suffered by their religion under Western rule became, in the messianic atmosphere of the *Buddha Jayanti*, the prime determinants of a process of change whose main thrust was the extension of the predominance established by Sinhalese Buddhists in the political sphere into all other areas of activity. Inevitably pressure for a closer association of the state with Buddhism and for the declaration of Buddhism to be the state religion were intensified. The Christian minority came under attack because of the prestigious and influential position they continued to enjoy, the most conspicuous evidence of which lay in the impressive network of mission schools they controlled.

Despite the education reforms of the 1940s the Christian schools retained much of the prestige they had enjoyed in the days of British rule, while the preponderance of Christians and other minorities in public life, especially in the higher bureaucracy, professions and business, remained intact although under greater pressure than in the past. The balance, however, was inevitably shifting in favour of the Sinhalese Buddhists, but Buddhist activists were dissatisfied with the pace at which this change was taking place. More ominously, they attributed the survival of Christian and minority privileges to the resistance of powerful vested interests which the government, through a lack of concern for Buddhist interests, was reluctant to challenge or upset.[8]

On the whole, S.W.R.D. Bandaranaike's government was much more cautious in handling matters relating to the interests of the Christian minority than it was over the language issue. It was a matter of prudence and priorities. The language struggle took precedence over all else, and there was no desire to add to the problems of the government by taking on an issue which was potentially just as dangerous. While Bandaranaike was in favour of restoring the traditional patronage accorded to Buddhism, he stopped well short of endorsing the demand that Buddhism be declared the state religion. After his assassination his widow took over the leadership of his party. Mrs Bandaranaike, unlike her husband, was not unwilling to handle two inflammable issues simultaneously. She was not interested at this stage in the more complicated issue of the status of Buddhism in the Sri Lankan polity, but a renewed commitment to press ahead with the language policy initiated by her husband's government — without the concessions to the Tamils he had promised to introduce — was accompanied by a policy of calculated opposition to the Roman Catholic minority over the mission schools.

On this issue, unlike on the language question, her government was supported by Marxist and radical groups within and outside the national legislature. All of them welcomed state control of education

—the Marxists and radicals because they viewed it as a matter of social justice, and secularisation of education as an end in itself, the Buddhist activists because it would redress a long-standing grievance of theirs and eliminate what they continued to regard as the main instrument of conversion to Christianity under Western rule as well as the basis of Christian privilege in contemporary Sri Lanka. There was a more practical consideration. Implicit in state control was the prospect of increasing Buddhist influence on education, both at the national and grassroots level. The fact that the vast bulk of mission schools were almost totally dependent on government finances, while in all but a handful of them the majority of students were Buddhists, made it nearly impossible to meet the arguments of the advocates of state control. There was also the zealous care with which all denominations of Christians avoided recruitment of non-Christians to the teaching staff in the schools, although the salaries were provided largely if not entirely by the state.

Once again it was the Roman Catholics who led the resistance and bore the brunt of the attack. Though all the religious groups — including the Hindus and Muslims, not to mention the Buddhists themselves — were affected by the decision to bring the state-aided secondary schools directly under state control, the Roman Catholics were the biggest losers. Most of the state-aided mission schools accepted the painful decision to be absorbed by the state. A few big schools, mostly Roman Catholic institutions in the urban areas, decided to retain their independence by becoming private institutions without the benefit of state aid. Deprived by law of the right to levy fees from their students, they maintained a precarious existence under very severe financial handicaps.

The Constitution afforded no protection to the minorities against the changes in language and education policy, though they were adversely affected by both. The constitutional obstacle of Section 29 (2) (b) would not operate as long as legislation was so framed that there might be a restriction in fact but not in legal form, and the restriction was made applicable to all sections of the community and not to a specific group. (When S.W.R.D. Bandaranaike's Official Language Act[9] was introdcued in the House of Representatives in 1956, the Speaker ruled that it was not a constitutional amendment and therefore required only a simple majority.) Nevertheless, the proven ineffectiveness of Section 29 (2) (b) as a check on encroachments on the interests of the minorities did not make that clause any more palatable to Buddhist activists. They continued to view it as an ostentatious concession to minority influence, and persisted in agitating for its elimination.[10]

The state transformed

The consequences of this transformation of nationalism for the processes of state-building may be outlined as follows. First, the concept of a poly-ethnic polity ceased to be politically viable any longer. In Sinhala the words for 'nation', 'race' and 'people' are practically synonymous, and a multi-ethnic or multi-communal nation or state is incomprehensible to the popular mind. The emphasis on Sri Lanka as the land of the Sinhalese carried an emotional popular appeal, compared with which the concept of a multi-ethnic polity was a meaningless abstraction.

Secondly, the abandonment of the concept of a poly-ethnic polity was justified by laying stress on the Western concept of a democratic sanction deriving its validity from the clear numerical superiority of the Sinhala-speaking group. At the same time the focus continued to be an all-island one, and Sinhalese nationalism was consciously or unconsciously treated as being identical with a Sri Lanka nationalism. The minorities, and in particular the Tamils of Sri Lanka, refused to endorse the assumption that Sinhalese nationalism was interchangeable with the larger Sri Lanka nationalism.

Similarly, the association of Buddhism with the state and the simultaneous reduction of Christian influence, especially after 1970, were integral features of the abandonment of the concept of a poly-ethnic polity. The political leadership in both major national parties, the SLFP (Sri Lanka Freedom Party) and the UNP, successfully held out against the agitation to elevate Buddhism to the status of the official religion of the state. However, with the adoption of a new Constitution when the island became a republic in 1972, the position changed.[11] Chapter II of that Constitution laid down that: 'The Republic of Sri Lanka shall give to Buddhism the foremost place and accordingly it shall be the duty of the state to protect and foster Buddhism while assuring to all religions the rights granted by Section 18(1) (d).' This same principle of a special status for Buddhism was also embodied in the 1978 Constitution which superseded the old one.

Third, linguistic nationalism was a populist nationalism. The masses —especially the rural masses—had entered the political arena, and no longer could political activity be confined to the elite. Linguistic nationalism had an appeal which cut across class interests, and it evoked as deep a response from the Sinhalese working class as it did from the peasantry and the Sinhalese-educated elite.

One of the notable consequences of this emergence of Sinhalese Buddhist populism was the setback it gave the Marxist movements. With independence and the first elections to the House of Representatives in 1947, they had emerged as the most potent challenge to the government of the day, if not yet a credible alternative to it. Their aspiration to this status of the alternative government was now thwarted by the emergence of linguistic nationalism and the populist form it took in the mid-1950s. The cosmopolitan outlook of the Marxists and their enlightened advocacy of a multi-ethnic, secular polity proved to be profoundly disadvantageous, and they were compelled to compromise on these issues without, however, any substantial political benefits. It is in this regard that the coalition between the SLFP and the left, established in 1964, becomes deeply significant. In joining the SLFP in a coalition, the Marxist left abandoned their opposition to the former's language policy and were no longer as strongly committed to a secular state as they had been in the past. They were protecting their mass base from further erosion by the attraction of linguistic nationalism to their supporters. As a result they were reduced in time to the status of appendages of the populist SLFP. In retrospect it would seem that the two Bandaranaikes between them established a new equilibrium of political forces within the country to which their supporters and associates, as well as their opponents, have had to accommodate themselves. The primary feature of this new balance of forces was an acceptance of the predominance of the Sinhalese and Buddhists within the Sri Lanka polity, and a corresponding reduction in status and significance of the ethnic and religious minorities.

Although the Buddhist movement was generally hostile to Marxist ideology, it had no strong opposition to the adoption of a socialist programme. Since plantation enterprise, nascent industry and the island's import and export trade were dominated by foreign capitalists, and the minorities were seen to be disproportionately influential within the indigenous capitalist class, Buddhist pressure groups viewed socialism as a means of redressing the balance in favour of the majority group. Every extension of state control over trade and industry could be and was justified on the grounds that it helped curtail the influence of foreigners and the minorities. The Sinhalese Buddhist section of the capitalist class was not averse to socialism as long as its own economic interests were not affected. This ambivalence towards state control over the economy was also reflected in the inner circles of the populist SLFP, by its attempt to reconcile a commitment to a hazy socialism with an advocacy of the interests of a section of the indigenous capitalist class — the Sinhalese Buddhist segment of it.

But it meant that resistance to state control over the dominant sectors of the national economy was so much weaker than it may have been if economic interests in themselves had prevailed over the divisive forces of ethnicity and religion. The result was that in Sri Lanka the economy was dominated and controlled by the state to a far greater extent than in other parts of South Asia. This state domination of the economy has persisted despite all attempts, since 1977, to liberalise the economy.

The salience of the complex problems of decentralisation in Sri Lanka's contemporary politics begins in the post-independence period. The political structure of Sri Lanka was a highly centralised one — indeed, an over-centralised one. The processes of centralisation encouraged and deliberately pursued by the British in the nineteenth century proved to be a formidably stable legacy. The early proponents of decentralisation were Sinhalese: Bandaranaike himself argued in favour of federalism in 1926 and for a form of provincial councils in the 1940s and the early years of independence; representatives of Kandyan opinion had advocated a three-unit federal structure for Sri Lanka in the late 1920s and thereafter. After independence the main, if not the sole, demand for devolution of power through federalism or a regional councils scheme was from Tamil political groups beginning with the Federal Party from its establishment in the late 1940s. All the island's governments since the mid-1950s have had to confront strong popular opposition to any tampering with the country's unitary political structure because of suspicions that the demand for federalism was only the thin end of the wedge of a separatist movement. Those in the forefront of the agitation for a federal state contributed greatly to this situation of pervasive suspicion by being vague, deliberately or unconsciously, in the terminology they used in their arguments, blurring the distinction between provincial autonomy, states' rights in a federal union and a separate state. As a result the island's successive governments since the 1950s have been reluctant to concede legitimacy to the political activity involved in the agitation for a federal state. The antipathy to separatist agitation, naturally, has been even more pronounced.[12]

Thus linguistic nationalism has exalted the state, contributed powerfully to state control over the dominant sectors of the economy, and acted as a brake on all attempts to deviate from the excessively centralised structure inherited from the British. At the same time, linguistic nationalism in its Tamil version provides the most potent threat to the integrity of the Sri Lankan polity and this persistent tension between two conflicting forms of linguistic nationalism is thus the root cause of Sri Lanka's current political crisis.

Notes

1. For discussion of this see K.M. de Silva, *Social Policy and Missionary Organizations in Ceylon. 1840–1955* (London: Longmans, Green and Co., 1965). See particularly pp.64–137.
2. Ibid.
3. K..M. de Silva, 'Christian Missions in Sri Lanka and their Response to Nationalism, 1910–1948'. in P.L. Prematilleke, *et al.,* eds., *Senerat Paranavitana Commemoration Volume: Studies in South Asian Culture,* (Leiden: Brill, 1978), V, 221–33.
4. K.M. de Silva, *A History of Sri Lanka* (London: Oxford University Press, 1981), pp.339–55.
5. De Silva, 'Christian Missions in Sri Lanka'.
6. On linguistic nationalism and its impact on Sri Lanka, see K.M. de Silva, *Managing Ethnic Tensions in Multi-Ethnic Societies: Sri Lanka, 1880–1985* (Lanham, MD: University Press of America, 1986), pp.196–226.
7. On the background for this period, an outstanding study is W. Howard Wriggins, *Ceylon: Dilemmas of a New Nation* (Princeton, NJ: Princeton University Press, 1960). See also D.E. Smith, ed., *South Asian Politics and Religion* (Princeton, NJ: Princeton University Press 1966).
8. For an excellent exposition of the viewpoint see, D.C. Vijayavardhana, *Revolt in the Temple* (Colombo: Sinha Publications, 1953); and *The Betrayal of Buddhism,* report of the unofficial Buddhist Committee of Inquiry (Balangoda, Sri Lanka, 1956).
9. The Official Language Act No. 33 of 1956. An Act to prescribe the Sinhala Language as the One Official Language of Sri Lanka and to enable certain transitory provisions to be made.
10. One of the reasons why an autochthonous constitution was adopted in 1972, rather than a comprehensive revision of the Soulbury Constitution, was the need to eliminate this clause.
11. On the processes of constitution-making, see K.M. de Silva, 'A Tale of Three Constitutions: 1946–8, 1972 and 1978'. *The Journal of Historical and Social Studies* (new series), 7 (2), pp.1–17.
12. For discussion of this theme see de Silva, *Managing Ethnic Tensions,* pp. 373–5.

5 MINORITIES IN BURMESE HISTORY

Ronald D. Renard

Of all the countries in South-east Asia, Burma faces the most perplexing minority problems. Out of a total of 35.3 million inhabitants in 1981, there were 28.3 million Burmans, 3.14 million Shans, 1.55 million Arakanese, 2.40 million Karens and other, smaller, groups such as the Kachin, Chin and Wa. Historically, the response to the existence of many different ethnic groups was always to intermingle freely. As the historian, Victor Lieberman,[1] has shown, political and ethnic units were distinct from one another in pre-British Burma. The Burman kings, who might be part Mon or part Shan, of, say, the Toungoo dynasty, had retainers who were Burman, Mon, Karen and Shan. The Mon kings of Pegu, who might be part Burman, part Karen, or part Shan, had retainers who were Burman, Mon, Shan and Karen. Three factors, according to Lieberman, were paramount in building loyalty among the different ethnicities. Patron-client bonds and the moral legitimacy of Buddhist kings were two. The third, negative, factor was the difficulty of welding regional unity. In a country where successors to the throne were known to kill all rivals, including brothers and uncles, losing factions readily aligned themselves with rival claimants or fled to other states where groups of other ethnic backgrounds lived. How, then, did the phrase 'minority', as used in Burma, come to denote ethnic minorities? What has so changed the state of relationships in Burma that Shan and Karen rebels are fighting for autonomy? There is no record of such ethnic unity in pre-British Burma, yet many of these rebels claim that never in the past did Burmans co-operate or intermingle with Burmans.

To answer these questions, an examination of British influence on the Burmese consciousness of minorities is necessary, since minorities only became a topic of concern to the residents of Burma after the first Anglo-Burmese War of 1824–6 and the ensuing contact with the British. At the beginning of the nineteenth century, the very notion of racial minorities was new in England. The British were influenced by the romantic nationalism, popular at that time in Europe, which extolled the people of their respective nations. Romantics and nationalists, including Lord Byron and Giuseppi Mazzini, believed that nations possessed a mythical individuality based on a shared heritage and common culture. They advocated the overthrow of old empires such as Austria-Hungary and the creation of new nations such as Italy and Germany which would enable the genius of the particular nationalities to express itself fully.

This process was encouraged by the invention of more accurate mapping techniques. Improved theodolites, allowing for more accurate angle measurements with portable instruments, made it possible for a country territorially to define its limits with accuracy. As time passed, residents of the various European countries came to believe that one nation ought to include only members of that nation and non-members should belong to others. Irredentism was a natural outgrowth as many countries, not just Italy, seeking their 'unredeemed', tried to bring their fellow nationalities into the same country. This line of thought, however, when pursued to its extreme, makes international co-operation impossible — a fact that the current unharmonious situation among different ethnic groups indicates.

Robert Taylor,[2] Victor Lieberman, E.R. Leach[3] and I[4] have shown how the British introduced these concepts of 'nation' and 'boundary' to Burma so that in many ways they have been internalised by the local residents who now deny the existence of any former way of thought. What scholars have not explored so fully is the definition of 'minority' in traditional Burma, the topic of this chapter. To arrive at a satisfactory definition appropriate for pre-British Burma, new concepts must be proposed.

This exploratory work examines new ways of conceptualising minorities in Burmese history which may be used instead of contemporary definitions. Taylor and Leach have shown how different ethnic groups operated in what is now Burma. Taylor discusses its comtemporary implications, and Leach shows that Shans and Kachins interacted in one area. No one, however, has looked for themes and methodologies operative in the whole of what is now Burma. In this chapter, I outline one way of defining minorities in Burma, and discuss some implications of that definition.

Definition of 'minority'

Minority means 'a racial, religious, political, national or other group regarded as different from the larger group of which it is part'. But in political terms, this definition is inadequate and clearly does not reflect current usage. Whites in South Africa, members of the royal family in the United Kingdom and Communist Party members in the USSR comprise only a small portion of the populations of those countries, but these groups are not disadvantaged or estranged. Minority has wider connotations than merely the numbers implied by the word's dictionary definition.

The study of minority groups, mostly by American scholars, has reached the point where one sociologist, Graham Kinloch has proposed a theory of minority group relations. According to Kinloch, minorities are *created* by majorities. In the process of nation-building, during which, for example, the notion of minority in Burma changed, as one group defines itself as a nation those outside the group become minorities. Kinloch states that a minority is 'any group that views itself and/or is defined by a majority power elite as different and/or inferior on the basis of assumed physical, cultural, economical, and/or behavioural characteristics and is subject to exploitation and discrimination.'[5]

In pre-British Burma, there were no racial minorities in Kinloch's terms. Racial minorities were created in the eighteenth and nineteenth centuries as European colonial elites moved on to other continents. Utilising biological theories common in the early-nineteenth century, the British and other Europeans concluded that certain groups of peoples and races shared physiological characteristics so that some races were more capable than others. Although historians of pre-British Burma have studied ethnic groups, they have not studied minorities in Kinloch's terms. G. H. Luce examined different ethnic groups in Pagan, but he tried more to say what peoples populated Pagan rather than consider which groups were alienated or disenfranchised.[6]

There were, of course, minorities in traditional Burma — people close to the power elite who considered themselves superior and people estranged from the power elite who were considered inferior. These criteria for establishing majorities (who might in fact be a small portion of the population as, say, white people in South Africa today) were not based on race or even ethnic group, but on access to power. Minorities, thus, are those people with poor access to power.

In order to determine who comprised the power elite majority of traditional Burma, a new look at this country's traditional governance must be taken. An examination of traditional Burmese life must separate those groups with access to power and those without. Only by doing this can an accurate assessment of majority and minority be made.

One immediate problem is that in pre-British Burma there has rarely been one centre of political power. Only at the height of the Toungoo Dynasty (1486–1597) and the Konbaung Dynasty (1753–1886) did one power dominate most of what is now Burma. For most of Burma's history, the different states competed for power. The Mon-ruled kingdom of Pegu remained a power in the Burma delta from as early as 825 until 1757. Arakan in the west was an independent kingdom from perhaps the second century until the last king was deposed in 1785. Various Shan states competed for power from the thirteenth century until the British accession, some defying even the power of the Konbaung kings. Besides these states, there were numerous mountain peoples who, for most of their lives, were essentially free of control by lowlanders. Mountain dwellers were not necessarily less powerful than valley dwellers. Leach aptly shows that in some places the Kachins in fact wielded more power than their supposed lowland overlords. As a result, there rarely was a Burmese state with one ruling centre and one set of minorities; usually a variegated pattern prevailed.

Further complicating the question of minority groups in pre-British Burma is the underpopulation that characterised Burma at that time. As is true for all mainland South-east Asian countries, the high birth-rate of the local people was offset by a high mortality rate, resulting in low population numbers. The main purpose of fighting wars was to take prisoners of war back to the victor's heartland. Thus, the many wars that characterised pre-British Burma created a high population mobility in which entire segments of a state's people were uprooted and moved elsewhere. This created high mobility in terms of status as well. Today's elite in one state losing a war would become tomorrow's alien minority in the winning state. Similarly, in pre-British Burma there was much voluntary movement. If a ruler displeased his subjects, they might easily decide to move.

The consequence is that pre-British Burma had large groups of people undergoing acculturation. For example, the descendants of prisoners brought back by Bayinnaung and settled near Ava would eventually become Burmese. Than Tun notes that after one or two generations the ancestry of such people had generally been forgotten. However, Than Tun points out that in pre-British Burma different notions of ethnic relations were held. He says men from Ayutthaya brought to Burma as prisoners of war and assimilated into Burmese life, 'could not be adjudged unpatriotic for completely severing their links with Ayutthaya (or Thailand) because they would not understand patriotism as we know it today'. Thus many individuals in Burma can identify with more than one ethnic group. Maha Bandula, for example, the great general in the first Anglo-Burmese War, is believed by Burmans to have been a Burman but Kachins assert he was Kachin.[7]

Instead, then, of looking for minorities in relation to one central dominant power, might there be a set of minorities in parallel locations in the structures of the different states? There were quite a number of unifying factors in the states of pre-British Burma. Two were that all these states were ruled by kings generally upholding Indic concepts of kingship and all were Theravada Buddhists in principle (after the fall of Pagan).

Power in pre-British Burmese states

Kings of pre-British Burma—whether Burman, Mon, Shan or belonging to another ethnic group—ruled using various Indic rites and guidelines. In symbolic terms, kings upheld the Dhamma (sacred law), were patrons of Buddhism and, by sitting at the 'centre of the universe', served as microcosmic Indras, absorbing the powers of the god himself and ruling as strongly and benevolently as he. From the palaces of the kings of Burma emanated power and authority that diminished in proportion to distance from the centre. Myriad practical factors —rival rulers, physical obstacles, internal politics and warlike neighbours—kept the kings from controlling all of their domain. Indeed, in the Shan state of Mogaung in the nineteenth century, Kachin uplanders were prevented from entering the city after dark because the titular rulers feared they could not control the Kachins. The powers of kingship worked regardless of the king's ethnicity; Mon, Shan and Burmans all confronted similar opportunities and problems. And when the occasional Wa or Kachin or Kayah became a ruler of a lowland state, he inevitably took on the trappings of Buddhist kingship even when not a Buddhist.

Buddhism in Burma, however, was not doctrinally the same as early Buddhism. Just as, for example, the Code of Manu was Burmanised[8] when it came to Burma, so too was Buddhism. The Buddha's methodology for avoiding suffering on earth remained essentially almost the same, but when Buddhism was adopted by different Southeast Asian peoples, their previously held beliefs influenced parts of the Buddha's message. Animistic practices emerged. The folk Buddhism of pre-British Burma varied between the different states. An emphasis on power led to a recognition of various forms of power: political, spiritual and magical. Political power in the Buddhist sangha generally was centred in the major states with famous patriarchs, such as Saddhamatthiti under King Naeapati of Burma who is customarily associated with royalty.

As with political hierarchies in pre-British Burma, leadership did not descend from the top in an unbroken line. Different factions and schools gained ascendancy for various periods of time with the result that, even in one centre, no one group dominated for long.[9] At its worst, this competition degenerated into power struggles.

Spiritual power, although closely related to high-ranking monks, also had strong links with forest ascetics who were supposed to lead a pure life. Tracing their origins to the early monks of India, forest ascetics repeatedly led reforms of Buddhism in the major centres. Living in rural areas away from the corrupting influences of the big centres, these monks were widely believed throughout pre-British Burma to be purer morally and spiritually.

Magical power rested with those spiritually strongest and with those having links with the forests. Rural dwellers and hill folk who lived in the forests were often considered more adept in the ways of magic. Monks who passed *vassas* (rains retreats) in the hills close to these upland Karens, Was, Chins and others learned how to deal with the spirits, and in addition to their spiritual powers also became powerful in the use of magic.

Hierarchies developed, with temples, abbots, patriarchs, different orders and schools in competition and disagreement over textual details, points of ritual and doctrinal interpretations. In all the Buddhist communities in Burma, a hierarchy existed with *sangharajas* or *thathanabaings* at the top and the monks, novices, nuns and lay helpers below them. In addition, 'temple slaves' often took care of monasteries and their grounds. These people, sometimes prisoners of war or retainers of a rich man donated to the monarchy, were considered somewhat inferior in status to freemen (*phrai ahmu dan*).[10] However, being a temple slave meant freedom from having to worry about many problems besetting one's neighbours. Temple slaves did not have to serve as soldiers or pay taxes. Those who were temple slaves often did not wish to change their status, and non-temple slaves often tried to change theirs. Although in terms of Kinloch's definition temple slaves could be considered a minority, they suffered little and were, in some cases, the envy of their majority neighbours.

Peoples of states and stateless peoples

If there were no groups readily equated as religious minorities in the cities of Buddhist societies, there certainly were on the fringes. Considerable status was attached to being Buddhist as opposed to not being Buddhist. Similarly, those who had been Buddhist longer were more prestigious, as the Mons were in comparison to the Burmese whose Theravada Buddhism came from Sudhammavati (Thaton), according to Burman chronicles of 1057. With it came various aspects of Indic civilisation—its art, literature and writing scripts. These Indic features that came with Buddhism blended with earlier Hindu borrowings to create a society with many aspects in law, kingship, architecture and music. This resulting 'Buddhist' civilisation contrasted with many non-Buddhist societies in the hills and in the extreme lower Irrawaddy delta. Just as Buddhists of longer standing were considered more prestigious than more recent converts, so too were Buddhists considered to be better persons than non-Buddhists. When, for example, the founder of Mon Hariphunichai, the *rishi* Vasudeva, was unable to find a suitable ruler for his new city among the indigenous Lawa (calling them 'forest creatures of the race of fools'), he invited the princess Cammadevi from the Dvaravati town of Lavo to become the new ruler.

The process by which uplanders and lowlanders diverged took centuries, but probably became obvious at the time when Indic civilisations were appearing in the lowlands during the first centuries. By the time these states were formed, lowland rice cultivation had been possible for centuries[11] and various groups in the lowlands were making a sufficient surplus from their agriculture so that they could engage in activities beyond those necessary for mere survival. As these states grew, they came to dominate upland communities; Cammadevi, for example, defeated the ruler of the Lua, Vilangka, soon after the former's arrival at Hariphunchai. As the lowland states developed, more elaborate structures, monuments, temple/monastery complexes and irrigation works were built. Trade developed, and these states supported increasingly large populations.

On the outside of these states lived uplanders and those in the far reaches of the lowland valleys. Trade closely bound those ruling the states and those on the margins, and numerous rituals emerged linking the two. In the East India Company's Gazette of 1926 British officials noted that Karens were the Burma delta's principal agriculturalists, supplying the market with fruits, vegetables, cotton and sesame. Similarly, Leach has noted that Shans and Kachins were always in close political relations[12] and the Karens were similarly close to the Mon, Burman and Shan lowlanders.[13]

What these marginal peoples did not share with the leaders of the state was religion. There is no indication that uplanders absorbed Hinduism or Buddhism from lowland centres. Although pagodas are occasionally found in the hills, they are usually in upland valleys, not on remote peaks and far from Buddhist centres. The recently discovered burial sites on the Thailand–Burma border near Tak Province have, for example, yielded perhaps only one Buddhist relic.[14] Despite the presence of bronze and iron artefacts, and magnificent Ming Dynasty, northern Thai, and perhaps some Burmese pottery indicating the wealth of those responsible for the sites, there is an absence of Buddhist or Hindu religious items.[15] Remote groups in the lowlands were also non-Buddhists — these included Karen, Wa and other groups such as the Kachin. Long ago there were members of major groups such as Thais and Burmans who were also non-Buddhist, but in Burma there were apparently none. Some such non-Buddhist groups, like the Tai Ya (related to Tai Nua of Xishuang Ban Na in Yunnan), lack a written script, elaborate architecture, Indic notions of kingship and many other attributes of Buddhist civilisations.

Non-Buddhist groups rarely adopted Indic elements of civilisation that came with Hinduism and Buddhism. Much of the language borrowings coming with the new religions did not, of course, reach non-Buddhists. Nor did the architecture, since many of the structures Buddhists built were religious edifices which those without universal religions (such as Hinduism and Buddhism) did not build or palaces which were found only in large states. For lack of manpower, uplanders built few stone structures. Nor would there have been a written script, an Indic calendar, law codes like those of Manu or other such importations.

When these groups did manifest actions evidencing Indic — which in many ways in pre-British Burma was equated with civilised — influences, they were garbled and significantly different from the already modified South-east Asian versions of the Indic original. Thus millinerial cults, which customarily originated in mountainous or otherwise remote areas, combined all manner of custom and practice. The nineteenth-century Ywa Telakhon cults of the Karens in eastern Burma combined political dissatisfaction with lowlanders, millenarial aspirations (the Karen's white, long-absent brother will return with the book of divine wisdom and lead the Karens to greatness), powerful weapons, and magic rites—derivations from Buddhism, practices reflecting Indic kingship and indigenous arts.[16] Although sometimes led by disaffected lowlanders—such as a Mon fisherman in 1782[17]—equally as often they were led by marginal peoples and most of the followers were also from marginal areas.

All these features—lack of Buddhism, the absence of states or no more than very small ones, illiteracy, low-level architecture and confused Buddhist practices—caused majority peoples to look upon these others with disdain. In so doing, lowlanders regarded marginal peoples as uncivilised ruffians who were in all probability inferior human beings. When, for example, Christian missionaries began preaching to Karens in the early nineteenth century, a Burman official objected that the Karens were too ignorant to know right from wrong and could be easily deceived.

> This is the way you do, is it? You come and fight us and get away part of our country, and now you wish to turn away the hearts of the poor ignorant Karens...but if you gave these books to the Burmans who know too much to be carried away with their nonsense it would not matter: but what do the poor ignorant Karens know?[18]

These Karens who lived mainly in forests were supposed to take on attributes of their environment, considered a dangerous place, with diseases to which non-forest dwellers were uniquely susceptible.[19] In Tai, Burman and probably Mon areas, people spoke of city folk (*khon muang mrou tha*) and hill folk (*chao khao chao doi chao loi taungthu*). Forest residents were called *yain* (wild) or *kha* (slave, savage) by Burmans and Tais who deplored their 'uncivilised' ways.

Backwoods people were considered better hunters, with longer endurance and a better sense of smell. They were also feared for their death magic. As the evidence from the history of Hariphunchai indicates, these beliefs in the superiority of city folk is of long standing. Vasudeva told that the inferiority of the Lua came from their having been born in the footprints of elephants, rhinoceroses, buffaloes, other animals and phantom creatures of the forest. Vasudeva added that the Lua 'wild men' lacked the ability to distinguish right from wrong and, although called men, were incapable of holding royal power. The oft-cited Burman injunction against Karens becoming Buddhist monks before the time of King Mindon (1853–78) shows that this way of thinking endured until recent times.[20] Similarly, when Burmans or Shans referred to uplanders, they would use derogatory phrases: for example, 'two Karen animals' or 'a beastly Kachin'.[21]

Burman, Shan and Mon chronicles rarely mentioned uplanders. Mon chronicles, although probably seeing Karens on a daily basis, 'never' used the word 'Karen'. Today Karen rebels nostalgically recall years of Mon–Karen friendship. In 1948, Karen nationalists petitioned the British for the establishment of a Mon–Karen autonomous state: 'The Mons and the Karens [are] traditionally brothers and sisters having always had the highest regard for each other',[22] read the statement. In fact, however, when representatives of the Mon court responsible for writing chronicles looked at the Karens, the latter group were considered unimportant. Burman and Shan chronicles similarly ignore Karens, Kayahs and other uplanders. Only in small states such as Mong Yawng (north-east of Kengtung), near powerful uplanders such as the Kayahs, are there references.[23] When lowlanders in pre-British Burma wrote chronicles, they wished to glorify the state and Buddhism — not to make ethnographic notes. Chronicles did not believe marginal people brought honour to the recounting of lowland state history because they considered them semi-civilised rustics. When chronicles did refer to uplanders it was to prominent individuals who were usually identified by lowland Indic titles and whom the chronicles identified as lowlanders.[24]

Burman and other city dwellers often scorned uplanders, considering them unintelligent, shabbily dressed and malodorous, god-forsaken wild men of the jungle who could not speak clearly.[25] Lowlanders believed that these wild men ate food unfit for human consumption such as monitor lizards, rats, vultures, coucals and a remarkable dish prepared from dusky leaf monkey — in which the fur was singed off and, after removing only the portion of the large intestine with hard stool, the rest of the animal, chyme and all, was curried.[26] Lowlanders also deplored highlanders; probably the cold water caused illnesses, but this rationale was lost on the city dweller. Divergent practices led to the belief that uplanders were insusceptible to diseases deadly to lowlanders, as Rambo[27] has shown for Vietnam.

These beliefs, it should be noted, were not based on ancestry: the Burmans (Shans and Mons) had no objection to people with Karen (or Kachin or Chin) blood from becoming monks. They were, however, opposed to people *living like* Karens from becoming monks. A number of Burman or Mon princes are known to have fled to the hills after unsuccessful struggles for power. One, for example, was Maung Maung Pon, who changed his name to Papaw Gyi and became a prominent leader of the Kayah state, Tharawaddy, in the early nineteenth century. As far as can be told, he 'became' a Kayah.

Although he may well have entered the monkhood himself for a short time in his youth, the Burmans surely would not have allowed his descendants to be monks. Rulers of states granted marginal peoples considerable autonomy in their daily lives, making few attempts to incorporate them into states. Marginal people considered themselves overlords of the marginal peoples, and utilised them as spies, porters and guides. Kings bought rice, but sometimes also simply requisitioned it.[28] Backwoods peoples were also taxed in kind for jungle produce and crops such as cotton, but rarely for cash.

The case of Papaw Gyi indicates a trend in the history of Burma which is perhaps as old as the eighth or ninth centuries, when the Burmans themselves moved out of the hills. They met the Mons in the lowlands and began the transformation from upland peoples to inhabitants of states.[29] As non-majority groups gained enough power to create their own states, they did so on the model of extant Buddhist states. Thus, the Pa-o, a Karennic ancestral group, have borrowed numerous Shan customs, and many Pa-o deny that they and the Karens share anything in common. By South-east Asian standards this is true; race as a distinction between groups is an invention of the West. Traditional groups in Burma did not classify people in this way. When the Pa-o elevated themselves to become state rulers, governing such small statelets as Hsa Htung, Wan Yin, Loi Long and Bawnin,[30] and adopted Buddhism, they ceased thinking of themselves as uplander or marginal Karen and began to think of themselves as lowlander or majority Shans. When the Kayahs established their own states, they too considered themselves rulers of powerful states, one step above the Karens whom they considered their vassals by presumptive right. Similarly, the Wa and Palaung who ruled states such as Mang Long and Tawngpeng adopted many adornments of lowland Buddhist states, and developed similar relations with marginal peoples around them. Even the physical and political situations went against this pattern, as Leach has shown, and when the uplanders were more powerful than the lowlanders, the uplanders paid homage nevertheless to the lowlanders 'as if' the lowlanders were the more powerful. Occasionally, too, marginal peoples moved into close contact with a major state, and paid taxes and offered services on the same basis as other residents of the lowland states.[31]

Once, however, a person changed from an upland or lower delta person and became a resident of a civilised state, that person was considered to have become another kind of human being. Leach and other students of ethnic groups[32] have shown how readily individuals could change ethnic affiliation in pre-British Burma. But once these changes were made, residents of the societies involved considered the change as total. In a parallel case about 75 years ago in Mong Hai of the Xishuang, Ban Na, a man of Akha descent, moved to Mong Hai where he became a high-ranking official. Quite a few residents of at least one Akha village no longer recognised this man as having been an Akha. In another case, noted above, the prisoners of war brought from Thai areas whose descendants became Burmans had a different understanding of patriotism and heritage.

Minorities in pre-British Burma

What existed in pre-British Burma was a world wherein identity was based on environmental habitat. Lowland wet-rice agriculturalists almost always, particularly in the seventeenth, eighteenth and nineteenth centuries, lived in states; upland swiddeners or hunters and gatherers were considered stateless and less civilised. The distinctions between marginal peoples and those in the states were most pronounced in the great centres. And since the Burman capital was usually the grandest such centre, the most extreme differences were there. Relations between Shans and Mons and the marginals, although sometimes inamicable, were generally smoother. This is implied in the ritual unity of Kachin–Shan dealings and in Karen memories of the adequate Mon–Karens dealings: 'Relations between the Mons and Karens must have been adequate,' said one Karen leader, 'the elders have nothing to say about it.' He added that Karens hold grudges; if problems between the Mons and Karens had existed, the Karens would have remembered.

In so far as minorities existed in these states, the main group of minorities were these marginal peoples living on the fringes of civilised states. These people were minorities estranged from power. The majority peoples looked down on them mainly because they considered the backwoods peoples uncivilised and a lower form of humanity. Where the states were smaller and distinctions between majorities and minorities less defined, relations were more amicable. Where the states were bigger, distinctions and animosities were the most pronounced.

The fact that upland groups such as the Karens and Kachins were ethnically different and numerically inferior to the Burmans, Shans, and Mons, and thus would be considered minorities today, is conceptually coincidental and irrelevant. In pre-British Burma, minorities were not members of the great states and did not have many Indic cultural attributes. In British and post-Independence Burma, minorities were and are numerically inferior groups. They are considered minorities because they were ethnically different from the majority people. An understanding of how this change occurred might be a first step on the way to reconciliation between the Burmans and all the many ethnic minority groups in Burma who believe they have reason to fight the majority. Without recognising traditional patterns and how they have been transformed during the British period, one cannot foresee any end to the present Burmese minority problems short of total conquest by the majority or total separation for these minorities.

Notes

1. Victor Lieberman, 'Ethnic Politics in Eighteenth-Century Burma', *Modern Asian Studies, 12* (3), 1978: *idem, Burmese Administrative Cycles, Anarchy and Conquest, 1580-1760* (Princeton, NJ: Princeton University Press, 1984).
2. Robert H. Taylor, 'Perceptions of Ethnicity in the Politics of Burma', *Southeast Asian Journal of Social Science, 10* (1), 1982.
3. E. R. Leach, *Political Systems of Highland Burma* (Boston: Beacon, 1954).
4. Ronald D. Renard, '*Kariang* History of Karen Tai Relations from the Beginnings to 1923' (PhD dissertation, University of Hawaii, 1980); idem, 'The Delineation of the Kayah States Frontiers, 1809–1894', paper presented at the 9th Conference of the International Association of Historians of Asia, Manila, 1981.
5. Graham Kinloch, *The Sociology of Minority Group Relations* (Englewood Cliffs, NJ: Prentice Hall, 1979), p.180.
6. G.H. Luce, 'Old Kyaukse and the Coming of the Burmans', *Journal of the Burma Research Society, 42*, 1959. Gavin Daws, 'Looking at Islanders: European Ways of Thinking about Polynesians in the Eighteenth and Nineteenth Centuries', *Topics in Culture Learning, 2*, 1974, describes a similar transformation in the South Pacific where Polynesia was 'invented or perhaps better created for the West in 1768', when Bougainville's ship reached Tahiti. Previous visitors to Polynesia had not seen the islanders as much other than ordinary people, but the French created the notion of the 'noble savage'.
7. Jaitun Chao, interview with Shan from Hsipaw living in Chiang Mai, 1977.
8. Aye Kyaw, 'The Origin and Growth of Customary Law in Thai Burmese Societies', paper presented at the 9th Conference of the International Association of Historians of Asia, Manila, 1983.

9. B.J. Terwiel, *Monks and Magic: An Analysis of Religious Ceremonies in Central Thailand* (Bangkok: Scandinavian Institute of Asian Studies Monograph no. 24, 1975).

10. *Phrai*, a Thai term not much used outside the Chao Phraya valley, refers to 'freemen' who owed service to the king. Similar practices existed in areas outside of Ayutthaya under Thai/Tai control, although this term was not always used. *Ahmu-dan* also owed service directly to the kings of Burman states. *Phrai luang* and *ahmu dan* resemble each other closely, but are not identical.

11. Joyce White, 'The Ban Chiang Tradition: Artists and Innovators in Prehistoric Northeast Thailand' in Joyce White, ed., *Discovery of a Lost Bronze Age*, Ban Chiang (Philadelphia: University of Pennsylvania, 1982).

12. Leach, *Political Systems of Highland Burma*.

13. Ronald D. Renard, '*Kariang* History'.

14. John Shaw, 'The Tak Hilltop Burials' (Chinag Mai: mimeo, 1985).

15. Ibid.

16. Theodore Stern, '*Ariya* and the Golden Book: A Millenarian Buddhist Sect Among the Karen', *Journal of Asian Studies*, 27 (2), 1968.

17. Michael Symes, *An Account of an Embassy to the Kingdom of Ava in the Year 1795*, 2 vols (Edinburgh: Constable, 1827).

18. C.H. Carpenter, *Self-Support Illustrated in the History of the Bassein Karen Mission from 1840 to 1830* (Boston: Rand Avery, 1882.)

19. For example, the Karen border chief of Sangkhlaburi in the nineteenth century had the Thai-Indic title Phra Si Suwannakhiri, which gives no indication that this man is a Karen.

20. Stern, '*Ariya* and the Golden Book'.

21. James George Scott, *Burma and Beyond* (London: Grayson & Grayson, 1932).

22. Ba U Gyi Saw et al., 'Annex A to the Minutes of the Third Meeting of the Karen Affairs Subcommittee, November 13', presented to the Chairman of the Regional Autonomy Enquiry Commission (Rangoon: 1948).

23. Sawangpannyakun Thawi, trans., *Tamnan Muang Yawng* (Mong Yawng Chronicle) (Chiang Mai: Chiang Mai University, 1984).

24. Karens, who are not native speakers of Burmese, often omit aspiration: *hlei* (boat) is often mispronounced *lei* (wind), and *hli* is notoriously misspoken *li* (penis).

25. A. Terry Rambo, 'Environment and Development: The Place of Human Ecology in Southeast Asian Studies Programmes' in Tunku Shamsul Bahrin, Chandran Jeshurun and A. Terry Rambo, eds., *A Colloquium on Southeast Asian Studies* (Singapore: ISEAS, 1981), tells that when Vietnamese settlers moved into the uplands, they built their houses on the ground with their cooking fires outside. The uplanders in those areas built their houses on stilts and kept domestic animals underneath. They also cooked in their houses. This discouraged the presence of malaria-carrying mosquitoes which stayed lower to the ground where they were distracted by the animals. The Vietnamese newcomers, however, without these acquired defences against malaria, suffered a much higher rate of infection.

26. Benny Gyaw, interview with former Burmese civil servant, Karen now living in northern Thailand, 1976.
27. Rambo, 'Environment and Development'.
28. Lieberman, *Burmese Administrative Cycles*.
29. G.H. Luce, 'Note on the Peoples of Burma in the 12th and 13th Centuries', *Journal of the Burma Research Society, 42*, 1959.
30. James George Scott and A. P. Hardiman, *Gazetteer of Upper Burma and the Shan States*, 5 volumes in 2 parts (Rangoon: Government Publication, 1900–1).
31. Lieberman, *Burmese Administrative Cycles*.
32. Charles Keyes, ed., *Ethnic Adaptation and Identity: The Karen on the Thai Frontier with Burma* (Philadelphia: ISHI, 1979).

6 NATIONALISM AND THE STATE IN THAILAND*

Likhit Dhiravegin

Introduction

Nationalism comes with the formation of a nation state. But this does not necessarily mean that all nation states have to be nationalistic. The argument posited here is simply that nationalism is different from ethnocentrism. Ethnocentrism implies a sense of superiority of one ethnic group over others, whereas nationalism denotes a high degree of national consciousness by exalting one's own nation above other nations. In this sense, nationalism can only exist in a nation state. Traditional China is a case where a sense of cultural superiority existed, but China was far from nationalistic. Indeed, nationalism in the modern sense of the term did not exist in China until the May 4th Movement of 1919. Even then it took a long time before nationalism took root in a country where the idea of a nation state was alien. China saw itself as the Middle Kingdom and its relations with other states were based on the tributary system.

In the case of Thailand, modern nationalism was non-existent until the campaign of King Rama VI, who tried to instil into the Thai a sense of nationalistic feeling with anti-Chinese sentiments as the stimulant. However, one can argue, as mentioned above, that the foundation of nationalism starts with the formation of a nation-state. In this regard, due credit has to be given to King Chulalongkorn who, through his reform programme, brought about a Thai nation state in lieu of the traditional kingdom. The process was a long and painful — but peaceful — one involving a number of courageous and astute policies. Such policies included, among other things, a centralised administrative system in national administration, a fiscal system, military organisation and, most important of all for a modern nation state, a centralised educational system.[1]

*   This study was undertaken as part of a project by the Association of Local Leaders. This project would not have been possible without the support of Mr Prida Kanoknark, Secretary to the Minister attached to the Prime Minister's Office. My thanks also go to the officers of the Office of the Prime Minister who facilitated the collection of data.

The greatest contribution of King Chulalongkorn was the creation of a Thai nation based on a more of less common culture, with Bangkok culture being dominant. The great monarch was able to transform the concept of the Thai nation based on the Thai or Tai ethnic group into a Thai-cultured Thai. This was done by two significant steps. The first was to incorporate the ethnically different outlying areas of the south, north and north-east into a new Thai nation state. Second, attempts were made to assimilate — and in certain cases integrate — the different ethnic groups into the mainstream of the new Thai nation state based on Bangkok dialect, Buddhism, and the metropolitian culture of the capital city. The Bangkok dialect became the official language and a *lingua franca* and was the only medium of instruction allowed in schools, government or the private sector. The assimilation of the other ethnic groups into the Thai nation state was indeed a success, but perhaps too successful in that it stifled local identity, creativity and pride. If the creation of a modern Thai nation and a Thai nation state is taken as a start, it was King Rama VI who gave the Thai nation state the dynamism of nationalism.

What King Rama VI did was to stir up nationalistic feelings among the Thai by espousing an anti-Chinese ideology. The monarch's attitude towards the Chinese can best be seen from his book, *The Jew of the East*, patterned upon Western anti-semitic tracts. King Rama VI turned the concept of the 'yellow peril' into the Chinese peril to fit it into the Thai social context of his time. It is beyond the scope of the present paper to analyse the underlying motives of the monarch, which could be described as a combination of factors — the most important of which was a political campaign against the elements, many of them of Chinese origin, who were antagonistic towards the absolute monarchical system of the time and, second, an anti-Chinese campaign to serve as a foundation for the creation of nationalistic feelings among the Thai. Organisationally, King Rama VI made use of the 'Wild Scouts', a paramilitary organisation to serve such a purpose. The 'Wild Scouts' also served as a force to counterbalance the military organisation under certain powerful princes. The relevant and significant point to be noted here is that King Rama VI continued where King Chulalongkorn, his father, left off. If anything, King Rama VI was instrumental in bringing about a complete process of creating nationalism in the modern Thai nation state.[2]

It should be clear that nationalism in Thailand is only a recent phenomenon. It came with the creation of the modern nation state of the Thai, reinforced by King Rama VI's anti-Chinese policy. In spite of its rudimentary nature, it served as the basic psychological foundation for the Thai's vigorous indoctrination with nationalistic sentiments in the modern period, a point which we will discuss later.

The main focus of this chapter is to discuss nationalism in relation to Thailand as a nation state. Following this introduction, we will discuss the nationalistic policy of Field Marshal P. Pibulsongkram. Then we will deal with the nationalistic feelings of a group of local leaders, whose views were derived from a field survey conducted in late 1984. The findings from the field survey should give a picture of the degree of success of the governmental policy in its campaign. The figures derived from the research project should reveal significant political findings and implications, many of which were probably the result of Pibulsongkram's campaign, a point to which we may now turn.

Rathaniyom or 'statism'

One of the most memorable and most controversial policies of Field Marshal Pibulsongkram was that of *Rathaniyom* or 'statism', implemented in a series of movements by Pibulsongkram, who was Prime Minister at the time, most notably in the late 1930 and early 1940s. The motive was to stimulate the Thai people to develop nationalistic feeling. This was in response to the perceived necessity at that time for a strong Thai state to meet the challenges of the international situation. Pibulsongkram envisaged a Thailand with a strong pride in its historical past and a refined culture, a populace with a good education and appreciation of the 'civilised' culture of the West. One of the more ludicrous orders he gave the nation was for men to kiss their wives before going to work. All Thai were expected to wear a hat as a sign of civilisation. Many of the instructions issued by the government only reflected the attitude of the government leaders of the time. The Thai as a people were probably viewed by Pibulsongkram as 'uncivilized' in comparison to their Western counterparts. As a result, there was a great need and urgency to get rid of this stage of backwardness. An examination of the announcements of Pibulsongkram will give a clear picture of both the situation of the society at the time as well as the leader's attitude to the Thai people.[3]

Nationhood and national identity

King Rama VI's nationalistic campaign was mainly based on anti-Chinese sentiment. Pibulsongkram's *Rathaniyom* sought to combine two elements, anti-Chinese policy—which came out in the form of laws reserving certain occupations for the Thai people, thus excluding aliens, most of whom were Chinese, from engaging in these occupations—and a positive nationalist campaign, one aspect of which was the attempt to create or improve the Thai nationhood and national identity. To be sure, King Chulalongkorn and his son, Rama VI, had laid the foundation for a Thai nation state, but the sentiments had yet to take root. The campaign needed to be intensified to complete this process. First and foremost was the need to create a new Thai nation. The name of the country was changed from Siam to Thailand, as announced in *Rathaniyom No. 1* on 24 June 1939. The Siamese people and nationality were to be referred to as Thai. Some held that the change of the country's name was related to Pibulsongkram's grandiose scheme of turning the country into an empire by incorporating lost territories such as Laos, part of Burma, and Cambodia where there were ethnic Thai, into Thai-land. Whatever the reason, this move was to transform the country into an assimilated Thai (mainly Bangkok) culture and leadership. One of the purposes was to put an end to primordial sentiments, characterised by an identity based upon regional and ethnic loyalties. This was to be seen from *Rathaniyom No. 3*, dated 2 August 1939. It suggested that such names as Thai Nua (northern Thai), Thai Isan (north-eastern Thai), Thai Tai (southern Thai), and Thai Islam (Thai Muslim) were not appropriate for a country like Thailand, which was a unitary state. It suggested that the word 'Thai' should be used instead. This point was again emphasised in *Rathaniyom No. 9*, dated 24 June 1940, item 3 of which said that the Thai people should not take place of birth or domicile or accent or dialect as a sign distinguishing one group from another. The people should feel that anyone born Thai has the same bloodline and speaks the same language. One important practice which was suggested and has now become part of the Thai culture was to stand up to pay respect to the national anthem and flag when it was hoisted in the morning and when it was taken down in the evening. The flag would be raised and lowered while the national anthem was being played. This policy was announced in Rathaniyom No. 4, dated 8 September 1939. It set the tone for statism, national pride symbolised by paying respect to the 'tricolour', blue standing for monarchy, red for the nation and white for religion. The policies contained in these various announcements were aimed at creating a strong nationhood for the Thai, a Thai national identity transcending primordial sentiments, and at least symbolic display of loyalty and nationalism by paying respect to the national flag and anthem. It sounds almost like a military state, but the motive is clear: to create a Thai nation state with a common identity and loyalty toward one common political unit, a Thai-land.

National security and public interest
The second theme of Pibulsongkram's nationalism campaign was in the areas of national security and public interest. This is contained in *Rathaniyom No. 2*, announced on 3 July 1939. The essence of this policy includes the following guidelines:

1. Thai citizens must not carry out any activities which do not take into consideration national interest and national security.
2. Thai citizens must not reveal any secret which would be harmful to the country and must not reveal it to foreign nations because such an act constitutes an act of treason to the country.
3. Thai citizens must not act as agents for foreign nations without due regard to the interest of the Thai nation. They must not side with foreign nations on issues which are in dispute with Thailand; those who do so are considered to commit acts of treason.
4. Thai citizens must not buy land on foreigners' behalf because such an act is harmful to the national interest and is an act of treason.
5. Whenever one sees someone who commits treason, he is duty-bound to put a stop to it.

It can be seen from the above that the policy laid down in Rathaniyom No. 2 is phrased in strong terms. It demands great commitment and loyalty to the Thai nation. At the same time it probably reflected Pibulsongkram's fears that his enemies might do things contrary to governmental policy. However, what is clear is that it demands a strong commitment to Thai national interest.

Economic nationalism
Economic nationalism is also an integral part of the *Rathaniyom*. The objectives were to encourage support for local products and to encourage the Thai people to become industrious by engaging in productive economic activities, not idling away their time and energy. This policy, announced in *Rathaniyom No. 5*, dated 1 November 1939, stipulated the following guidelines:

1. Thai people should consume foodstuffs produced in Thailand.
2. Thai people should wear clothes made from materials manufactured in Thailand.
3. Thai people should support their country by patronising agriculture, commerce, industry and other professions of the Thai.
4. Any public utility operated by the Thai government or the Thai people should be patronised by the Thai.
5. Those working in agriculture, commerce, industry and other professions which are given support by the government must try to improve quality and maintain a good standard, and should pursue their livelihood with honesty and integrity.

In *Rathaniyom No. 7*, announced on 21 March 1940, the government urged the Thai people to engage in work which would be economically productive for the country. Working was equated to rendering help in nation-building. The Cabinet promulgated a resolution which said:

> Every Thai with an able body must help in the process of nation-building by having an occupation. Those who do not work are those who do not play their part in helping build up the Thai nation, and they do not deserve any respect from the Thai people in general.

The economic nationalism mentioned above is reflective of the government's policy, as well as reflective of a situation considered by the government to be unhealthy. It is common knowledge that the Thai people, when compared to the Chinese, are not so energetic, especially in earning a livelihood. The government was probably frustrated over the situation and tried to encourage the Thai to undertake any job which would earn them some income. As a policy to stimulate the Thai to become nationalistic economically, it is in line with a policy to increase foreign reserves and to promote Thai products, agriculture and industry. But, of equal importance, it was aimed at creating a sense of pride and identity among the Thai.[4]

'Social' nationalism

For lack of a better word, the term 'social' nationalism is used to denote a policy to create a Thai nation characterised by people with an education, good ethics and civilised manners. This is reflected in *Rathaniyom No. 9*, announced on 24 June 1940, which encouraged the Thai people to be proud of the Thai language, to go to school in order to learn how to read and write Thai, and to encourage literacy in the Thai language. The Thai people were also required to carry out the duty of a good citizen and to instruct those who do not know this duty to be aware of what should be done and what duty to perform.

Pibulsongkram, in a note to the Minister of Finance dated 3 May 1940, urged the Thai people to learn good manners, to become gentlemen. The Minister of Finance was to encourage all civil servants of the ministry to learn the manners of the civilised world. The note also mentioned unbecoming and selfish behaviour of the people, such as failure to line up for the purchase of tickets at theatres, not knowing how to show courtesy to ladies, the sick and the elderly, not refraining from smoking at places where it is annoying to others, destroying public property, and so on. The Thai people were also asked to use the proper kind of dress, to have civilised manners and to show courtesy in public, and to spend their time to useful purpose (*Rathaniyom No. 10, 11 and 12*). Later, a detailed campaign for a civilised culture was announced in the National Cultural Maintenance Act of 1940 and 1941, among others.[5]

All the above were aimed at creating a Thailand with a culture befitting a civilised nation. It also reflected the concern and frustration of the leaders who were aware of the situation which needed to be rectified. However, it could also be taken as part of a comprehensive *Rathaniyom* or 'statism', The overall policy encompassed the building of nationhood, national identity, national security and public interest, economic nationalism and culture. It was indeed a formidable task, difficult even to imagine. The policy was at times ridiculed by critics. But given the situation of the time and given the trend of taking Westernisation as civilisation and given the necessity of having a modern nation state in which the citizens could be counted upon to play a contributory role imbued with a sense of civic obligation, political consciousness, national identity and cultural pride, the efforts of Pibulsongkram—although some of them might appear to be too demanding or too dictatorial—should be viewed with a more objective eye. One should also bear in mind that similar movements, such as that of Atatürk, or the New Life Movement of Chiang Kai Shek, took place elsewhere, and indeed it is suspected that the *Rathaniyom* policy could have been inspired by these movements. Whatever the evaluation of the *Rathaniyom*, it could be taken as a step toward the creation of a modern Thai nation state which combined a sense of nationalism, cultural pride and 'civilised' patterns of behaviour with the anti-Chinese policy discussed earlier. The *Rathaniyom* policy was a policy of nationalism put into operation. Indeed, much of today's nationalistic sentiments could be traced back to the mobilisation program engineered by the *Rathaniyom* policy. It has laid down the psychological foundations of present-day Thai nationalism and the nation state, an aspect of which we now turn our attention to.[6]

The nationalism of Thai local leaders

The nationalistic sentiments of the local leaders to be discussed in this part of the chapter will be based upon empirical data derived from a study conducted in late 1984. On 17–20 December 1984, a meeting of the representatives of local leaders at the *tambol* (commune) and village levels was held for the first time in history. It was organised by Mr Charn Manutham, Minister attached to the Office of the Prime Minister. The main purpose was to sound out the opinion of these local leaders (who were invited to participate in a three-day seminar and sightseeing of places of interest and significance in Bangkok) regarding the establishment of an Association of the Federation of Local Leaders in Thailand. In order to reap the benefits of the presence of such a big group of local leaders representing the five regions of Thailand, a field survey of the group was undertaken. The total number of participants was 360, including the *tambol* leaders or *kamnan*, village leaders and deputies, the *tambol* medics or doctors, and *kamnan* assistants. A ten-point questionnaire was used to find out these local leaders' nationalistic sentiments. The questionnaire was handed out to each of the local leaders during lecture breaks and collected from them two hours later. A total of 294 questionnaires were returned from the 360 local leaders (81.7 per cent). Sixty-six local leaders did not return their questionnaires because they did not finish filling them out and had to leave the conference early. The data were then fed into the computer for analysis and cross-tabulation. However, it was found that there was not much difference among the local leaders with regard to nationalism, national pride and attitudes towards foreigners. This may stem from the fact that the group is rather homogeneous.

General characteristics of the local leaders
Of the total number of 294 respondents, 31.0 per cent came from central Thailand, 23.5 per cent from the North, 17.7 per cent from the South, 23.1 per cent from the North-east and 4.8 per cent from the East. As for their positions, 23.8 per cent of the local leaders were

kamnan, 37.8 per cent village headmen and deputies, 17.7 per cent *kamnan* assistants, 20.4 per cent *tambol* medics or doctors, with 0.3 per cent giving no answer. In terms of religious denomination and sex, the group was also very homogeneous. The majority of the local leaders were Buddhists (95.2 per cent), only 0.7 per cent were Christians, 3.7 per cent were Muslims and 0.3 per cent gave no response. The majority of them were male (96.6 per cent) while 2.4 per cent were female and 1.0 per cent did not respond. As for occupation, 71.5 per cent were engaged in rice farming, cash-crop planting and orchard-keeping, 17.3 per cent in trading or business, 3.7 per cent in wage labour, 1.0 per cent in fish and shrimp farming, 0.3 per cent in orchard-keeping and trading, 4.4 per cent in 'other' occupation, and 1.7 per cent gave no answer. It can be seen from the above that the local leaders under study as a group are very homogeneous in their background, religious belief, sex and occupation.

Two important variables are age and educational level.[7] This is because age and education are found to influence attitudes and values, especially classic liberalism and conservatism. The great majority (70.7 per cent) of the local leaders were aged between 41 and 55. Those aged between 41 and 60 constituted about 80 per cent. While the mean age, 47, can be considered as young, the age factor, which was expected to bring about variation in the local leaders' attitudes, may have been affected by the education variable, education not being at a very high level.

The majority of the local leaders (almost 80 per cent) received only primary education. Only 16 per cent had an education beyond primary level, and an insignificant number were holders of junior degrees or bachelor's degrees. These findings are to be expected, because so many of the local leaders were engaged in agricultural occupations and the majority were tied to the village. There is thus no compelling reason for them to undergo a high level of education. This somewhat low level of educational achievement could be expected to affect the local leaders' nationalistic feelings and attitudes towards foreigners; they were likely to be on the conservative side. Moreover, the majority of the local leaders' nationalistic sentiments and pride in the Thai nation could be expected to be in line with governmental policy or propaganda. The ideas of the local leaders are expected to be conventional, in accordance with the schooi curriculum for such subjects as civics and moral lessons.

National pride and nationalistic sentiments of the local leaders

National Pride. National pride and nationalistic sentiments are often, though not necessarily always, related. In our study, it was found that national pride among the local leaders was high. The majority (82.3 per cent) of local leaders, when asked, if they had a choice, what nationality they would want to be born into, said that they would choose to be born Thai. In another similar question, we asked whether they would want to be born Thai in the next life (reincarnation in Buddhist belief), to which the vast majority (94.2 per cent) said they would. Although these responses indicate that the local leaders are proud of being Thai, one can also look at the situation in a different light. First, these local leaders may have been caught by surprise by these two questions. They might never have thought about the matter and thus what they answered could have been a conditioned reflex. Second, given the low level of education, and given the absence of opportunity to interact with foreigners — except the people of the border areas, Laotians, Cambodians, Burmese and Malay, in addition to the Chinese and Indian residents of Thailand — it is difficult for the local leaders to visualise being born as nationals of another country. On the other hand, the absence of knowledge of another country, or familiarity with other nationals, would compel the local leaders to cling to their ethnicity. This would make them feel attached to their national identity more than those individuals who are more international in outlook because of a higher level of education. One respondent said he would like to have been born a Scandinavian: he held a master's degree from abroad.

In order to find out what contributed to the national pride of the local leaders, they were asked to name three things which make them proud of being Thai, to which nearly half (49.3 per cent) mentioned the trilogy of the Thai nation, its religion (Buddhism), and the monarchy, with 63.8 per cent mentioning one or more of the three elements of the trilogy. A small number mentioned democracy (2.4 per cent) and 1.0 per cent mentioned the country's prosperity. The role of the trilogy in sentiments of national pride is striking. Indeed, if there is any ideology to speak of, the trilogy may be said to be the major political ideology of the Thai. The question is whether these answers reflect 'formalized national pride' as a result of a governmental campaign policy, or the genuine situation. No definitive answer is possible without further investigation. But given the positive role played by the monarchical institution regarding the welfare of the

people, and given the visits made by the King and other members of
the Royal Family into even remote villages, there are good reasons to
argue that the sentiments expressed by the local leaders reflect what
they really feel.

Much of national pride may be the result of what one thinks about
national history. To be sure, most nations glorify their past. This is an
inevitable and necessary first step in nation-building. The case of Thai
history is no exception. History lessons in schools focus on the
glorious past of the Thai kingdom, the great leaders and heroic wars.
Whether the description of history is true or not is irrelevant here.
What is important is that pride in one's national history is instilled by
the socialisation process at school. When asked if they thought the
Thai nation had in the past been a great nation or just a small one,
61.9 per cent said that the Thai nation had been great while 28.6 per
cent said it had been a small, ordinary nation. This reflects the fact
that pride in the history of the Thai nation is part of the political
socialisation process contained in the school curriculum. It suggests
that the national pride campaign of the Ministry of Education has
been rather successful.

However, when the local leaders were asked if they thought of
themselves as Thai, or as other people based on regions, such as a
southerner or a northerner, their answers were noteworthy. Although
the majority thought of themselves as Thai (68.4 per cent), there was a
small but significant number who thought of themselves as nationals
of the region. This may reflect the remnants of regionalism or localism
which outweigh the national Thai identity. Others mentioned both
Thai and other identities, suggesting either a lack of understanding of
the question or the phenomenon of 'dual identity', which should
perhaps be construed as thinking of oneself as Thai. If so defined, the
number who thought of themselves as Thai would be 85.4 per cent, a
proportion suggesting that the nation-building process has been
successful.

Nationalistic sentiments

Nationalistic sentiments can be generated in two ways: first, positively, by inculcating a sense of national pride and loyalty towards the
nation, a point which we have already discussed; second, arousing
negative sentiments against certain groups or people, usually minority
groups in the country or peoples of different ethnicities in the
neighbouring countries where some form of conflict—such as a border

dispute — has already become an issue. This negative nationalism is most noted in developing countries because of the need to bring about national unity by finding a common enemy. On the other hand, sentiments against other ethnic groups can serve as a means to divert the attention of the people from policy failures on the domestic front. Sometimes this had led to war as a means to externalise internal problems. Historical cases of such wars abound.

In our study, we found that nationalistic sentiments in Thailand stem from a combination of the positive and negative approaches.

Positive Nationalistic Sentiments. The local leaders were asked two questions regarding their nationalistic attitudes. The first was whether they would want to emigrate to another country. The second was whether they would volunteer to fight against an enemy which attacked Thailand. The answers given are impressive. The majority of the local leaders said they did not want to emigrate to other countries (91.8 per cent), and the majority (92.5 per cent) also said they would volunteer to fight for the country. While these answers can be interpreted legitimately as reflecting the positive aspects of the local leaders' nationalistic sentiments, — emotional attachment to the motherland and the willingness to sacrifice their lives for the country in times of war — it can also be taken as a pro forma or formalistic answer or conditioned reflex, just like the cases of national pride. While the second interpretation may be valid, one can also argue that, judging from the historical record of struggles against such national enemies as Burma, the Thai people's loyalty and commitment to the motherland is not lacking. What the local leaders said may truly reflect their nationalistic attitudes. What should be noted is the 7.5 per cent who did not respond to the question about volunteering to fight against an invading enemy. It may reflect the fact that they were not sure about their answer, or it may reflect an unwillingness to volunteer which they did not want to express.

Negative Nationalistic Sentiments. Negative nationalistic sentiments are characterised by negative attitudes about other groups, usually of different ethnicity. To measure this aspect of nationalistic sentiment, three questions were asked of the local leaders. One question was whether they thought the Japanese, Chinese, Indians, and so on, could be trusted. A Likert-type question with a five-point response scale was used. The second question was patterned after the Bogardus scale of social distance, inquiring whether the local leaders would vary in their relationships with a number of foreigners, with marriage ties being designated as the closest type of relations. The local leaders were then asked in a third question to name foreigners whom they disliked.

Nationalities whom the local leaders 'distrust' or 'distrust strongly' are the Burmese, Vietnamese, Cambodians and Laotians. The Burmese are a case which can be explained easily. Being a traditional enemy in history, bitterness against Burmese has been instilled into the minds of the Thai. As a result, distrust of Burmese is to be expected. As for Vietnamese, Cambodians and Laotians, this can be explained by the fact that the three Indochinese states have not been on good terms with Thailand since the mid-1970s. Campaigns against these three countries have become both a foreign policy stand as well as a domestic mobilisation. If anything, it shows that the campaign policy of the government has borne fruit, or that the local leaders simply toed the line of the government. However, this attitude is reinforced by the degree of relationship the local leaders would want to extend to foreigners. The numbers of those who want to associate with Burmese, Vietnamese, Cambodians and Laotians only at the level of acquaintance are high: 51.4, 50.3, 54.1 and 51.5 per cent respectively.

Those who would like to co-operate in work with the four groups of people mentioned above or take them as close friends or enter into a close or intimate relationship with them constitute only a small fraction of the survey population. At this level they were more favourably disposed towards the Chinese, Japanese and Westerners, with the Chinese proving the most popular of these three groups. This may stem from the long and close relationship between the Chinese and the Thai and the increase in intermarriage.[8]

A very high percentage of the local leaders expressed their dislike for three groups of people: Vietnamese, Cambodians and Laotians (36.1 per cent). Almost 80 per cent expressed dislike for the Vietnamese; 56.5 per cent expressed dislike for Cambodians, and 50 per cent for Laotians. Again, one can explain this situation by taking into account the governmental policy campaign against the three Indochinese states as the underlying factor contributing to such an attitude. At the same time, it can be argued that the border war refugee problems and the communist regimes in the three Indochinese states could also serve as a reason for the development of such an anti-Indochinese sentiment among the local leaders.

Conclusion

Nationalistic sentiments or nationalism in Thailand, as we have briefly discussed, may be said to have passed through three stages: the stage of formation of the modern nation state during the reign of King Chulalongkorn, followed by the stage of anti-Chinese nationalism during the reign of King Rama VI and the government of Field Marshal Pibulsongkram. Then came the present stage of anti-Indochinese nationalism. The question is whether this anti-Indochinese sentiment reflects nationalism or is just a conditioned reflex resulting from government policy and campaign. Dislike of foreigners can be interpreted in terms of nationalistic feeling, but it can also be interpreted as ethnocentric sentiment without coalescing into nationalism as generally understood. In the case of Thailand, it seems to be a mixture of the two.

It may be concluded that while a good foundation for nationalistic sentiments has been laid down by past leaders, development into full nationalism with a positive approach, such as dedication to national interest, pride in Thai culture — but not blind adherence to outdated customs and traditions — rational analysis of the objective situation of the country rather than emotional assessment of the situation clouded by dogmatic belief and emotional commitment to an outlandish goal, must be attempted.[9] This type of rational, emotionally mature nationalistic sentiment is yet to be developed in Thai society. The ground has been prepared, but it needs to be further nurtured for the tree of nationalism to grow healthily. This may be a most painful process and a herculean task to undertake.

Notes

1. For a discussion of the reforms of King Chulalongkorn, see, among many others: Detchard Vongkomolshet, 'The Administrative, Judicial and Financial Reforms of King Chulalongkorn, 1868-1910', (unpublished MA thesis, Cornell University, 1958); Tej Bunnag, *The Provincial Administration of Siam 1892–1915* (London: Oxford University Press, 1977); David Wyatt, *The Politics of Reform in Thailand: Education in the Reign of King Chulalongkorn* (New Haven, CT: Yale University Press, 1969).
2. For a discussion of King Rama VI's nationalism campaign, see Walter Vella, *Chaiyo! King Vajiravudh and the Development of Thai Nationalism* (Honolulu: University of Hawaii Press, 1978).
3. For an English translation of the *Rathaniyom* Announcements, see Thak

Chaloemtiarana, *Thai Politics, 1932–1957 (Extracts and Documents)*, vol. 1 (Bangkok: Social Science Association of Thailand, 1978), pp. 244–54.

4. This economic nationalism has been revived by the government of General Prem Tinasulanonda in 1985, and has been dubbed 'Premanomics' by some people.

5. Chaloemtiarana, *Thai Politics*, pp. 255–60.

6. Even today, Pibulsongkram's nationalistic sentiments are often mentioned with admiration. Indeed, if anything, his inspiration has given the Thai a sense of direction, regardless of its merits or otherwise.

7. Likhit Dhiravegin, *Political Attitudes of the Bureaucratic Elite and Modernisation in Thailand* (Bangkok: Thai Watana Panish, 1973), pp. 39–44.

8. One statement which has now become a cliché is that the Thai and the Chinese are nothing less than brothers.

9. During the Thanin Kraivixien regime in 1977 which came to power after the coup of 6 October 1976, ultra-conservative campaigns were launched. All the programmes, although born of good intention, became a political nightmare for the Thai people.

PART III: BUDDHIST INSTITUTIONS AND MINORITIES

7 BUDDHIST RESURGENCE AND CHRISTIAN PRIVILEGE IN SRI LANKA, C. 1940-1965*

K.N.O. Dharmadasa

Introduction

This chapter deals with a very significant phase in the long-drawn out encounter between Sri Lanka's once powerful Christian minority and its Buddhist majority. Earlier stages in this encounter are surveyed in an outstanding study by K. Malalgoda[1] in which the reader will find an absorbing review of the eighteenth-century revival of Buddhism, and an account of the emergence of the present institutional structure of the Buddhist order, its various sects (called *nikayas*) and the failure to evolve a central organisation. The same author provides a trenchant analysis of the issues involved in the Buddhist–Christian confrontation of the last quarter of the nineteenth century[2] in which we see the emergence of two new centres of Buddhist learning established in the 1870s, the two *pirivenas* of Vidyodaya (1873) and Vidyalankara (1875) in the suburbs of Colombo. In the present chapter the Vidyalankara *pirivena* and its alumni play a central role.

For the political background to the mid-twentieth century conflict between a resurgent Buddhism and Sri Lanka's Christian minority, the reader could turn to the works of W. Howard Wriggins[3] and K.M. de Silva.[4] It would be superfluous, therefore, to go in any great detail into this background in the present chapter, which will confine itself to a brief review of some of the issues that emerged at this time, to some of the key personalities involved in the principal controversies of the period, and to a look at an emerging shift in the balance of power within the Buddhist institutional framework. It will also demarcate some of the stages by which the erosion of Christian privileges was successfully achieved.

In Chapter 5 of the present volume, K.M. de Silva makes the important point that while the Christians, both Roman Catholic

* I gratefully acknowledge the help I received from Professors K.M. de Silva and C.R. de Silva in the preparation of this article.

and Protestant, were less than a tenth of Sri Lanka's population, they were a privileged minority wielding considerable power and influence. By the 1940s this influence and power, if not yet the prestige of the Christian minority, were in decline.[5] The Buddhist activists, bhikkhus as well as laymen, were unwilling to countenance the continuance of Christian privilege, and were intent on effecting a further substantial reduction of these, if not their total eradication. For this purpose they focused their attention on the schools which they regarded as the source of Christians' dominance of public life. The Roman Catholics were the dominant influence in the education system through their efficiently run network of schools. They were, at this stage, the principal defenders of the status quo in education which by the 1940s was under systematic attack by Buddhist activists.

The Vidyalankara *pirivena* and the political bhikkhu movement

The Buddhists' campaign was spearheaded in the 1940s by the bhikkhus of the Vidyalankara *pirivena*, which at that time became the centre of an unusual religious ferment: unorthodox and essentially political in outlook, anti-colonial, and socialist if not Marxist. Many of their alumni who went to India for higher education were deeply influenced by the Indian nationalist movement and quite often by the latter's Marxist component. Of the bhikkhus who thus went to India in the 1930s and 1940s, five are important in the agitation we review in this chapter: Udakandawela Saranankara (1902–66); Naravila Dhammaratana (1900–73); Hadipannala Pannaloka (1903–53); Walpola Rahula (b. 1907), who had the distinction of being the first bhikkhu to graduate from the University of Sri Lanka; and Bambarande Siri Sivali (1908–85). On their return to Sri Lanka they turned to political activity with the Marxist party, the Lanka Sama Samaja Party (LSSP), established in 1935, and other radical forces.

Drawn into the struggle against the continued Christian dominance of the school system, they were soon among the most ardent supporters of the education reforms initiated in the late 1930s. The most controversial and far-reaching of these reforms came after 1943 following the publication of the truly epoch-making *Report of the Special Committee on Education* in 1943.

There were three main issues: first, that education should be in the student's mother tongue, Sinhala or Tamil, instead of in English; second, that education should be made 'free', that is to say no tuition fees be charged at all levels of education — primary, secondary and tertiary — with the state paying for it all; and third, that a change be effected in the system of grants-in-aid to schools run by missionary organisations and other religious bodies. K.M. de Silva explains why these proposals were so controversial:

> While the reforms proposals envisaged the continuation of these mainten-
> ance grants by the state, they went well beyond the conventional grants-in-
> aid system by making provision for payment of salaries of teachers in
> the denominational schools provided, however, that tuition fees were
> abolished. The Christian missions viewed these proposals with deep
> suspicion. The dilemma they faced was that while the payment of teachers'
> salaries would relieve them of a heavy burden, entry into the new scheme
> of 'free' education posed the danger of increased state intervention in, if
> not bureaucratic control of, their schools. Yet to opt out of the scheme was
> to lose the maintenance grants on which the vast majority of these schools
> depended for survival. Only the few elite denomination schools could
> survive without grants-in-aid from the state.[6]

The Roman Catholic church in Sri Lanka led the opposition to these changes. Ranged against them were a wide variety of forces: a section of the board of ministers intent on carrying out these reforms quickly; a majority of legislators; Marxist and radical forces in the country; and, spearheading the campaign, were the Buddhist activists.

Our concern here is with this last group, the Buddhist activists and, in particular, the bhikkhus. The Vidyalankara bhikkhus saw themselves as spearheading a campaign in which they had two objectives: to reform the existing school system which they saw as 'a bastion of Christian privilege', and 'to widen the range of conflict to bring the Sri Lankan political elite, the emerging establishment led by D.S. Senanayake, within the scope of the struggle for elite displacement'.[7] While they had wide support in regard to the first objective, they had to defend their position in regard to the second.

Most Buddhists were distinctly uncomfortable to see bhikkhus engaged in political activity. Lay Buddhists were very vocal in their opposition. These critics had most of the newspapers of the day on their side, and articles and editorials came out against bhikkhu involvement in politics. The bhikkhu activists in turn felt it necessary to convince the Buddhist public that political activity was not incompatible with their religious calling. They fell back on Buddhist tradition and the Pali chronicles of ancient times, the *Mahavamsa* in particular, for precedents for what they sought to do. They began with the Buddha's injunction to bhikkhus to 'roam in the world for the good and comfort of the many' and sought to show how the Buddha himself had sometimes taken part in *mahajana sevaya* (service to the people) by attending the sick, advising householders on how to utilise their income, counselling kings on kingly virtues, and even acting as peacemaker when conflicts seemed imminent.[8]

Moving on to the history of Sri Lanka, they were on even surer ground. Various instances of bhikkhu involvement in affairs of state from the earliest times in the island's long recorded history were cited: the part they played in the choice of heirs to the throne, reconciling factions in civil wars, administering civil justice and training heirs apparent.

The Venerable Walpola Rahula's first book, *Bhiksuvage Urumaya* (1946), drew material from scriptures, commentaries and historical chronicles to present an impassioned case for the 'political' bhikkhu. His principal argument was that historically the bhikkhu had always played an active role in the life of the community. The modern bhikkhu, Rahula asserted, was acutely aware of that *urumaya* (heritage), and when confronted with the reality of contemporary decline in national and religious life considered it his duty actively to help arrest that decline. *Bhiksuvage Urumaya* became a manifesto of the 'political' bhikkhus.

As we have seen, the key figures in this movement were on the teaching staff of the Vidyalankara *pirivena*, by then the most dynamic institution of monastic learning in the country. Historically, Vidyalankara and its slightly older sister institution, Vidyodaya, had been parent institutions to most of the 124 *pirivenas* that had sprung up in various parts of the island by 1947. The latter had been founded by alumni of these two institutions and generally looked up to Vidyodaya and Vidyalankara for leadership and guidance in academic and other matters. These peripheral *pirivenas* provided the Vidyalankara bhikkhus with a ready network of connections in many parts of the island.

There was no ready acceptance of this new model of the bhikkhu, the bhikkhu as political activist, within the sangha itself where more orthodox views on the bhikkhus' role in society were strongly entrenched. The 'political' bhikkhus at first did not make any great impact on the established institutional structure of contemporary Sri Lankan Buddhism with its three main *nikayas* or sects: the orthodox or conservative Siyam *nikaya* and the rival Amarapura and Ramanna *nikayas*. So they resorted to improvising an organisation of their own, one of the first modern associations of bhikkhus in Sri Lanka, the Lanka Eksath Bhikkhu Mandalaya (LEBM), or United Bhikkhu Organisation of Lanka. It was a small but very articulate group, whose membership cut across the traditional *nikaya* divisions.

Many of the prominent members of the LEBM came from Vidya-lankara; these included the five leading figures mentioned earlier. All of them belonged to the Siyam *nikaya*, the preserve of the dominant *goyigama* caste, and thus one may not impute their thrustful spirit to the assertiveness of bhikkhus from non-*goyigama* castes. There is one notable consideration, however: they hailed from relatively poor temples in the coastal areas. The Vidyalankara bhikkhus were at loggerheads with the *nikaya's* hierarchy in Kandy and other bhikkhu dignitaries appointed by that hierarchy. They regarded these personages as being slavishly submissive to the colonial government and the emerging Sri Lankan political establishment led by D.S. Senanayake.

While the hierarchy at Malvatta and Asgiriya, the headquarters of two chapters of the Siyam *nikaya*, would not appove of the radicalism and unorthodox style of the Vidyalankara group, there was one point on which they both saw eye to eye: the bhikkhus' historical prero-gative to be heard on matters of public concern. An example of this is seen in the foreword to a polemical work of this period by D.C. Vijayawardhana, a close associate of the Vidyalankara bhikkhus, written by Pahamune Sumangala, the *Mahanayaka* of Malvatta from 1927 to 1945. In it he argued that:

> The claim of the Sangha today to be heard in relation to social, political and economic problems and to guide the people is no new demand but a re-assertion of a right universally exercised and equally widely acknow-ledged up to the British occupation of the country.[9]

To return to the education reforms and legislation of the mid-1940s, D.S. Senanayake, the most powerful of the political figures of the 1940s, and soon to be the island's first post-independence prime minister, pointedly declared his opposition to them. Indeed, the Board of Ministers was sharply divided on this controversial legislation. Fortunately for the advocates of education reform the constitutional structure of that period — the Donoughmore Constitution — gave individual members of the Board of Ministers and even 'backbench' legislators much greater independence than under a cabinet system; the result was that while Senanayake did not conceal his opposition to this Bill, he was unable to prevent either its presentation in, or its approval by, the legislature and its implementation if adopted by it. But he could attempt to delay the debate on it and could and did use his powerful influence to soften its impact.

Delaying tactics were devised in the hope that once the elections to the first Parliament were held in the last quarter of 1947, there would be a new minister of education, and that in any case there would be cabinet government and cabinet discipline, and with a new government and a new minister there could be a new Bill less inimical to the interests of the status quo in education than the one piloted by C.W. W. Kannangara, the then Minister of Education. If its opponents within the legislature were intent on postponing the discussion of this Bill, its supporters took the issue to the public in a well-organised campaign. Three groups were involved in this campaign: lay Buddhists led by Professor G.P. Malalasekera, President of the All Ceylon Buddhist Congress, and Dr E.W. Adikaram, a leading Buddhist educationalist; Marxist and radical groups; and bhikkhu activists led by the LEBM. The Roman Catholics who led the resistance were confronted by a Central Free Education Defence Committee representing Buddhist interests.

This campaign had the desired effect. Most members of the legislature were intent on contesting a parliamentary seat later in the year, and as prospective candidates they did not wish to be seen supporting moves to postpone discussion of a Bill which had wide public support, much less to vote against it. Indeed when the time came to vote on the Bill on 15 May 1947 no one opposed it, not even D.S. Senanayake, and the bill was adopted unanimously. The role played by the bhikkhus in ensuring the bill's triumph was handsomely acknowledged by V. Nalliah, a Tamil state councillor:

> If today we are here, in a spirit of calm resignation discussing this Education Bill, we owe that fact to the politically conscious section of the Buddhist clergy. This is the first victory they have won, and that is why I say this Bill will go down in history, not because of any intrinsic merit in it, but because of the manner it will go through this Assembly...This Bill marks the first great indication of a political awareness, of an awakening, among the masses of this country.[10]

While supporters of the Bill celebrated a hard-won victory, their opponents had extracted a significant concession — 'assisted' denominational schools which did not wish to join the new scheme were to receive grants-in-aid on the old basis until 30 September 1948, after which all aid would cease. The deadline was subsequently extended after independence under a new minister of education. (Kannangara lost his seat at the parliamentary elections of 1947 to a powerful independent.) In 1949, an expatriate British Roman Catholic, Dr H.W. Howes, was appointed director of education. It was a controversial appointment both because the claims of Sri Lankans to hold this prestigious post had been overlooked and because of the insensitivity to Buddhist fears of a strengthening of Roman Catholic influence in the education system. To Buddhist critics of D.S. Senanayake, this appointment was symbolic of his continued opposition to the free education system. He could not prevent passage of the Bill, but he could control the process of its implementation.

The general election of 1956 and the triumph of Sinhalese Buddhist interests

At the general election of April 1956, the UNP was decisively defeated by the Mahajana Eksath Peramuna coalition led by S.W. R.D. Bandaranaike, who had broken away from the UNP in 1951. Language and Buddhist religion were the major issues in the election, and the two main demands from the Sinhalese Buddhist interests were the adoption of Sinhala as the sole official language and the 'restoration of the rightful status' of Buddhism.

One is struck by the concentration of attention on the language issue, and the distinct shift of emphasis away from Buddhist causes *per se* to the larger issue of ethnic rights. This affected the activities of all major Buddhist pressure groups. For example, the Sinhala Jatika Sangamaya, founded by the Venerable Baddegama Wimalawansa as a pressure group for Buddhist causes, was now committed to the advocacy of Sinhala as the sole national language. A similar shift of focus is also seen in the activities of the older All Sri Lanka Buddhist Congress, which by now was primarily a Sinhalese ethnic organization. A third organisation, the Bauddha Jatika Balavegaya (BJP), established in the mid-1950s by L.H. Mettananda, often set the pace in political activity on the language issue.

By now laymen and lay organisations, such as those mentioned above, were among the principal spokesmen for Buddhist causes.

Prominent among them were Professor Gunapala Malalasekera, President of the All Ceylon Buddhist Congress for 18 years until he resigned in 1957 on appointment as Sri Lanka's first ambassador to the Soviet Union; L.H. Mettananda, Principal of Ananda Vidyalaya, the premier Buddhist school on the island during the period 1945–55, and, as noted above, founder of the BJP in the mid-1950s; D.B. Dhanapala, principal of Gurukula Vidyalaya, a school attached to the Vidyalankara *pirivena*, in the 1940s, who resigned his post in that school in support of the 'political' bhikkhus, and later became editor-in-chief of the Sinhalese newspapers of the Times of Ceylon group; and N.Q. Dias, a senior public servant, a member of the elite Sri Lanka Civil Service, who was a key figure in setting up Buddhist societies among public servants, and who in 1954 established the Congress of Buddhist Organisations in the Government and Local Government Services. These strategically-placed laymen began a campaign for a series of far-reaching changes: the imposition of total prohibition; a state-controlled education system; and the payment of compensation by the state for the damage inflicted on properties of Buddhist and allied institutions under colonial rule.

The bhikkhu element in Buddhist activism was undergoing change. Unlike in the 1940s when only a small group of young bhikkhus from one institution — the Vidyalankara *pirivena* — were politically active, there was by now much wider participation in political activity, with bhikkhus from all *nikayas* (Siyam, Ramanna and Amarapura) appearing on political platforms. By the 1950s, they were no longer on the defensive in indulging in political activity. The campaign to establish Sinhala as the national official language and to ensure the primacy of Buddhism in the Sri Lanka polity established the bhikkhu as an unmistakably legitimate opinion leader.

Many of the new bhikkhu leaders of the 1950s held strategic positions in the ecclesiastical 'hierarchy' as heads of *viharas* (temples) which gave them a solid base and a regular network of relationships with younger bhikkhus and lay devotees to work with. In the case of some other bhikkhus, notably the Venerable Baddegama Wimalawansa, Henpitagedera Gnanasiha and Talpawila Silawamsa, the role of head of temple coalesced with that of *pirivena* principal, expanding their influence network.

Their organisational network was widened further to link up with other Buddhist activists. On 4 September 1954, the Panca Maha

Bala Mandalaya (a grand coalition of five resurgent social forces) was formed, bringing various strands of Sinhalese Buddhist interest groups into one federated whole. As the organisers of the Bala Mandalaya saw it, the five forces were *Sanga-veda-quru-qovi-kamkaru* (bhikkhu-Ayurvedic physician-teacher-farmer-worker). The chairmanship of the Bala Mandalaya was offered to an influential senior bhikkhu, the Venerable Kiriwattuduwe Prajnasara who, at that time, was head of Vidyalankara *pirivena*. The potential political importance of the associational mobilisation of these influential sections of the population became evident by the mid-1950s.

In a symbolic mixture of the traditional and the modern the Panca Maha Bala Mandalaya organised a motorcade, on 29 October 1955, from Colombo to the ancient city of Anuradhapura, where an oath was administered to, and enthusiastically taken by, the vast crowd gathered there, to commit themselves to the struggle to establish the primacy of the Sinhala language and Buddhist religion in the Sri Lanka polity. The oath was taken at the foot of the statue of King Dutthagamini, the great Sinhalese national hero of ancient Sri Lanka.

On the eve of the general election of 1956, Buddhist activists published a spate of pamphlets and a host of broadsheets mostly directed against the UNP. The Venerable Baddegama Wimalawamsa was one of the most prolific pamphleteers of the day, as the author of a series of these on the emotive theme of *Dharma Yuddhaya* (War of Righteousness), with titles such as *Aanduwa Ha Missionary Balaya* (The Government and the Power of the Missionaries), *Ada Budd-hagama* (Buddhism Today), and *Pujaka Wada* (The Activities of the Christian Priests). He also edited a newspaper called *Rodaya* (The Wheel). The burden of his campaign was that Buddhism, which had suffered greatly under colonial rule, continued to be handicapped even after independence, while Christians continued to hold an advantageous if not prominent position in the school system, health services and state employment in general. Mettananda was another indefatigable pamphleteer, castigating the baneful influence of what he termed 'Catholic Action' in Sri Lankan public life. Through pamphlets such as *Catholic Action in Sri Lanka*, *Aanduwa Bauddhayawa Ravatuwaa* (The Government Cheated the Buddhists) and *Aanduwa Kristiyanita Bauddhayawa Bilidiima* (The Government Sacrifices the Buddhists to the Christians), Mettananda charged the UNP government with being irresponsibly oblivious to the advantages enjoyed by Christians, at the expense of Buddhists.

In retrospect the mid-1950s was a period of emerging political consciousness among the people. The general election of 1956 stands out as a watershed political change 'effected by the cumulative choice of hundreds of thousands of individual voters',[11] in which voters demonstrated a surprising maturity in eschewing sectarian considerations for party policies. Indeed one is struck by the enormous contribution made by Buddhist activists in stimulating and leading popular political participation, acting as links between the political centre and the periphery, and impressing upon large sections of the population, who were generally indifferent to political issues, an awareness of their rights and privileges as members of a democratic polity. In this way these activists, among whom the bhikkhus were a major element, made a significant contribution to the politicisation of the masses on the island.

The Sinhalese Buddhist intelligentsia also represented another, less savoury, development, in sponsoring sectarian — that is, exclusively Sinhalese Buddhist — interests at the expense of larger national concerns. For example, most of them would brook no compromise on a rigid Sinhala-only language policy and no concessions that would in any way be seen as diluting the 'Sinhala only' formula. They were also strong opponents of all proposals to decentralise administration, and devolve power to regional units of administration.

Even their major achievements such as the establishment of two bhikkhu universities, Vidyalankara and Vidyodaya, and setting up a Ministry of Cultural Affairs during Bandaranaike's administration marked the triumph of a sectarian policy. The Vidyodaya University and Vidyalankara University Act of 1958 specifically state that these institutions were established to work for 'the advancement and dissemination of knowledge and for the promotion of Sinhala and Buddhist culture'. Furthermore, it was stipulated that they were to maintain Buddhist traditions, their vice chancellors were to be bhikkhus and that all statutes made by their governing councils were to be in accordance with *Vinaya* rules, the Buddhist laws of discipline for the bhikkhus.

The Ministry of Cultural Affairs, the third of the important new institutions created by the new government, underlined a commitment to promote indigenous literature, traditional arts and crafts. Under the leadership of N.Q. Dias, who was to play a key role in that ministry as its first director of cultural affairs, the priorities of this ministry were clearly the encouragement of Sinhalese and Buddhist literature, traditional arts and Buddhist activities above all else.

Buddhist institutional reform was an altogether more difficult proposition. In its most familiar form, that of defining Buddhism's 'place' in the Sri Lankan polity, and elevating it to the status of the state religion, it posed almost insuperable difficulties. A committee of inquiry, appointed in 1955 by the All Ceylon Buddhist Congress, consisting of eminent Buddhist lay leaders and a number of important bhikkhus, prepared a report on the state of Buddhism. The report was published on 4 February 1956, just before the general election of that year. It contained a detailed exposition of what the committee saw as the perilous state of Buddhism. Throughout the report there were demands for a stronger link between Buddhism and the state. Bandaranaike had committed his coalition of parties to implementing most of the recommendations in the report. After his government came to power, he appointed the Buddha Sasana Commission in February 1957 to examine the implementation of the principle of according Buddhism 'its rightful place' in the country. The Commission was also asked to make recommendations for a reform of the sangha. This commission consisted of ten leading bhikkhus and five lay Buddhist leaders. Its report was presented to Prime Minister Bandaranaike in mid-1959. But he did not live to see it published or to see the issues it raised taken up for discussion. The short caretaker government which succeeded him upon his assassination had the report published, but was politically too weak to take any follow-up action.

The three-and-a-half years of Bandaranaike's administration marked the peak of bhikkhu involvement in politics and public affairs, and the peak as well of their influence. Two powerful bhikkhus, the Venerable Mapitigama Buddharakkhita and Talpavila Silavamsa, were executive committee members of the SLFP, while Henpitagedera Gnanasiha, mentor of N.Q. Dias, was ubiquitous as a power broker. Mapitigama Buddharakkhita, the most prominent bhikkhu politician of this period was a charismatic figure, more political boss than pious bhikkhu; for a time he succeeded in bending the Prime Minister to his will and forced the latter to curb the radicalism of three Marxist or left-wing members of his cabinet. But hubris came when the Prime Minister himself was assassinated by a bhikkhu in a conspiracy hatched by Buddharakkhita — a conspiracy in which lust for power was mixed with sordid commercial greed and accusations of sexual misconduct as well.[12]

The assassination of Bandaranaike brought in its wake strong, if diffused, public criticism of dussila (impious) bhikkhus, while bhikkhu involvement in politics was roundly condemned. For some time bhikkhus thought it politic to keep away from public functions other than strictly religious ones. Significantly, at the two general elections of 1960, in March and July, there was a complete absence of bhikkhus on political platforms. In course of time, however, bhikkhus returned to politics. But it could be said that bhikkhu politics never recovered from the terrible misdeeds of that September of 1959.

The consolidation of Buddhist supremacy

During the 1960s, Buddhists made notable advances in their campaign to erode the entrenched position of Christians; they also consolidated their supremacy with the general support of all political parties, including the Marxists.

During the first government of Mrs Sirimavo Bandaranaike (1960–5), there was a reappearance of bhikkhu political involvement, although on a smaller scale than during the previous decade. Several issues propelled bhikkhus and other Buddhist opinion leaders into political action, demonstrating that despite the very real loss of prestige suffered by the bhikkhus after the assassination of S.W.R.D. Bandaranaike, they still wielded influence which could be effectively channelled into political activity.

The central issue during the early-1960s was the completion of the process of state control over education begun by Kannangara. Prime Minister Bandaranaike and his Minister of Education, W. Dahanayaka, had preferred to leave the status quo in education undisturbed.[13] With the Assisted Schools and Training Colleges (Special Provisions) Act of 1960, the new government under Mrs Bandaranaike went ahead with extending state control over the 'assisted schools' system largely controlled by Christians. The Roman Catholic hierarchy put up a resolute opposition to the move, and there was a period of acute tension which fortunately did not lead to any serious outbreak of violence. With the state takeover of schools, the Christian minority lost the power of patronage over appointments of teachers and support staff to these schools as well as the admission of students.[14] In practical terms the Buddhists could now expect an increase of their own influence over the educational system under state control. The long-drawn-out Buddhist agitation in a vital sphere of public life had at last achieved its goal.

Christian groups suffered a further erosion of influence to the advantage of the Buddhists with an abortive *coup d'etat* led by Roman

Catholic and Protestant officers in the armed forces and police in 1962.[15] Any support the government may have lost in its tough stand on the schools takeover was now recouped in its struggle against a still formidable set of opponents. More important, this incident provided the justification for the government to support Buddhist activists in a propaganda campaign against the Christians, and in particular the Roman Catholics.

Governor-General Sir Oliver Goonetilleke, an Anglican, was suspected of complicity in the coup attempt, and was replaced by William Gopallawa, a Sinhalese Buddhist and kinsman of the Prime Minister. A Sinhalese newspaper acclaimed his appointment as 'the first appearance of a Sinhalese Buddhist Head of State since the days of the ancient kings of Lanka'.[16] Other noteworthy consequences that followed the abortive coup were the appointment of General Richard Udugama ('whose political Buddhism the plotters had despised')[17] as commander of the army, and the purge of the armed forces under the direction of Buddhist activist N.Q. Dias who then held the powerful position of permanent secretary to the Ministry of Defence and External Affairs.[18]

Thus during Mrs Bandaranaike's first term of office the primacy of Buddhism and Buddhists in Sri Lanka's political system and public life became a hard reality. This transformation of public life on the island was achieved largely by lay Buddhists both within the government and outside it. Bhikkhus played a very limited role here, which was not surprising because the sangha in general had lost much prestige with the assassination of S.W.R.D. Bandaranaike.

Elite displacement: the triumph of the orthodox bhikkhus

We have seen how, in the aftermath of Bandaranaike's assassination, politically active bhikkhus confronted the general disapprobation of the Buddhist public. During the mid-1960s political activism among bhikkhus enjoyed a revival, but on the whole they were unable to recover the influence on public policy which they had in the mid- and late 1950s.

The first issue on which the bhikkhus, particularly those who had been conspicuous in the political arena, were thwarted came up with the attempt at institutional reform by Mrs Bandaranaike's government in 1960. The Buddha Sasana Commission had recommended far-reaching reforms which would bring bhikkhus of all *nikayas* under the administration of a central authority; place all temple property in the hands of a central trusteeship under government supervision; and ensure strict adherence to the *vinaya* rules by such measures as prohibiting bhikkhus from entering lay professions such as teaching and their involvement in party politics.[19] Given the general mood of disenchantment with 'political' bhikkhus at this time, it seemed opportune to implement a thoroughgoing reform of the sangha.

The government began implementing some of the reforms recommended by the Commission, starting with an attempt to ban bhikkhus from working for pay. When this ran into opposition from a predictable source, the bhikkhus who stood to lose by the change, the government backed down. These opponents, apart from being habitual political activists, had been supporters of the SLFP. There was also the opposition from the more conservative bhikkhus headed by the *Mahanayakas* of Malvatta and Asgiriya who had opposed the appointment of the Buddha Sasana Commission *ab initio* as an unwarranted attempt to usurp their traditional authority by new religious authorities wielding administrative control over bhikkhus and temple property. They were opposed to the implementation of the recommends of the Commission.

On the other hand, several prominent bhikkhus publicly expressed their support for the envisaged reforms. Among these were the Chairman of the Commission, the Venerable Kalukondayawe Prajnasekera of the Siyam *nikaya*, and the Venerable Henpitagedera Gnanasiha, the SLFP-orientated political activist. Most Buddhist lay organisations were generally in favour of these reforms. Among those who supported them were the All Ceylon Buddhist Congress and the Young Mens' Buddhist Association.

While the opposition of vested interests among bhikkhus succeeded in forestalling *sasana* reform, the outcome of this prolonged controversy did little to improve their image in the country. In the eyes of laymen, the opposition of the bhikkhus to *sasana* reform appeared to rest on sordid motives: the desire to continue in wage-earning professions, indulge in politics and control temple property. And then in April 1966 the Venerable Henpitagedera Gnanasiha, an advocate of *sasana* reform, was arrested along with several officers and other ranks of the armed forces on suspicion of complicity in àn attempted *coup d'etat* against the UNP-led coalition government. Although the charge was not proved, the bhikkhu was kept in remand custody for the duration of investigations and trial, which took three years.

With such heavy odds against them, the influence and prestige of the politically-active bhikkhus continued to decline while the *Mahanayakas* of Malvatta and Asgiriya, with their tradition of non-partisanship, were seen to be more acceptable spokesmen for the Buddhists. The disrepute suffered by politically active bhikkhus thus had the far-reaching consequence of contributing to the enhancement of the prestige of the orthodox and conventional bhikkhu leadership.

During the years 1965–70, a policy of consciously elevating the *Mahanayakas* to a position of national significance began. The aim was to accord them honours befitting the highest religious dignitaries of the Buddhists. Two official residences in Colombo were allocated to the two *Mahanayakas*, a gesture that was symbolic not only of their new status as the two chief Buddhist religious dignitaries, but also of their elevation to a position of pre-eminence among all religious dignitaries of the country. Thus the activism of the 'political' bhikkhus had had the end result of buttressing the position of the traditional leadership of the sangha. The 'political' bhikkhus had succeeded in reducing the influence of the Christian minority enjoyed in Sri Lanka's life, but the beneficiaries of this process of elite displacement were not those who initiated it and fought most vigorously for it, but the traditional bhikkhu leadership.

Notes

1. Kitsiri Malalgoda, *Buddhism in Sinhalese Society 1750–1900* (Berkely: University of California Press, 1976).
2. Kitsiri Malalgoda, 'The Buddhist Christian Confrontation in Sri Lanka, 1800–1880' *Social Compass, 20* (2), 1973, pp.171–200.
3. W. Howard Wriggins, *Sri Lanka: Dilemmas of a New Nation* (Princeton, NJ, Princeton University Press, 1960); K.M. de Silva, *Managing Ethnic Tensions in Multi-ethnic Societies: Sri Lanka 1880–1985* (Lanham, MD: University Press of America, 1986); see also Chapter 4 of the present volume.
4. For a discussion of this, see K.M. de Silva, 'Christian Missions in Sri Lanka and their Response to Nationalism, 1910–1948' in L. Prematilleke, K. Indrapala and J.E. Van Lohuizen-de Leeuew, eds., *Senarath Paranavitana Commemoration Volume* (Leiden: Brill, 1978), pp.201–233.
5. De Silva, *Managing Ethnic Tensions*, op.cit, p.72.
6. Ibid., p.73.
7. These points were cogently argued in bhikkhu Walpola Rahula's polemical work, *Bhiksuvage Urumaya* (Colombo: Swastika Press, 1946, in Sinhalese). This book has been translated into English as *The Heritage of the Bhikkhu* (New York: Grove Press, 1974).
8. K.M. de Silva, *Managing Ethnic Tensions*, op.cit, pp.144-52.

9. Foreword to D.C. Vijayawardhana, *Revolt in the Temple* (Colombo: Sinha Publishers, 1950), pp.17–19.
10. Hansard [State Council debates] 1947, col. 1665.
11. Wriggins, Sri Lanka, p.327.
12. See *The Report on the Assassination of Prime Minister S.W.R.D. Bandaranaike*, Sessional paper III of 1965 (Colombo: Government Press, 1965).
13. See de Silva, *Managing Ethnic Tensions*, pp.196–200.
14. See S. Arasaratnam, 'The Christians of Sri Lanka and National Politics; in G.A. Oddie, ed., *Religion in South Asia* (Delhi: Manohar, 1977), pp. 177–9.
15. For details see Donald R. Horowitz, *Coup Theories and Officers' Motives: Sri Lanka in Comparative Perspective* (Princeton, NJ: Princeton University Press, 1980).
16. Editorial in the *Davasa*, 2 March 1962.
17. Horowitz, *Coup Theories*, p.211.
18. Ibid.
19. See *Buddha Sasana Komisama Vartava* (Colombo: Government Press, 1959), 18: 'Vani Sasi Vartava'.

8 IMPACT OF THE DHAMMACARIK BHIKKHUS' PROGRAMME ON THE HILL TRIBES OF THAILAND*

Sanit Wongsprasert

The hill people living in the remote valleys, uplands and highland areas of northern and western Thailand numbered in 1985 some 400,000. They are distributed over 20 provinces. They are dry-rice and livestock raising farmers. They are made up of nine tribes: the Karen, Meo, Lahu, Lisu, Yao, Akha, Lua, Htin, and Khmu. The largest of these groups is the Karen and the smallest is the Khmu. The Karen are found in 15 provinces and the Htin live only in Nan Province. The others are dispersed throughout the country. Initially, the Dham-macarik Bhikkhu Programme (DBP) was set up to strengthen the government policy of integrating the hill tribes, enabling them to become first-class, self-reliant Thai citizens.

The programme was established in 1965 with money provided by the Asia Foundation. It is administered by a chairman, the abbot of Wat Benjamabophit in Bangkok. The Department of Public Welfare, Ministry of Interior, act as co-ordinator and prepares the formal request for money. In 1970, Her Royal Highness the Princess Mother laid the foundation stone for the Monk and Novice Training Centre at Wat Srisoda, situated in the foothills of Doi Suthep, Chiang Mai. Since then, a three-storeyed training centre has been constructed.

* This article is based on a field study of the Dhammacarik Bhikkhu Programme of Wat Srisoda, Chiang Mai Provinces, Thailand, carried out during the period January to September 1983. I was assigned by Mr. Wanat Bhruksasri, Director of the Tribal Research Institute, Chiang Mai, to lead the follow-up research team which included Sompop Larcharoj, Precert Chaipikusit, Saranee Thaiyanan, and Panop Satayopas. We visited several tribal communities in northern and western Thailand where the bhikkhus had been working. The information presented in the article was collected by direct enquiry. I am deeply grateful to Prakhru Nikhom Dhammaprasart, the abbot of Wat Srisoda. My thanks are due also to Dhammacarik bhikkhus and the tribal people who allowed me to carry out the follow-up research amongst them. I acknowledge with thanks the advice and assistance of Mr Peter Hoare, former Adviser to the TRC, and Dr John McKinnon, TRI-ORSTOM Project, during the writing of this report.

Objectives

The objectives of the government and private foundations are: to facilitate the work of the Dhammacarik bhikkhus responsible for spreading the teachings of the Buddha; to promote mutual understanding between hill tribes and Thai people; to develop and provide welfare to alleviate urgent problems faced by hill villagers; and to train them to follow the Buddhist way of life.

The programme

In 1965, a survey team consisting of bhikkhus from Wat Benjama-bophit and the staff of the Department of Public Welfare visited Meo and Yao villages in Phetchabun Province in search of a way to prepare the DBP. A pilot programme was then set up in 1965 and a permanent programme inaugurated in 1966.

Ten teams, each consisting of 50 bhikkhus, were assigned to work among the Meo, Lahu, Akha, and Karen of Chiang Mai, Chiang Rai, Mae Hong Son, Tak, and Phetchabun provinces. Each team worked in its trial village for one month. This experience was a success, as 12 young tribesmen asked to enter the sangha.

Between 1965 and 1983, 2,143 youngsters, over 100 per year, have entered the sangha and undergone an elementary and Dhamma education. Since 1966, the DBP has involved the education of over one-third of the total tribal population.

When working in the field, a Dhammacarik bhikkhu is granted 750 baht[1] per month for his upkeep. Each bhikkhu works with an average of 1,440 villagers. Every year many bhikkhus from all over Thailand come to Wat Srisoda to apply to become Dhammacarik bhikkhus. The senior Dhammacarik bhikkhus evaluate each case and select bhikkhus on the following criteria:

1. They must have been monks for a period covering more than two *vassas* (rainy seasons).
2. They must hold at least a second level (*Nak dham tho*) in Dhamma education.
3. They must behave according to *Vinaya*.
4. They must have a good level of general knowledge and ability.
5. They must be able to guide and perform religious ceremonies.

In 1983, 42 bhikkhus were selected to attend the Dhammacarik

Bhikkhu Training Centre before being assigned for service in the field. A little over 50 per cent of these bhikkhus were in the 20–29 age group. About 15 per cent were between 13 and 20 and the rest were over 29, with about 10 per cent over 60. As at 1983 there were 152 DBP alumni from 11 ethnic groups, with almost half of the total being Karen (Table 8.1).

Table 8.1 Bhikkhus in Wat Srisoda by Ethnic Group, 1983 ($n = 437$)

Ethnic group	Monks	Novices	%
Karen	7.0	40.0	47
Yao	1.0	11.0	12
Htin	2.0	8.0	10
Meo	0.4	5.6	6
Lahu	0.2	3.8	4
Akha	0.0	4.0	4
Lua	0.0	2.0	2
Lisu	0.0	2.0	2
Khmu	0.0	1.0	1
Shan (or Thai Yai)	0.3	4.7	5
Thai	1.5	5.5	7
	12.4	87.6	100

Source: DBP

Duties and responsibilities of Dhammcarik bhikkus

A Dhammacarik bhikkhu team work-unit consists of two or three monks. Each team may service a cluster village, or two to seven tribal settlements. Their duties ard responsibilities are to:

1. emphasise development, and, through an understanding of belief and teaching, wisdom, morality and culture;
2. act as co-ordinators between villagers and various development agencies;
3. promote and co-ordinate communal activities;
4. urge villagers to understand and co-operate in development projects;

5. assist in the amelioration of hill-tribe health problems by providing primary health care;
6. provide elementary education to children in villages where government schools have not yet been established; and
7. report on special problems in the area of their assignment to the chairman of the Dhammacarik Bhikkhu Committee for consideration.

Recently, some Karen have realised that many of their endemic problems could be solved by Dhammacarik bhikkhus performing religious rites designed to chase away evil spirits. Another common problem is that when the soul of a dead person causes them trouble, they cannot enjoy peace until a proper cremation ceremony has been performed by the monks.

Activities

The Dhammacarik bhikkhus' activities in the highlands can be classified into two levels of implementation: individual and household level, and the community level. At the individual and household level the Dhammacarik bhikkhus provide primary health care and help villagers and hill people to deal with the local administration in matters such as taxes, registration of births and deaths, and so on. For example, the DBP reported that in 1983 about 5300 individuals and 1600 households were assisted by the programme in health matters and about 700 individuals in administrative matters. At the community level, Dhammacarik bhikkhus have been active in establishing farm co-operatives, youth groups, providing veterinary care and in the development of infrastructure facilities such as roads, school buildings and wells.

Another essential Dhammacarik bhikkhu service is the spread of Buddhist teachings and guiding highlanders on how to gain merit at nearby Buddhist temples. They encourage tribal Buddhists to visit holy places such as Dio Suthep temple in Chiang Mai, and even further afield in the north-east of Thailand. These pilgrimages are a source of pride to the Dhammacarik bhikkhu.

The Dhammacarik bhikkhu alumni

Table 8.2 records the employment in secular society of the 152 alumni of Wat Srisoda Dhammacarik bhikkhu. Typically, hill people engage in shifting or slash-and-burn cultivation. Thai lowlanders believe that this practice is detrimental to the ecosystem in the north and west of the country. Among the Dhammacarik bhikkhu alumni, 85 per cent adopted modern agricultural techniques[2] and the remainder returned to follow traditional practices. Only 9 per cent[3] of the hill people accept family planning. This figure rose to 50 per cent among the Dhammacarik bhikkhus. On average, alumni had families with 2.1 children.

Table 8.2 Occupations of the Dhammacarik Bhikkhu Alumni, 1983

Occupation	%
Returned to their villages to become farmers	18
Continuing higher education	7
Working in the private sector	6
Private businesses	4
(jungle tour guides; tribal dancing showmen, traders)	
Government employees (teacher; border patrol police;	65
radio announcers; soldier; and village headman)	

Source: DBP

Religions of the hill tribes

Other reports have been prepared on Dhammacarik bhikkhu activities,[4] but none concern themselves with the nature of tribal religious beliefs and practices. Thai textbooks mention Buddhism, Christianity and Islam as major religions and some minority group religions such as Hinduism and Sikhism. Discussions of highlander religions, however, need to be made available if we are to come to an understanding of how either acculturation or integration are to proceed.

Religious beliefs vary from one hill tribe to another. Supernatural beings play a part in every aspect of their myths, be they deities, spirits, or whatever. In order to divine the will of supernatural beings, ritual activities are practised to secure practical outcomes rather than abstract souls. I will outline the major characteristics of the Karen, Meo, Lahu, Lisu, Yao, Akha, Lua, Htin, and Khmu religions.

The Karen centre their belief on spirits and impersonal powers.

Organised religious movements are inspired by prophets and are of a nativistic character. They have been syncretistic, combining in various degrees indigenous, Buddhist and Christian elements.[5] The Meo, Yao, Lisu, Akha, Khmu and Htin are primarily animists whose beliefs are based on ancestors and spirits.[6] The Lahu are theistic animists.[7] The Lua, on the other hand, are, like the Thai, animistic Buddhists.[8]

A great variety of spirits and souls of ancestors are believed to exist. Spirits inhabit trees, water, mountains and swiddens. Other spirits are patrons of the activities of village headmen, religious leaders and blacksmiths. These spirits and souls live in an empirical realm, and behave as human beings. The Meo, Lahu, Yao, and Akha greatly fear and respect such supreme spirits.

Supernatural beings of the Lisu, Htin, and Khmu are spirits of ancestors; they inhabit the jungle, earth, water, wind, mountains, villages, houses, and there is also a lightening demon.

The Karen believe in an otiose creator who inspires messianic content. Supernatural beings include local spirits with human characteristics who exercise some control over human events and malevolent spirits.[9] All of the supernatural beings, the evil ones and spirits of ancestors, are potentially troublesome and must be appeased regularly.

The priest-exorcist, the shaman, and spirit or religious specialists are ascribed a status, except for the female shaman of the Yao. The practitioners communicate with spirits, go into trances, interpret omens, foretell the future, and exorcise evil spirits. Usually they do not engage in black magic or sorcery. They lead villagers in sacrifices and ceremonies held in honour of supreme and local gods, and some of them participate in marriage ceremonies.

The New Year's festival is the most important annual ceremony. Domestic animal meat, rice cakes, beeswax candles, and crops are offered to several significant spirits. A common ritual is frequently performed when there is some loss. The spirit specialist may restore the patient to health with herbs and the sacrifice of a domestic beast. More elaborate rituals are performed to deal with a severe illness considered to be caused by angry spirits, in which case this ceremony is usually performed by several specialists.

The Meo, Yao, red Lahu, Lisu, Lua, Khmu, and Htin bury their dead. Cremation is practised by the Karen and black Lahu as well as the Thai. Some food is offered for the soul of the deceased. The body is kept on a mat wrapped in a white cloth or placed in a wooden coffin for one day or more. Those who die a violent or unusual death are buried at once in the jungle. After death, a person's soul is reborn in the form of the next child born in the village. Souls of ancestors not yet reborn are ceremonially informed to move and migrate with the group concerned. Periodic ceremonies are held for the souls of deceased ancestors. Immediately following death these may be performed quite frequently to enable them to enter the spirit world.

Highlanders are religiously observant and closely follow traditional beliefs. Their religious rules require strict discipline. The hill tribes do not attempt to proselytise others to change their religion. However, missionary activity is acceptable, and in the case of Buddhism may ease them out of traditional constraints. They feel that Dhammacarik bhikkhus' teachings provide an opportunity rather than an exclusive alternative like Christianity.

Advantages of the Dhammacarik bhikkhus' services

We collected data from 28 sample villages and interviewed 366 male and female household heads. The composition of our sample is presented in Table 8.3. Most informants who had been in contact with Dhammacarik bhikkhus expressed their appreciation of the opportunity to learn the teachings of the Buddha. The second most favoured reason given for acceptance was the private relationship they had formed with the bhikkhus. The least enthusiastic response made reference to the agricultural extension service provided. Table 8.4 indicates that highlanders expect bhikkhus to deal with religion rather than practical matters such as agricultural extension. Agricultural extension work is already taken care of by the Department of Public Welfare. However, the Dhammacarik bhikkhu alumni considered this to be the most appropriate source of help.

As noted in Table 8.1, individuals from many different ethnic groups participate in the DBP. When hill people were asked what ethnic group they preferred their bhikkhus to come from, 77 per cent said they preferred Thais because tribal monks often created problems. In particular Thai bhikkhus were preferred as teachers of appropriate behaviour. Only 10 per cent of the sample villagers preferred to have their own people as bhikkhus because they felt it was more convenient to relate with them in the traditional way.

Table 8.3   Tribal Informants

Tribe	No. of villages	Informants No.	%
Karen	13	165	45
Meo, Yao and Akha	7	92	25
Lahu	2	30	8
Lisu	2	28	8
Htin and Khumu	4	51	14

Source: Author's survey, 1983

Buddhist religious rites and the tribal adopters

When judged by the fact the highlanders had invited monks to per-form religious rites, it can be said that about one-third of all such people exposed to Buddhist teachings have nominally adopted Buddhism. Most highlanders still look at bhikkhus with some reservations, and many did not want to express an opinion. In particular, the Karen, Htin, and Khmu are quite doubtful about the Thai nature of the DBP. However, we also found that these same people are less guarded about allowing monks to be present at their religious rites.

Highlanders are, on the whole, quite poor and often produce insufficient food for consumption. However, once they have an established relationship with a Dhammacarik bhikkhu teacher they contribute food and provide bowls of cooked rice. Several tribal groups donate food to bhikkhus throughout the year. The Lisu, Htin, and Khmu are exceptions to this. These latter folk are busy with their swiddening during the mid-rainy season and this keeps them away from the village for a long period of time.

Another way to gain merit which is noteworthy is to visit sacred temples. This is most often practised by tribal followers with the exception of the Meo, Yao, Akha, and Lisu, who use what free time they have available to search for new cultivable lands.

Many senior hill folk require their sons to enter the sangha in order to have a chance to learn about the outside world. All realise that the discipline means their children cannot eat after midday. Others with only one son would otherwise have given permission, but felt it was more important that he stay at home.

Table 8.4   Principal Advantages Gained from DBP as Identified by Participants (%)

Tribe	Buddhist Teachings and morals	Private relationship	Health and sanitary	Infrastructural improvement	Teaching in school	Local administration guidance	Agricultural extension
Karen	55	41	27	18	4	6	6
Lahu	57	66	30	17	13	9	0
Meo							
Yao							
Akha	38	39	18	17	31	3	1
Lisu	86	35	38	54	32	21	6
Htin	66	46	22	24	19	12	12
Khmu							
Average	60	45	27	26	18	10	5

Source: Author's survey, 1983.

Problems and obstacles

There are many problems and obstacles facing the DBP, some of which are important and others not. The fiscal budget, personnel and equipment are continuing problems. A number of Dhammacarik bhikkhus are not yet well qualified.

Generally the Thai language is used to address men. Females and elderly villagers do not speak Thai, and this greatly inhibits effective communication. Daily conversation is no great problem. However, it is difficult to explain Buddhist philosophy in tribal languages.

The major problem faced by bhikkhus living in villages is where food is in short supply. The presence of a bhikkhu can place an unwelcome demand on village resources. Temples in the city secure extra food to feed the temple boys. The bhikkhus in tribal villages have no other choice but to share their food with hungry children. Furthermore, hill people prepare food to suit their palates, and many bhikkhus complain that the food is too hot, salty or oily for them.

Some Dhammacarik bhikkhus do not have a strong educational background and also have too little experience to deal with problems that are quite numerous and quite different from those of the average Thai peasant. Highlanders often expect monks to know how to solve all their problems and are disillusioned when they cannot do so.

Impact

Dhammacarik bhikkhus are principally trained to spread the teachings of the Buddha among the hill tribes. They are given a basic elementary and Dhamma education. Such elementary knowledge is not sufficient to convince highlanders to give up their religions which are closely integrated into their culture, and to that extent they remain inflexible. The hill folk are most likely to accept Buddhist teachings, which enable them to escape from traditional obligations and constraints, rather than because it is a superior belief system. The specific impact may differ from one ethnic group to another. Karen, who are not wealthy enough to send their sons to school, see it as a chance to gain an elementary education in temple schools. The Lahu, Meo, Yao and Akha are interested in learning about Thai culture from the bhikkhus in order to secure their civil rights, such as citizenship. The Lisu perspective is also one of convenience: knowledge gained in such a programme helps them to deal with local officials. The Htin and Khmu are less interested than other tribes in allowing their sons to enter the sangha.

About four-fifths of the Dhammacarik bhikkhu alumni become salary earners, the rest return to their villages. These returnees bring skills and knowledge back to their homes which enable them to make a significant contribution to their communities.

Notes

1. 26 baht = US $1.
2. For example, wet-rice cultivation, use of ox carts, and so on.
3. 'Hill Tribes Denied Mee Chai', *Daily News,* 13 July 1983, P. 3.
4. *Report on the Spread of Buddhism to the Hill Tribes in the North (1966),* by the second contemporary Dhammacarik Bhikkhu, Department of Public Welfare (Bangkok: 1969, mimeo); *Report on the Spread of Buddhism to the Hill Tribes in the North (1971),* by the seven contemporary Dhammacarik Bhikkhu, Department of Public Welfare (Bangkok: 1972, mimeo); *Monetary Report on Dhammacarik Bhikkhu Work between 1967–1972* (Chiang Mai: Tribal Research Centre, August 1973, mimeo).
5. Harry I. Marshall, *The Karen People of Burma: A Study in Anthropology and Ethnology* (Columbus: Ohio State University Press, 1922), pp.210–11 and 264–5.
6. Private communications with the Meo specialist, Khun Chupinit Kesmanee; the Yao specialist, Khun Mongkhol Junbumroong; the Lisu specialist, Khun Prasert Chaipigusit; and the Akha specialist, Khun Uraiwan Sangsorn of the Tribal Research Institute, Chiang Mai.
7. O. Gordon Young, *The Hilltribes of Northern Thailand* (Bangkok: United States Operations Mission to Thailand, 1961), pp.14–16.
8. Ibid., p.69.
9. Marshal, *The Karen People of Burma* pp. 210–33.

References

Wanat Bhruksasri, *et al.* (1983). Field-work Report No. 1, 'Evaluation of the Dhammacarik Bhikkhu Service among the Hill Tribes (Chiang Mai: Tribal Research Institute, mimeo, text in Thai).

Wanat Bhruksasri (1984). *Evaluation of the Dhammacarik Bhikkhu Service among the Hill Tribes* (Chiang Mai: Tribal Research Institute, Department of Public Welfare, Ministry of Interior, text in Thai).

Department of Public Welfare (1969). 'Report on the Spread of Buddhism to the Hill Tribes in the North' (Bangkok, mimeo, text in Thai).

Department of Public Welfare (1972). 'Report on the Spread of Buddhism to the Hill Tribes in the North' (Bangkok, mimeo, text in Thai).

W.R. Geddes, (1965). 'The Hill Tribes of Thailand', *SEATO Record* (Bangkok).

Dusit Khomkjumphan and Prasert Chaiphigusit (1973). 'Monetary Report on the Dhammacarik Bhikkhu Work, 1967–1972' (Chiang Mai: Tribal Research Centre, August, mimeo, text in Thai).

Harry I. Marshall, (1922). *The Karen People of Burma: A Study in Anthropology and Ethnology* (Columbus: Ohio State University Press).

J. McKinnon, and Wanat Bhruksasri, (1974). *Highlanders of Thailand* (Kuala Lumpur: Oxford University Press).

Sanit Wongsprasert, (1982). *Highland–Lowland Migration: a Study of Lahu and Meo Move Towards Majority Life* (Chiang Mai: Tribal Research Centre).

O. Gordon Young, (1961). *The Hilltribes of Northern Thailand* (Bangkok: United States Operation Mission to Thailand).

9   SRI LANKAN MONKS ON ETHNICITY AND NATIONALISM*

Nathan Katz

Introduction

Three assumptions underlie this report, two substantive and one methodological. Substantively, it is held, first, that Buddhist monks in Sri Lanka are capable of enormous political influence, a power which has lain virtually dormant for about two decades but which has shown· signs of reawakening in the aftermath of the traumatic 1983 ethnic violence; and, second, that the current ethnic conflict is the greatest crisis — politically, economically and religiously — which Sri Lanka has faced since independence. The methodological assumption involves the usefulness of surveys and statistical studies of Sri Lanka. Before presenting the data, a few words will be said in support of these assumptions.

The political significance of the Sri Lankan sangha

The pivotal role played by the Sri Lankan sangha in the 1956 elections is widely accepted today, due to the seminal study by Wriggins.[1] However, many observers see this high-profile political activism by the monks as an anomaly in Buddhist history. The view of Buddhism as essentially an other-worldly, reclusive system of individual purification, first propounded by Weber,[2] is still used to characterise Buddhism.

This characterization is but a crude caricature, as could be demonstrated on the basis of the three interrelated modes of inquiry. First, an unbiased reading of the canonical and post-canonical literature of Sri Lankan Theravada Buddhism clearly shows important teachings

*   Support for this research was provided by a sabbatical grant from Williams College, and the University of South Florida provided a Faculty Foreign Travel Grant to enable me to attend the Bangkok workshop, I am most grateful to both institutions.

about society promulgated by the Buddha of the Pali canon, both implicitly and explicitly, an emphasis embellished in such post-canonical writing as the *vamsa* literature, which presents the Sri Lankan narrative in a 'sacred history' framework, as well as in the *atthakatha* commentaries.

Second, an analysis of the discourse of early Buddhologists reveals the political context in which Buddhist studies in the West were and are carried out. In studying Western academic perceptions of Islam, Edward Said[3] found that derogatory stereotypes coincided with the rise of the Western imperialism, and similar structures inhabit academic thinking about Buddhism as well. To say that Buddhism is socially passive is, in effect, to justify the imperialist manipulation of the Sri Lankan economy and polity.

Third, a dialogical engagement of contemporary Sri Lankan monks clearly evokes strong and sincere concerns about the nature and direction of contemporary society. Coming to know some of these monks is more effective in dispelling the caricature of other-worldliness than any other mode of inquiry.

This fundamental misunderstanding of Buddhism as unconnected with society has led to as many dire practical consequences as academic conundrums. Attempting to understand a Buddhist country through the other-worldly discourse has led to unfortunate policy decisions. An example of the sorts of problem that emerge has been described by a former USAID worker, Arthur Niehoff,[4] in his analysis of the failure of a well-digging development project in Laos in the 1950s. Not including Buddhist monks in the planning and administration of the project inexorably led to its failure, which Niehoff attributed to the bureaucracy's stubborn adherence to the other-worldliness paradigm. With a suitable sense of irony, Niehoff described some monk-led anti-American demonstrations at Vientiane are in 1960, and proposed the image of the placard-carrying, rock-throwing monk as more appropriate than the image of the meditative social recluse. Similarly, an attempt to resolve or manage Sri Lanka's current ethnic crisis without enlisting the advocacy of the sangha is also doomed to failure.

Monks are neither recluses nor an inconvenient sector of the population who need be mollified to support various government policies. Monks have played, and continue to play, a role of leadership in Buddhist societies. Their exclusion from political power under imperialist rule and the disdain in which they are held by many contemporary development leaders antagonise the monks and doom any project under consideration. In terms of the current crisis, many observers have remarked that were the sangha to rise forcefully and unequivocally against the recurrent anti-Tamil violence, then it would be stopped. Perhaps they are the only group in Sri Lanka with the influence to effect such a response. To ignore or attempt to manipulate them is to assure that the crisis will not be settled.

The significance of the ethnic crisis for Sri Lanka

Two studies of the Sri Lankan economy have been published recently, studies remarkable for the divergence of their assumptions and conclusions. The first, by Dilip Bobb,[5] appeared in the March issue of *India Today*, a new Delhi weekly which presents an independent Indian perspective on issues. But the magazine is not entirely unfriendly to Sri Lankan concerns. (It was this journal which first documented the existence of terrorist training bases in Tamilnadu, much to the embarrassment of Delhi.) Its analysis of the Sri Lankan economy saw the ethnic crisis as the paramount factor frustrating development and prosperity there. Due directly to the ethnic crisis, Sri Lanka's national debt has been increasing at alarming rates; Tamil professionals have been leaving Sri Lanka in such numbers as to create a crisis in her health-care systems and in governmental and private sector bureaucracies; foreign investment, so essential for President Jayewardene's open economy strategy, has dwindled; and costs for humanitarian relief and anti-terrorist military operations have stretched the budget to breaking point. The picture there presented is grim.

Only six weeks later, the conservative American think tank, the Heritage Foundation, published a glowing economic report by Devindra R. Subasinghe.[6] In its eleven pages, only two paragraphs are devoted to the ethnic crisis, claiming it could be quelled by American military assistance and by increasing the private sector of the economy because, as Subasinghe puts it, 'A free economy and private enterprise do not discriminate' against minorities.[7] Just as Bobb's analysis of the economy focuses almost exclusively on the ethnic crisis, Subasinghe virtually ignores it.

It seems that the analyses of *India Today* and the Heritage Foundation reflect more their respective ideological commitments than any objective view of the situation. The influential *New York Times*[8] opined in an editorial that the problem in Sri Lanka, in essence, is ahistorical, one of ethnic prejudice, quite separable from ideology or economics: 'Bigotry in Sri Lanka has defeated left and right. It is a fearful symmetry that beggars optimism' — a view which generally reflects international opinion on the question.

The impact of the current crisis on Sri Lanka's economy is, I think, incontestable and obvious. Its impact on the moral fabric of the society is less obvious but perhaps more pernicious.

Methodological questions

The data for this report on the attitudes of Sri Lankan monks on ethnicity and nationalism were gathered from September 1983 to February 1984. Thirty-seven monks who reside in monasteries in and around Peradeniya consented to in-depth interviews on a range of issues of social, political and religious interest.[9] (A copy of the questionnaire, which comprised only a part of these interviews, is appended.)

In these interviews, extensive data were collected on the background of the monks. Their age, length of service as a bhikkhu (fully ordained monk) and as a *samanera* (novice), the location of the interview, their profession (and degree of status commensurate with that profession), their sect (*nikaya*), data on their socio-economic background (father's occupation, amount of land owned by the family, and so on), whether English or other foreign languages were known, educational background and whether there had been travel or pilgrimages abroad — all these factors were duly collected and noted.

One-sixth of the interviews were conducted in English and the balance were held in a mixture of Sinhala (for which a translator, Mr Maneesha de Silva, was used) and Pali (which the investigator understands). Most of the interviews were conducted at Buddhist temples, a few of which are well known (such as the Getambe Vihara), but mostly in village temples. Some were held at the university, some over tea at cafés and some at the investigator's residence.

Unfortunately there is no reliable information as to the composition of the Sri Lanka sangha upon which to base a scientific sample. The records, kept by the Department of Buddhist Affairs in Colombo, which were consulted for this purpose, are woefully out of date. In the utter absence of foundational data, then, monks were selected as interview subjects on the basis of the location of their temple, their relative status within the monastic community, their sect, and so on, relying on several years' experience working with monks on a variety of questions. While not strictly a scientific sample, the background information gathered indicates that a wide cross-section of the monastic community has been consulted. The present work is to be understood as exploratory rather than confirmatory, as would have been possible had a scientific sample been possible to obtain. What is claimed of this study is that the monks represented come from a variety of backgrounds, that their backgrounds are analysed such that this exploratory survey should serve as a basis for further research. Those familiar with the Sri Lanka sangha are invited to corroborate or falsify these findings on the basis of their experience with these monks.

The relatively small sample size does not necessarily impinge upon the usefulness of these findings. The problem was one of resources. It seemed wiser to proceed with in-depth and open-ended interviews with a smaller number of monks, rather than to try and get larger numbers and therefore more superficial interviews restricted to the question-naire, especially given the common wisdom that questionnaires are of limited value in a South Asian context.[10] Each interviewee had a great deal to say about almost all of the questions, and I wanted to listen. This is a very time-consuming way of gathering data, but it is felt that this humanistic interview method provided richer results than sole reliance on a questionnaire. These are the methodological assumptions made about this adaptation of the interview–questionnaire–statistical approach to the subject.

The background data on our sample, then, are as follows. In terms of age, one-third attained intellectual maturity before 1952, which is to say they were educated when Sri Lanka was still a British colony. One-fifth attained maturity between 1953 and 1975, during the 'Buddhist renaissance', an era marked by a high degree of political activism on the part of the sangha. More than 40 per cent were educated since the watershed events of the Colombo Non-aligned Summit (1976) and the election of the centre-right UNP government (1977).

As for profession, one-fifth work in an undistinguished profession, such as a *pirivena* instructor. Another fifth have distinguished professions, such as head of a temple or university lecturer. One-third are university students, a high-status position but treated as a separate category for the purpose of this analysis. One-quarter have an irrelevant professional status: they may not hold a renumerative position or may be 'retired'. This last group probably best reflects the character of monks in Sri Lanka as a whole.

Two-fifths are members of the Siyam Nikaya, based in Kandy, the largest, oldest and most prestigious of Sri Lanka's three monastic fraternities and open only to young men from high-caste (*goyigama*) families. One-eighth are of the Amarapura Nikaya, and two-fifths are of the Ramanna Nikaya. There is unfortunately no reliable information as to the proportions of the sangha as a whole belonging to these three groups.

Based on their fathers' occupations and amount of land held by their families, one-sixth were judged to be from disadvantaged economic backgrounds. One-sixth gave ambiguous responses or declined to respond to questions about economic background.

Nearly a third had university degrees, just over a third were pursuing university degrees and just over a third did not have higher education. More than four-fifths had never been out of Sri Lanka, a tenth had been to India on pilgrimage and a twentieth had been to America, Europe or Japan. One-sixth had some competency in English while more than four-fifths spoke only Sinhala and the canonical languages.

This is the composition of our sample. Efforts were made to avoid talking only with 'big' monks, those to whom Western scholars routinely have access and/or who are most often quoted in local newspapers. The sampling thus obtained is felt to be reasonably representative of Peradeniya, a university town.

After gathering this background data, a series of 30 statements was read and monks were asked to register their disagreement or agreement (on a one-to-five scale). The statements were intended to discern the monks' opinions regarding society and to focus specifically on their views of various domains of socio-political involvement. Often these interviews would evolve into extended discussions of politics and society, both in theoretical and quite specific aspects. In the most general terms, I was seeking to learn how Buddhist monks envisioned society and especially about their thoughts on what role monks ought to have in actualising that vision.

The context for the present data

Nationalism and ethnicity was only one of five attitudinal domains about which opinions were solicited. The other were ideology, ecumenicalism, 'cultural insularity', and women's issues. In addition to these structures of attitudes, monks were asked about the propriety of monastic involvement in development, education, 'Gandhi-style' activism, and the political process. Before reporting the findings on attitudes about nationalism and ethnicity, a brief review of the data in these other areas is appropriate.

Ideology

Ideology was reflected in six of the questions posed. Monks were asked about the compatibility of Buddhism and Marxism, democratic socialism, capitalism, the free-market economy (of the current government), the controlled economy (of previous governments) and sympathy for the goals and methods of the Sarvodaya Shramadana movement.

There was unambiguous consensus on two of these issues. Ninety per cent agreed with the compatibility of Buddhism and democratic socialism, an ambiguous term. Similarly, 90 per cent disagreed with any compatibility between Buddhism and capitalism. These two issues seem to be the moorings of contemporary monastic ideological thought. A Buddhist-Marxist *rapprochement* was thought desirable by three-tenths; half felt they were incompatible views, indicating that Buddhist-Marxist syncretism in Sri Lanka, thought to have been so instrumental in the post-independence period, is on the wane (if, indeed, it ever did enjoy broad popular support).

Turning to more immediate manifestations of the left and right in the Sri Lankan body politic, monks were asked whether they supported the free-market policies of the current government. Most did not. Half felt the free market was contrary to traditional values, while only a fifth gave it support. A good deal of concern was expressed about the rising national debt associated with free-market policies, while others were concerned about the consumerism and greed such policies seem to invite.

Nearly three-quarters of the monks expressed support for the Sarvodaya movement, while one-twentieth expressed disapproval and a quarter were either of a mixed view or declined to answer.

We shall see whether and how these ideological factors weigh upon attitudes regarding nationalism and ethnicity.

Ecumenicalism

Four statements on ecumenicalism were put to respondents, two dealing with the monks' appraisal of the rival Mahayana ('The Mahayana is an authentic form of Buddhism' and 'The Mahayana is a compromised, degenerate form of Buddhism') and two with 'other religions' more generally ('The *Buddhadharma* is the only path to *nibbana*' and 'All religions lead to the same goal'). Not only were opinions on this issue volatile (in the sense of having a high standard deviation) but, as we shall see, this issue impinges interestingly on attitudes towards nationalism and ethnicity.

There is a consensus, albeit not one without volatility, towards a critical view of the Mahayana. More than three-fifths disagreed with the statement that the Mahayana is an authentic form of Buddhism. One quarter agreed. When the question was put inversely (the Mahayana as a 'compromised, degenerate' form of Buddhism), consistency was evident. A clear majority (nearly three-quarters) agreed with this negative characterisation, but a significant minority opinion (one-quarter) emerged.

The views on "other religions" did not fall into so nearly symmetrical a pattern. When asked whether Buddhism was the 'only path to *nibbana*', a canonical formulation (from the *Satipattahana Sutta*), 90 per cent agreed, with only 10 per cent in dissent. Yet, when asked whether 'all religions lead to the same goal', more than half agreed and only a third disagreed. This seems to reveal a tendency for monks to affirm liberal attitudes toward other religions when the question is put in such a way that agreement is possible, which is to say when the question is not put into terms which would contradict the Theravada sacred canon. Interestingly, it seems easier for a monk to accept the religious legitimacy of 'other religions' than of Mahayana Buddhism.

'Cultural insularity'

Theoretically, it would seem that 'the Tamil question' and the ecumenical issues are connected with a vaguer sense of looking inward versus looking outward culturally. This tendency to look inward could be termed 'cultural insularity' and it was approached through three questions put to the monks: whether tourism has only corrupting influences on society; whether one should look to classical times to address current social problems; and whether one should look to all quarters for alternative solutions to current social problems.

The question about tourism reflects the 'popular wisdom' of the media and politicians in contemporary Sri Lanka. Tourism, of course, is a major foreign exchange earner, as it is in many Third World countries. The press often sensationalise tourists' nudity, recreational use of drugs and active sexual behaviour (including much-publicised instances of prostitution, homosexual and otherwise, involving young Sri Lankans) as in violation of traditional social values. Indeed, an anti-tourism climate exists which is reflected in the majority of monks' attitudes. Three-quarters agreed with the strongly negative evaluation of tourism, yet one-sixth did not, some claiming that tourism had 'mixed results, some good, some bad'. These interview subjects wanted to distinguish between types of tourist. Some ('the hippies') were felt to have an unambiguously negative impact, while other tourists— those who visit sacred sites, become introduced to meditation or who buy books about Buddhism—were felt to have a positive impact.

This sense of 'cultural insularity' was also tested by the questions on approaches to current social, political and economic issues. Should one approach these issues through a study of classical Sinhalese culture? In general, the 'big' monks—or at least those so often cited in the local press—do so. The *Mahavamsa*, for example, is often read as a blueprint for public policy. Such a view represents an 'inward lookingness', yet such a view was not advocated unambiguously by the monks. Three-fifths agreed with this approach and a quarter disagreed. When the converse of this statement was read—that one ought to look to all quarters for guidance—100 per cent agreed. It seems that while classical expressions continue to exercise considerable influence on the monks, this influence is by no means exclusivistic. The Sri Lankan sangha, judging from this data, is quite open to beneficial influences from all quarters. It is this 'outward lookingness' which Niehoff[11] observed in Laos and which is corroborated in this study. Clearly, Sri Lankan monks are not culturally insulated, nor do they wish to be. In this respect the sangha does not resemble the 'clergy' of some other countries who uncritically seek to resacralise the social order.

Women's issues

Only one women's issue, albeit a controversial one, was raised: whether the monk supports the reintroduction of the bhikkhuni sangha (ordination lineage for nuns) in Sri Lanka. The order was inaugurated by the Buddha in the sixth century BC, introduced to Sri Lanka by Sanghamitta Theri in the third century BC, and died out in the twelveth century AD. In recent years, several thousand women have styled themselves *dasa sil mathas*, or 'mothers of the ten precepts', traditionally a lay status. By donning the saffron robes, however, they assume the status and functions of nuns, much to the dismay of the 'big' monks.[12] The data show that these women enjoy more support within the sangha than either common wisdom, the local and international press, or the "big" monks would lead us to believe. Three-fifths supported their aspirations, while 30 per cent did not. Even among those who did not support the nuns, sympathy for them was often expressed: 'If there were a proper way to do it, that would be fine. But since the *parampara* (the lineage of ordination dating back to the Buddha) is broken, there is no way to do it properly.' Those in support seemed to be untroubled by the legalistic technicalities of the Vinaya. 'It's only fair', as one monk succinctly put it.

Socio-political involvement

Twelve aspects of monastic involvement in social and political processes were raised with the interview subjects. Issues about explicitly political involvement, involvement in national development, in education and in (for want of a better term) 'Gandhi-style' activism were raised. In general, the monks favoured educational and developmental involvements unambiguously and overwhelmingly.[13] While pluralities supported 'Gandhi-style' activism, there was some dissent. The most telling results, however, emerge from the data on political involvement. Monks overwhelmingly approved of a monastic role in advising governments and clearly (though not so overwhelmingly) disapproved of identification with a political party. The other political domains — holding an appointed governmental position, engaging in electoral politics and standing for elected office — show a movement from relative positive consensus to dissensus to something approaching a negative consensus.

The monks' attitudes on ethnicity and nationalism

Many observers feel that 'the Tamil question' poses the most serious threat to Sri Lanka's aspirations for development and national integrity. This issue was all the more immediate as the interviews were conducted in the wake of the July 1983 anti-Tamil programmes (but before the recent escalation of terrorist activity). Two questions relating to this issue were raised: whether the sangha should defend the Sinhalese-Buddhist identity of the nation; and whether the Tamils have some legitimate grievances against the government.

Only 10 per cent disagreed with the sangha's role citing the *Mahavamsa*, the fifth-century Pali epic by Mahanama which defines the 'sacred history' or 'national covenant' of the Sinhalese people. The sangha was seen as a 'bastion of true culture'. Others, perhaps aware of the implicit contradiction between such a universalist theory as Buddhism and the limiting nature of any nationalism, pointed out somewhat apologetically that 'even the Buddha had a special love for his relatives'. More than a few replied that this identity should be defended 'without harming any other religion or nation', or that 'one must keep a balanced mind about these matters'. One monk who disagreed with the majority (and one active in the Sarvodaya movement) related at length how this role had been functional at some stages of Sri Lanka's history, but should now be discarded. Only the younger monks and university students tended to question this role for the sangha.

While most monks expressed genuine revulsion at the violence, here many opinions seemed hardened. Replies were given curtly: 'The Tamils have more privileges than the Sinhalese' and 'It is the Sinhalese who have the grievances; the Tamils have been privileged'. For analytical purposes, the coupling of these two positions — that the sangha should defend the Sinhalese-Buddhist identity of the nation and that the Tamils do not have any legitimate grievances against the government — shall be termed the 'hard-line' position.

Of the 37 monks, four strongly disagreed with the sangha's role in defending the religio-ethnic identity of the nation. Six felt the Tamils' claims had some justice. While 28 accepted the 'hard-line' position, eight went against the grain on at least one of these issues. Six other monks expressed less than ethusiastic support for the majority's position. When we look at those holding a minority (i.e. not the 'hard-line') view on these issues, patterns of subjective coherence begin to emerge.

The four monks who strongly disagreed with the sangha's role in defending the religio-ethnic identity of the nation diverge from the other 33 on nine issues surveyed. (Divergence is here defined as a mean score on an issue varying by one point or more). They are more likely to accept monastic involvement in party politics; they are more likely to agree that monks may both stand for elected office and identify with a political party. Ideologically, they are less likely to support free market policies and more likely to favour a controlled economy. They are also less likely to express sympathy for the Sarvodaya movement. They are less likely to feel that the Vinaya must adapt to historical circumstances than the majority, are less likely to advocate democratic socialism and, predictably, are more likely to feel that the Tamils have legitimate grievances. In terms of background factors, these monks are more likely to be young, university students, and from the Ramanna Nikaya.

Those five monks who strongly felt that the Tamils have some legitimate grievances also present intriguing divergences from the majority 32 (monks). These five diverge from the majority on the following issues: they are more likely to advocate monastic involvement in the political process than the majority. They are more likely to support direct monastic involvement in elections, to favour a monk's holding an appointed governmental office, and to identify with a political party. They are more favourable towards a monk's organising and leading a *satyagraha* campaign, but are more critical of the Sarvodaya movement. Predictably, they are more sceptical about the sangha's role in defending the nation's religious identity. They also are more likely to support the reintroduction of the bhikkhuni sangha, and are less likely to look to classical times for solutions to contemporary problems.

Background factors also seem to impinge on the monks' views of the legitimacy of Tamil grievances. Those expressing sympathy tend to be: of the middle or younger age-group; a student or of irrelevant professional status; a member of the Siyam Nikaya; and of disadvantaged economic background. While no single background factor unites these five, we do see that among those sympathetic to the Tamils, none is elder, of an undistinguished or distinguished professional position, of prosperous economic background, or has a university degree.

One must be very tentative in generalising from such a small data base to the general monastic population. However, this exploratory study indicates that the following theses ought to be tested by future work:

(1) The younger monks and those studying at the university are less likely to adopt a 'hard-line' position on 'the Tamil question'.

(2) The more politically involved a monk, the less likely he is to adhere to the 'hard line'.
(3) The 'hard line' is more likely to be rejected by those with reservations about the Sarvodaya movement, a surprising finding.
(4) Monks enjoying distinguished professional status are most likely to adopt the 'hard line'.
(5) Monks from disadvantaged socio-economic backgrounds are less likely to be 'hard line' than those from more prosperous backgrounds.

However, even among those adopting a 'hard line' on 'the Tamil question', there is mitigating evidence that this does not involve cultural insularity and an uncritical attitude towards the social order. As a whole, the monks demonstrate a high degree of openness to other cultures, ideas, religions and peoples.

Notes

1. W. Howard Wriggins, *Sri Lanka: Dilemmas of a New Nation* (Princeton, NJ: Princeton University Press, 1960).
2. Max Weber, *The Religions of India* (Glencoe, IL: The Free Press, 1958).
3. Edward Said, *Orientalism* (New York: Vantage, 1979). On the same theme, see Nathan Katz, 'Scholarly Approaches to Buddhism: A Political Analysis', *The Eastern Buddhist* (new series), *15* (1), 1982, pp. 116–21.
4. Arthur Niehoff, 'Theravada Buddhism: A Vehicle for Technical Change', *Human Organization*, *23* (2), 1984, pp. 108–12.
5. *India Today*, 15 March 1985.
6. Devindra R. Subasinghe, 'Now, A Sri Lankan Free Market Economic Miracle' (Washington, DC: The Heritage Foundation Asian Studies Center *Backgrounder*, no. 27, 7 May 1985.).
7. Ibid., p. 10.
8. 'Sri Lanka's Fearful Symmetry', *New York Times*, 29 May 1985.
9. The statistical analysis of these data is the work of F. Robert Stiglicz of the Political Science Department at Williams College, and the author is most indebted for his invaluable aid. Throughout this chapter, percentages have been rounded off.
10. This widely-held view smacks of a condescending attitude towards monks in particular and South Asian people in general.
11. Niehoff, 'Theravada Buddhism.'
12. Ellen S. Goldberg, 'Buddhist Nuns Make Comeback in Sri Lanka—To Monks' Dislike', *Christian Science Monitor*, 2 April 1984.
13. Issues of monastic involvement in socio-political arenas are the subject of an extended discussion in Nathan Katz and F. Robert Stiglicz, 'Social and Political Attitudes of Sri Lanka Monks: An Empirical Study', *South Asia Research*, *6* (2), November 1986.

Appendix: The Questionnaire

Interview No:
Date:

I. Background

Name:
Age:
Age at *pabbajja*:
Age at *upasampada*:
Location of interview:
Residence:
Profession (if any):
Occupation before *pabbajja* (if any):
Nikaya:
Home village:
Father's occupation:
If landowner, how many acres?
Other economic background:
English? Where/when studied:
Pali:
Sanskrit:
Other language(s):
Educational background:
Travel abroad:

II. Survey of social attitudes

Key: 5–agree strongly; 4–agree somewhat; 3–neutral or mixed; 2–disagree somewhat; 1–disagree strongly; 0–no opinion

_____ 1. *Vinaya* must adapt itself to historical circumstances.

_____ 2. A monk should limit his intercourse with the laity to *bana*.

_____ 3. The *sangha* should advise governments.

_____ 4. A monk may be engaged in elections and other political activities.

_____ 5. I support the free-market economy of the UNP.

_____ 6. I support a controlled economy.

_____ 7. Buddhism and Marxism are compatible philosophies.

_____ 8. Buddhism and democratic socialism are compatible.

_____ 9. Buddhism and capitalism are compatible.

_____ 10. Monks should participate in the economic development of the nation.

_____ 11. The *sangha* should defend the Sinhalese-Buddhist identity of the nation.

_____ 12. A monk could, under certain circumstances, participate in a *satyagraha*.

_____ 13. A monk could, under certain circumstances, organise and lead a *satyagraha*.

_____ 14. I am generally sympathetic to the goals and methods of the Sarvodaya Shramadana movement.

_____ 15. The Tamils have some legitimate grievances against the government.

_____ 16. Monks may hold appointed offices and positions in a government.

_____ 17. Monks may stand for elected office.

_____ 18. Monks may identify with one or another political party.

_____ 19. Monks may participate in agricultural development.

_____ 20. Monks may teach various subjects at universities and other schools.

_____ 21. Monks should restrict their teaching to the Dhamma.

_____ 22. The Mahayana is an authentic form of Buddhism.

_____ 23. The Mahayana is a compromised, degenerate form of Buddhism.

_____ 24. The *Buddhadharma* is the only path to *nibbana*.

_____ 25. All religions lead to the same goal.

_____ 26. I would support the reintroduction of the bhikkhuni sangha to Sri Lanka.

_____ 27. Meditation should be taught to the laity as well as to the sangha.

_____ 28. Tourism has only corrupting influences on our society.

_____ 29. Contemporary society, in order to solve its problems, should look to classical times for solutions.

_____ 30. In order to solve our problems, we should consider alternative solutions from all quarters.

PART IV: CASE STUDIES OF MINORITIES IN BUDDHIST POLITIES

10 THE INDIAN TAMIL PLANTATION WORKERS IN SRI LANKA: WELFARE AND INTEGRATION*

S.W.R. de A. Samarasinghe

Sri Lanka's multi-ethnic population of 15.6 million (1986) consists of 11.5 million (74 per cent) Sinhalese, 2.8 million (18.1 per cent) Tamils and 1.1 million (7.1 per cent) Muslims, and a number of other small ethnic groups each numbering less than 50,000.[1] The Tamil minority consists of two distinct subgroups: the Sri Lankan Tamils (2.0 million or 12.6 per cent of the total population) and the 'Indian' (or 'Plantation') Tamils (0.86 million or 5.5 per cent of the total population). The former came to Sri Lanka from South India in antiquity, and today form a part of Sri Lanka's indigenous population.[2] The latter came mainly as immigrant plantation workers over a period of more than a hundred years beginning about 1825.

The current ethnic conflict is almost entirely between the Sri Lankan Tamil minority and the Sinhalese. For reasons discussed later, the Indian Tamils have not been directly involved in it, although the dynamics of the conflict are such that they, too, are being increasingly drawn into the thick of it.[3]

This chapter describes the historical evolution of the Indian Tamils in Sri Lanka and analyses the process of integration of the community to the larger Sri Lankan polity while retaining their distinct cultural identity.

Origins

The Indian Tamil immigrants came to the country in search of employment and business opportunities created by the development of the plantation economy under British rule.[4] It was reported that by 1837 there were about 10,000 Indian estate labourers on the island.[5]

* The helpful comments made by K.M. de Silva and Michael Reich on a draft of this chapter are gratefully acknowledged.

Over the next 100 years their number grew steadily in step with the expansion of the plantations. The 1911 population census recorded 531,000 Indian Tamils (13 per cent of the population) and at independence in 1948 the number was about 800,000 (12 per cent of the population). There are some important features concerning Indian immigration to Sri Lanka during this period that are worth noting.

First, the bulk of the Indian immigrants were Hindu Tamils belonging to depressed (scheduled) castes from the present Tamilnadu state in South India. The majority of them came to work as unskilled labourers on the island's rapidly expanding plantations. These people were motivated to migrate partly because of poverty—famine, low income, unemployment ('push' factors)—at home, and partly because of the relatively attractive conditions—mainly an assured job and income ('pull' factors)—on the island. Moreover, among the immigrant destinations in various parts of the British Empire, Sri Lanka had the advantage of being the closest to South India and provided better prospects to maintain close ties with home or even return home.

Second, a significant number of Indian Tamil immigrants also found employment as unskilled and semi-skilled workers in the urban sector, especially in Colombo, in the harbour, railways, road construction, sewage and sanitary services, as well as numerous sundry occupations such as tailors, barbers and rickshaw pullers. Thus an official study estimated that in 1936, of a total Indian Tamil population of around 870,000, about 660,000 (76 per cent) were on estates and the remaining 210,000 (24 per cent) were outside the estates.[6]

Third, there was a small number of Tamils with some education who immigrated to Sri Lanka to take up employment in white-collar jobs such as clerks and teachers.

Fourth, there was a comparatively small but highly visible and important group of Indian immigrants who came to Sri Lanka for business. The immigrant labourers were mostly Tamils. The businessmen, however, were an ethnically mixed group that consisted not only of South Indians, including Malabar Moors and Natukottai Chettiars, but also Borahs, Sindhis and Memons from the western part of India.[7] Jackson estimates that in 1936, trader families would have accounted for a minimum of 20 per cent (i.e. 40,000) of the total Indian population outside the estates.[8] Indians dominated the import of goods from India.[9] They also claimed an important share of the wholesale and retail trade on the island. Moreover, until the Great

Depression in 1930–1 Natukottai Chettiars dominated money-lending outside the formal European-owned banking network.[10] Since access to the latter for native businessmen was highly restricted, this in effect meant that the Natukottai Chettiars were the island's foremost informal bankers.[11]

The period before 1900 was marked by a more or less *laissez-faire* attitude towards Indian immigration. Gangs of Indian workers, freely recruited by agents known as *Kangaanies*, were brought to the island. For the employers, this method ensured an assured supply of cheap labour.[12]

When Indian immigration commenced in the 1830s it was seasonal because Sri Lanka's first major plantation crop, coffee, did not require a large permanent resident labour force. Thus the bulk of the immigrants were adult males who returned to India each year. Tea, which replaced coffee after the 1860s, required a more stable resident workforce. Therefore, every encouragement was given by the employers for whole families to immigrate to settle permanently.[13] Consequently, what Jayaraman[14] recognises as the first phase of Indian immigration to Sri Lanka characterised by seasonal fluctuations, gradually came to be a more permanent type of settled immigration.

In the new situation, fluctuations were not seasonal but cyclical. Net immigration increased in boom conditions on the plantations, as it did during 1923–8, and dropped when a recession or depression occurred, as it did in 1929–33. However, the trend was decidedly upward, and with rubber also emerging as a major new plantation crop after 1900, the Indian Tamil immigrant population increased very rapidly in the first three decades of the twentieth century. By 1929 the estate Indian population alone was an estimated 740,000 and the non-estate population another 150,000, which totaled about 900,000 and accounted in all for about 15 per cent of the island's population.

The rapid growth of the Indian population was accompanied by a significant qualitative change in official attitudes and policy towards them, especially the estate labour force. The initiative for this change actually came from the Indian government, which passed the Indian Emigration Ordinance No. 7 of 1922 regulating all Indian emigration. In order to continue to receive Indian immigrants, Sri Lanka had to conform to certain basic requirements to improve the welfare of immigrant workers. This Sri Lanka did by passing the Labour Ordinance of 1923 which gave legal effect to several such provisions.[15] Perhaps the most significant step taken was the enactment of the Minimum Wage Ordinance of 1927 which specified minimum wage rates for plantation workers, who became the first group of workers to enjoy this privilege on the island.

A profile of socio-economic status

The Indian Tamils as a group stand out from the rest of the Sri Lankan population due to their overwhelming concentration in the plantation economy and comparatively low social status (Table 10.1). Around three-quarters of the Indian Tamil population live on estates, and over 80 per cent of the labour force in that community is employed in the plantation industry. Indeed, on the plantations even today all other Sri Lankans account for only 20 per cent of the jobs.

The national literacy rate is 86.5 per cent, but the Indian Tamil rate is only 66 per cent. Moreover, the Indian Tamils' infant mortality rate is estimated to be about twice the national average of 23 per 1,000. The median income per worker is only slightly above half the national figure. This comparative backwardness has had a lot to do with the traditional association of the Indian Tamils with the evolution of the plantation economy and the political configuration that emerged in Sri Lanka after independence. The interesting question — not only from the point of view of Sri Lanka's future as a nation, but also from a theoretical perspective — is the manner in which the Indian Tamil community will evolve in the future to take its legitimate place in the Sri Lankan polity.

Status, class and power

The historical evolution of Sri Lanka's Indian Tamil community and the current position it occupies in the island nation's society and polity, especially in the light of the current ethnic conflict, raise some interesting theoretical issues about social stratification in a developing pluralistic society. As a group the Indian Tamils have had a remarkable degree of internal social cohesion. If occupation is considered a criterion to distinguish social class, then as plantation labourers they occupy a clearly demarcated segment of society. In that position they have had very little in common with the Sinhalese in the areas where they lived. Almost all the major dimensions of social stratification — culture, religion, caste and occupation — have stood as barriers against any close links being formed between the two groups.

Even more striking is the fact that Indian Tamils and Sri Lankan Tamils never developed truly close bonds. As an ethnic group the Indian Tamils and Sri Lankan Tamils belong to the same South Indian Dravidian stock. They speak the same language, Tamil, and in each group about 85 per cent are Hindus and the rest Christians. However, for several reasons, until now these common factors have not served to promote an ethnic bond between the two groups. First, the mostly upper-caste Sri Lankan Tamils, considered the mostly depressed-caste Indian Tamils to be their social inferiors. Second, because of continued links maintained by many Indian Tamils with their home villages in South India, they have generally been considered to be temporary immigrants, in contrast to the permanently settled Sri Lankan Tamils. Third, there is a vast gap in education between the poorly-educated Indian Tamils and the generally better-educated Sri Lankan Tamils. Fourth, the former are predominantly working-class, whereas the majority of the latter consider themselves to be either farmer-class or middle-class. Fifth, the two groups occupy two different parts of the country. Most Indian Tamils live in the central region and south-west corner of the country where the tea and rubber plantations are located. With the exception of the Nuwara Eliya district, where the Sinhalese number only about 36 per cent, these are predominantly Sinhalese areas. Only 8 per cent of the Indian Tamils live in the north and east which are inhabited predominantly by the Sri Lankan Tamils. For these reasons, not only are the prefixes 'Indian' and 'Sri Lankan' used to distinguish between the two groups but, more importantly, few social or political bonds have developed between them. Socially, for example, between 1973 and 1978, only 2,678 marriages were registered that involved partners from the two communities. In contrast there were over 45,000 marriages in each group where both partners were from the same community.

The Sri Lanka Workers' Congress (CWC), the trade-union-based political party established in 1941, commands the unchallenged allegiance of the bulk of the Indian Tamils. The political cleavage between the two Tamil communities is starkly evident today when Sri Lankan Tamil groups were locked in a violent battle with President J. R. Jayewardene's government, in which the CWC leader, Sooriyamurthi Thondaman, holds a senior Cabinet appointment.

Thus when, Indian Tamils are recognised as a group with its own unique identity, the question that arises is the way they will relate as a group to the larger social dynamic of the Sri Lankan polity in the next two or three decades. There are two broad facets involved. First, how will they relate to the Sinhalese and the Sri Lankan Tamils in the context of the current ethnic rivalry? Second, what would be the processes and implications of the political and socio-economic uplifting and integration of the community to the Sri Lankan polity? In the rest of this chapter we shall look at the position of the Indian Tamils with a view to answering these questions.

Table 10.1 Indian Tamils: A Socio-economic Profile, 1981

Population (1981)		825,000
As a percentage of total population		5.56
Distribution of population, 1981 (%)		
Urban		7.3
Rural		16.1
Estate		76.6
Employment, 1981–2 (%)		
Estate		83.0
Other		17.0
Education, 1981 (%)		
Illiterate		33.1
Secondary or higher		8.6
Median monthly income per income receiver, 1981–2		
Indian Tamil	Rs 378	(US$ 18)
All communities	Rs 689	(US$ 34)
Infant mortality rate per 1,000 live births, 1984		
Average for Sri Lanka		23.1
Plantations only		over 50

Sources: Department of Census and Statistics, *Census of Population and Housing, Sri Lanka 1981* (Colombo: Department of Census and Statistics, 1981); Central Bank of Sri Lanka, *Report on Consumer Finances & Socio Economic Survey, 1981/82 Sri Lanka* (Colombo: Central Bank of Sri Lanka, 1984); Registrar General's Department, Colombo; Janatha Estate Development Board, *Orientation Seminar for Estate Superintendents on Formulation of Nutrition Intervention Programmes (Colombo: 1984), p. 4.*

Friction, conflict and uncertainties: 1930–64

As long as the Indian immigrants were sojourners living mainly in estate enclaves separated from the native population and taking jobs which the latter did not want, there was not much room for ethnic friction. Even the urban worker did not evidence a desire for permanent settlement. For example, in 1931 in Colombo, the male to female ratio in the Indian Tamil population was more than four to one, and among the 17,000 Malayalis there were only about 600 females. Indeed, the savings that were remitted home and the periodic visits made by the immigrants to India— it was reported that around 1930 about 120,000 or 16 per cent of the estate population visited India annually[16]— only served further to strengthen this non-permanent image of the Indian immigrant. However, the situation began to change in the inter-war period, especially in the 1930s, and the Indian community began to get embroiled in national issues. There were a number of reasons for this turn of events.

First, the sharp growth in the Indian population and the more settled and permanent character[17] it acquired after 1900 began to be felt by the native population. This was so especially in the two Kandyan provinces—Central Province and Uva[18]—where the estate population increased fivefold from 114,000 in 1871 to 585,000 in 1946, and the non-estate population increased almost threefold from 360,000 to 919,000 during the same period.[19] This population increase put tremendous pressure on land and made the Kandyan Sinhalese feel that the Indian estate Tamils were making a living off the land which should legitimately be theirs. Thus, the demand was made to acquire estates for distribution among the landless Kandyan peasantry.[20]

Second, the economic difficulties caused by the Great Depression had the unfortunate consequence of focusing attention on 'foreigners' who, it was alleged, took business and jobs away from natives, a sentiment also expressed elsewhere.[21] In Sri Lanka this attitude had two facets. One was the criticism levelled by Sri Lankan businessmen against the Indian businessmen and the Chettiar moneylenders who were accused of exploitation and usuary respectively. In popular perception this antipathy got extended by association to the Indian community as a whole.

Third, the economic recession of the 1930s, in the context of a rapidly rising population,[22] led to the demand that Indian immigration should be terminated to preserve jobs for the locals. An official enquiry did not find evidence of immigrants taking away jobs from the natives and refused to stop immigration.[23] Nevertheless, after 1930 there was a deliberate shift in government policy to give preference to natives in employment ('Sri Lankanisation'),[24] and no estate labourers were freshly recruited from India after 1937. Furthermore, under two schemes of repatriation begun in 1924 and 1937 respectively, over 135,000 Indian Tamil estate workers were repatriated over 1924–51.[25] Finally, in reaction to a Sri Lankan government decision to dismiss about 2,500 Indian workers in government service and repatriate them to India, the Indian government imposed a total ban on immigration of unskilled labour to the island with effect from 1 August 1939.

Fourth, fears were expressed that the Indian Tamils would undermine the position of the Kandyan Sinhalese if the former got voting rights under the Donoughmore Constitution (1931), which introduced universal franchise to Sri Lanka. At the behest of Governor Sir Herbert Stanley and the Sinhalese political leaders, the original recommendation of the Commision to give the right to vote to all who qualified on residence was modified to make it available only to those who have had a minimum of five years' residence. In the elections to the first State Council in 1931, the Indian Tamils (15 per cent of the population) had about 100,500 votes (6 per cent of the electorate) and elected two members to a house of 50. One of them became the minister of labour as well.[26]

The concern among some sections of the Sinhalese community regarding Indian voting rights was strengthened by the rapid increase in the number of Indian registered voters, from 100,500 in 1931 to 235,000 in 1939. As a defensive reaction the Sinhalese-dominated government decided, under the Village Committee Ordinance of 1937, to deny the Indian Tamils the vote in village committee elections, a disadvantage which was removed only in 1977. Moreover, regulations for registration of voters were tightened, which resulted in the number of registered Indian Tamil voters dropping to 168,000 by 1943.[27]

Attempts to resolve the citizenship and immigration problems in two rounds of Indo-Sri Lankan talks in 1940 and 1941 failed.[28] In the 1947 parliamentary elections seven Indian Tamil members (7 per cent of the total seats in Parliament) were elected from the Kandyan electorates. The Indian Tamil voters also influenced the results in another dozen or more seats. Consequently, two issues came up. One was the loss of parliamentary representation for the Kandyan Sinhalese in the constituencies where the Indian Tamils won. The other was the perceived left-wing preference of the Indian Tamil voters which displeased the then ruling right-of-centre United National Party (UNP). As a 'remedy' for both, the government enacted the Sri Lanka Citizenship Act of 1948 and the Indian and Pakistani Residents (Citizenship) Act of 1949 which stipulated stringent conditions under which citizenship could be obtained. Then by the simple device of restricting the vote to only Sri Lankan citizens, through the Sri Lanka Parliamentary Elections (Amendment) Act of 1949, the government disenfranchised the bulk of the Indian Tamils. Under the new regulations, 825,000 applied for Sri Lankan citizenship but only about 135,000 (16 per cent) were successful. In the first general election (1952) that followed under the new dispensation, no Indian Tamil was elected to Parliament.

Following Indian (1947) and Sri Lankan (1948) independence, the Indian Tamil issue was eventually resolved through two agreements.[29] The first, in 1964, was between Sri Lanka's Prime Minister Sirima R.D. Bandaranaike and Indian Prime Minister Lal Bahadur Shastri. In it, Sri Lanka agreed to confer citizenship on 300,000 stateless Indian Tamils and their natural increase. India agreed to accept 525,000 and their natural increase. The agreement was to be implemented over a 15-year period. The status of another 150,000 Indian Tamils who were left out of the 1964 agreement was resolved in the second agreement (1974) between Mrs Bandaranaike and Indian Prime Minister Indira Gandhi, in which each country undertook to accept another 75,000. However, only 506,000 applied for Indian citizenship. In February 1986, the Sri Lanka government settled the matter by granting Sri Lankan citizenship to the remaining 94,000. Under the Indo- Sri Lanka peace accord of July 1987 India will take the residual of about 100,000 people who have acquired Indian citizenship but still remain on the island.

From discrimination to integration: after 1964

The restrictions upon claims to citizenship and disenfranchisement of the Indian Tamils in 1948–9 denied them political power and blunted their ability to compete with other groups in the country. For example, being non-citizens, they were deprived of access to agricultural land under land-settlement schemes.[30] They were also ineligible for jobs in the state sector and the organised private sector.

After the mid-1950s the employment opportunities and welfare benefits provided on the plantations were also constrained by several factors. Extended periods of depressed commodity prices, coupled with heavy taxation on plantation crops, prevented the plantation workers from obtaining higher wages. For, example, between 1955 and 1973 real wage rates in the plantation sector declined marginally. Rapid population growth on plantations and the take-over of estates by the government for village expansion aggravated the unemployment and under-employment problem.[31] The nationalisation of plantations in 1972 and 1975, and its resultant realienations, caused considerable displacements among Indian Tamil plantation labor. These and other related conditions (see Table 10.1) persuaded Hugh Tinker to describe the Indian Tamils as 'permanently second class citizens...[an] under class...in powerless conditions...compelled to assume a ghetto identity'.[32] However, since Tinker wrote those words over a decade ago there are definite signs of improvement and, indeed, his very pessimistic prognostication appears to be increasingly irrelevant.

The granting of citizenship and the acquisition of voting rights have removed the principal political disability that confronted the Indian Tamils. The Sri Lanka Workers Congress (CWC), which severed its connections with the separatist Tamil United Liberation Front (TULF) in 1976, supported the UNP led by J.R. Jayewardene in the 1977 general election. The CWC also won one seat in parliament and its leader, S. Thondaman, who was elected, was given a Cabinet office.

The CWC's willingness to work with the government appears to be based on practical considerations. First, its leadership of the estate Tamils can be retained only if the distinct identity of the latter is preserved. Second, 90 per cent of the Indian Tamils live in the south among the Sinhalese. They have neither a strong territorial claim or attachment to a 'homeland' as the northern Tamils do. Third, the need to alleviate the socio-economic conditions of the Indian Tamils takes precedence over linguistic nationalism. Fourth, between the Indian Tamils and the Sinhalese there is not the same mutual suspicion and the intense competition for jobs, land, university places, and so on, as exists between the Sinhalese and the Sri Lankan Tamils. Fifth, the CWC obviously wishes to exploit the electoral power it has in the south for benefit of its supporters. Thus, notwithstanding the damage to person and property suffered by some Indian Tamils in the racial violence of 1977, 1981 and 1983, the CWC leadership has repeatedly declared its commitment to a united Sri Lanka and opposition to the separatist movement. Indeed, in the absence of the Sri Lankan Tamil political leadership from Parliament after August 1983, Thondaman has become an intermediary between the government and the Sri Lankan Tamil leadership.

The CWC and Mr Thondaman have used their position to win several political and economic concessions for the estate workers. The most notable political concession was granting citizenship to the 94,000 Indian Tamils who, in principle, should have gone to India under the Indo-Sri Lanka agreements. The most important economic gain has been wage increases for plantation workers. For example, the minimum nominal wage rate for an adult male unskilled tea estate worker has risen from Rs 4.36 in July 1977 to Rs 23.75 in April 1984 (445 per cent). From April 1984, breaking with a century-old tradition, female estate workers are being paid the same wage rates as males. A large number of plantation workers have received assistance from the Ministry of Rural Industrial Development, headed by Mr Thondaman, for small-scale dairying.

Social welfare forms an important part of the US$211.8 million 1985-9 medium-term investment programme in the plantation sector. In 1984 the Education Ministry recruited 1,000 teachers for estate schools and in July 1987 it was announced that another 2,000 will be recruited. According to the Public Investment Programme 1985-9,36.2 per cent (Rs 202 million) of the total sum (Rs 559 million) allocated to new projects in education will be for the development of the plantation schools. Around 50,000 new housing units are to be built for plantation workers by 1990.

The socio-economic gap which existed between the Indian Tamils and the rest of the Sri Lankan community began to narrow after 1970. Since the early 1970s the unemployment and underemployment rates on estates have been below those in the urban and rural areas.[33] The median income in the estate sector as a proportion of the all-island median income increased from 48.9 per cent in 1973 to 61.8 per cent in 1978-9 and remained almost unchanged at 61.4 per cent in 1981-2.[34] But even more importantly, owing to a female labour-force participation rate on the estates that is three times the national average and children who work, the crude activity rate on the estates is about 50–60 per cent higher than elsewhere. Thus, in 1963 and 1973 there was practically no difference between the average family income on the estates and the rural sector although by about 1980 the estate family income had dropped to around 70–75 per cent of rural family income. However, it is likely that the 1984 wage increase for estate workers would have reduced the gap. Illiteracy on the estates declined by about 16 per cent between 1953 and 1973 and by another 14 percent between 1973 and 1981.

The above gains notwithstanding,[35] much remains to be done before the Indian Tamils are fully integrated into the mainstream of Sri Lankan society. To complete that process the Indian Tamils have to emerge from the plantation enclave. They also need a strong middle class to assume a more normal social profile. The Indian Tamils are likely to mobilise their new-found political strength under the CWC to achieve these objectives. Although they are only about one-twentieth of the population overall, the CWC commands an important bloc vote in Sri Lanka's presidential elections. Moreover, they will be able strongly to influence future parliamentary elections in some districts in central Sri Lanka where they live in large numbers.

Conclusions

Sri Lanka is a country of immigrants and the Indian Tamils have been the most recent such large group. Native–immigrant conflicts are a common feature in most such societies. Viewed from that perspective, we can appreciate better both the plight of the Indian Tamils and the anxieties of the host community over the three phases — c. 1830–1930, 1930–64 and post 1964 — that we have identified. For over a century the Indian Tamils were essentially a community apart, economically, socially and culturally, and the question of integration never really arose. When it did in the 1930s, the fundamentals were resolved over a period of about 35 years, half of which was under a colonial administration when neither Sri Lanka nor India were totally free to reach a mutually acceptable settlement.

Buddhism in Sri Lanka, not having a proselytising tradition, has not been used as a means of assimilation of any recent immigrant community. Neither has Sri Lanka resorted to expulsion of immigrants, as countries such as Burma and Uganda have done to their own Indian immigrant communities. Even though the repatriation programme exerted a certain amount of pressure on the Indian Tamils to apply for Indian citizenship, in the final analysis there was no strict compulsion to do so, even to help achieve the target specified for India. Indeed, in 1986 Sri Lanka decided to absorb 94,000 Indian Tamils and their natural increase who should have gone to India under the Bandaranaike–Shastri agreement. This is particularly important in the context of the fact that undetected illicit immigrants from South India, roughly estimated to number anything between 100,000 and 500,000[36], if true, accounted for, perhaps, about 10 per cent of the Indian Tamil population in 1964. Moreover, Mrs Bandaranaike's proposal to place the Indian Tamils on a separate electoral register was also dropped after Indian and local criticism.

The recent bouts of ethnic violence have definitely interrupted the integration process of the Indian Tamils. Nevertheless, it is more likely that practical political and socio-economic considerations, and the essential affinities and humanism of Buddhism and Hinduism, will persuade the Sinhalese and the Indian Tamils to accept each other as integral parts of a larger Sri Lankan plural society.

Finally, it is useful to ask whether any conclusions of a more general and theoretical nature can be drawn from the experience of the Indian Tamil community in Sri Lanka concerning the nature and importance of ethnicity as a social force in the Third World. In my view, the experience recounted here offers an excellent example of a case where cultural identity, and political and socio-economic factors, reinforce each other to produce a strong ethnic subgroup identity. This case suggests that shared primordial factors, such as language and religion, powerful as they may be in promoting group identity, are not by themselves sufficient to overcome social class clevages that divide an ethnic group — Indian Tamils and Sri Lankan Tamils. This experience also shows that, even in a country poor in resources, an immigrant ethnic group can be peacefully integrated to the host society through judicious policies. What is required is the political will to do it and a mutual recognition of the sanctity of cultural identity of the two groups involved.

Notes

1. Nearly 94 per cent (10.8 million) of the Sinhalese are Buddhists and 69 per cent (1.9 million) of the Tamils are Hindus. Thus some see a religious angle (Buddhists versus Hindus) to the present ethnic conflict. However, it is generally felt that the Christian churches of the various denominations in which there are members of both communities are also divided to some extent along ethnic lines on this issue, and that religion does not enter the picture directly.
2. At present approximately 50 per cent of the Sri Lankan Tamils live in the Northern Province (13.5 percent of the island's land area), which they dominate. About 20 per cent live in the Eastern Province (15 per cent of the island), which they share with the Sinhalese and the Muslims. The remaining 30 per cent of Sri Lankan Tamils live in the south among the Sinhalese.

3. The conflict was further complicated when clashes occurred in April 1985 in the Eastern Province between the Tamils and the Muslims who until then were detached bystanders in the conflict.
4. On the development of the plantation economy, see Donald R. Snodgrass, *Sri Lanka: An Export Economy in Transition* (Homewood, IL: Richard D. Irwin Inc., 1966).
5. Government of Sri Lanka, *Report of the Committee Appointed to Consider the Medical Wants Ordinance and the Diseases (Labourers) Ordinance. Nos. 9 and 10 of 1912*, Sessional Paper XXI of 1930 (Colombo: Sri Lanka Government Press, 1930).
6. Sir Edward Jackson, *Report of a Commission on Immigration into Sri Lanka*, Sessional Paper III of 1938 (Colombo: Sri Lanka Government Press, 1938).
7. See Haraprasad Chattopadhyaya, *Indians in Sri Lanka* (Calcutta: OPS Publishers, 1979), pp. 140–69.
8. Jackson, *Report on Immigration*.
9. In the colonial economy India was Sri Lanka's second most important trading partner behind the UK. Sri Lanka's exports to India were negligible, but in 1924–9 23 per cent of the country's imports, mostly textiles, rice and other consumer goods, came from India. The Indian business houses in Colombo who had the appropriate business links in India and credit facilities from the Chettiar money-lenders had no difficulty in monopolising this business.
10. See Government of Sri Lanka, *Sri Lanka Banking Commission Report*, Sessional Paper XXII of 1934 (Colombo: Sri Lanka Government Press, 1934).
11. See W.S. Weerasooriya, *The Natukottai Chettiar: Merchant Bankers in Sri Lanka* (Colombo: Tisara Publishers, 1973).
12. From about the third quarter of the nineteenth century some legislation was enacted to provide basic education and health facilities and to regulate working conditions. However, these did not amount to much. See Visakha Kumari Jayawardene, *The Rise of the Labor Movement in Sri Lanka* (Durham, NC: Duke University Press, 1972); Chattopadhyaya, *Indians*, pp. 170–83; Government of Sri Lanka, *Report of the Committee appointed to consider the Medical Wants Ordinance and Diseases (Labourers) Ordinance Nos 9 and 10 of 1912*.
13. Whereas in the nineteenth century the adult male to female ratio on the estates was very high, by the mid-1930s this was almost one to one (Jackson, *Report on Immigration*).
14. R. Jayaraman, 'Indian Emigration to Sri Lanka: Some Aspects of the Historical and Social Background of the Emigrants', *Indian Economic and Social History Review, 4*,(4), December 1967, pp. 319–59.
15. S.U. Kodikara, *Indo-Sri Lanka Relations Since Independence* (Colombo: Sri Lanka Institute of World Affairs, 1965), pp. 8–9.
16. Government of Sri Lanka, *Report of the Committee appointed to consider the Medical Wants Ordinance and Diseases (Labourers) Ordinance Nos. 9 and 10 of 1912*, p. 3.
17. No definite estimate has been made of the permanent settler population. Kodikara, *Indo-Sri Lanka Relations*, p. 11) notes that the

Donoughmore Commission (1928) estimated it to be 40–50 per cent, the Jackson Report (1938) 60 per cent, and the Soulbury Commission (1945) 80 per cent. Although these may by rough figures, given the fact that they were an informed official opinion, the upward trend supports the view that the Indian Tamils were increasingly becoming a settled population.

18. These two provinces embrace the districts of Kandy, Matale, Nuwara Eliya, Badulla and Moneragala.

19. Government of Sri Lanka, *Report of the Kandyan Peasantry Commission*, Sessional Paper XVIII of 1951 (Colombo: Government of Sri Lanka Press, 1951).

20. Ibid., p. 18.

21. See, for example, Michael Adas, *The Burma Delta* (Madison: University of Wisconsin Press, 1974).

22. Between 1911–21 and 1921–32, the inter-censal population growth rate nearly doubled from 9.5 to 18.9 per cent.

23. Jackson, *Report on Immigration*.

24. Government of Sri Lanka, *Report on Labour Conditions in Sri Lanka*, Sessional Paper XIX of 1943 (Colombo: Sri Lanka Government Press, 1943), p. 11.

25. Commissioner of Labour, *Administration Reports 1951* (Colombo: Sri Lanka Government Press, 1951), Table XX.

26. In the 1936 election two were elected.

27. K.M. de Silva, 'The Minorities and Universal Suffrage' in K.M. de Silva, ed., *Universal Franchise 1931–1981. The Sri Lankan Experience* (Colombo: Department of Information, Ministry of State, 1981), pp. 85–6.

28. See Kodikara, *Indo-Sri Lanka Relations*, pp. 92–8.

29. See ibid., ch. IV.

30. The Land Development Ordinance of 1935 restricted state land lease under colonisation to Sri Lankans. This was only one but perhaps the most important of several such legislation enacted during the thirties.

31. Until the second quarter of 1971 repatriation under the 1964 agreement was very limited. Thus, in 1969–70 'very roughly... underemployment in the sense of short hours...amounted to about 10 percent of the employed manpower...Open unemployment [was] about the same possibly somewhat more'. See International Labour Office (ILO), *Matching Employment Opportunities and Expectations* (Geneva: ILO, 1971), p. 30.

32. Hugh Tinker, *The Banyan Tree—Overseas Immigrants from India, Pakistan and Bangladesh* (Oxford: Oxford University Press, 1977), ch. 2 and p. 50.

33. Central Bank of Sri Lanka, *Survey of Sri Lanka's Consumer Finances,* (Colombo: Central Bank of Sri Lanka, 1973, 1981–2).

34. Ibid.

35. Some observers do not concede that much has been done in the past decade to improve the living standards of the Tamil plantation workers. See, for example, Ronald Rote, *A Taste of Bitterness—The Political Economy of Tea Plantations in Sri Lanka* (Amsterdam: Free University Press, 1986), ch. IX.

36. Kodikara, *Indo-Sri Lanka Relations*, pp.155–6.

11 RELIGIOUS MINORITIES IN BURMA IN THE CONTEMPORARY PERIOD

Trevor O. Ling

Religious minorities and the events of 1961–2

In this chapter the contemporary period will be taken to mean the period of Ne Win's government, from 1962 to the present time. The religious minorities contributed significantly to events which led to the military take-over on 2 March 1962.[1] The state of affairs which made the coup necessary had developed out of the excitement and turmoil of the preceding decade, and the so-called 'Buddhist Revival' promoted by the government of U Nu and the Anti-Fascist People's Freedom League. Comprehensive accounts of the controversies and tensions which arose between the Buddhist majority and the non-Buddhist minorities in Burma during the years up to 1962 have been provided by D.E. Smith and Michael Mendelson.[2] After the euphoria of the *Buddha Jayanti* celebrations in 1956, which in Burma took the form of the building of a vast new 'cave' to serve as the assembly for the Sixth Buddhist Council and the setting up of a new Buddhist complex at Kaba Aye on the outskirts of Rangoon, some further culminating symbolic act seemed to be required, in Prime Minister U Nu's view. It took the form of a declaration by U Nu to the monks at the final full session of the council that consideration would be given to the possibility of making Buddhism the state religion of Burma, but he did warn the assembly of monks that there were, however, certain difficulties — the effect such an action would have on the unity of Burma; on neighbouring countries; and on non-Buddhist government servants in Burma.

D.E. Smith points out that U Nu shifted his ground in later public statements and 'seemed to regard the 1956 declaration as an unconditional promise which he was honor-bound to keep'.[3] After preliminary meetings with non-Buddhist religious leaders — Muslim, Christian and Hindu — to discuss the nature and effect of the contemplated legislation, U Nu became involved in bitter controversy with his own political party, the Anti-Fascist People's Freedom League. Such controversy was even more serious and damaging to national unity.

Therefore,

> With the threat of civil war hanging over the country, General Ne Win was
> installed as premier in October 1958. His caretaker government proved to
> be stable, honest and efficient; not a few Burmese greeted the prospect of
> general elections in early 1960 and a return to party politics with under-
> standable misgivings.[4]

But by the time the elections were held a great deal of campaigning on
the issue of making Buddhism the state religion had been carried out
by political monks and by lay supporters of U Nu's party. U Nu
himself had assumed the robes of a monk for a short period. He was
accused by his political opponents of deliberately using religion for
political purposes. It has also been said that he believed he would gain
religious merit by making Buddhism the state religion, and it could
therefore equally well be said that he was using politics for religious
purposes. In U Nu's way of seeing things the two were perhaps so
closely intertwined that success in one inevitably meant success in the
other. However, the political success was short-lived despite the fact
that amendments to the Constitution making Buddhism the state
religion of the Union of Burma became law in August 1961. This
faced strenuous objections from religious minorities. The Buddhist
monks soon had another grievance. Further legislation was proposed,
in which 'The Union government [promised to] protect the [minorities]
from all dangers including insult and false representation made by
words either spoken or written or by other means'.[5] September and
October saw a series of mass demonstrations by Buddhist monks and
laymen against the proposal to protect other religions,[6] which led to
violence between them and the Muslims in a suburb of Rangoon.

During the next four months, from November 1961 to February
1962, relations between the government and the non-Burman areas of
the country deteriorated further. The tension between them was
increased by the events of 1961; one of the immediate consequences
was the formation of the Kachin Independence Army. It was clear
that the coup of 1962 was to prevent further disintegration of the
Union of Burma; what was surprising was the swiftness and silence
with which it was carried out.

The religious minorities since 1962

This time Ne Win and the Revolutionary Council did not hand back the reins of government. No direct action was taken to reverse U Nu's State Religion Act but 'the coup was widely interpreted as a repudiation of U Nu's revivalism and medievalism in favour of a modern scientific approach to Burma's problems'.[7] The new government discontinued the practice introduced by U Nu of observing Buddhist sabbath days (which follow a lunar calendar) as public holidays and reverted to the more general practice of observing Saturday afternoon and Sunday as the weekend holiday, a change which was widely welcomed. In the interests of public health, U Nu's ban on killing insects, rodents and pests was also lifted. Fairly soon, in what amounted to a brief policy statement, the new government announced the right of every citizen to practise his or her religion without hindrance, and the government's intention to support every citizen's right to adhere to the ethics and traditions of the various religions. What was indirectly rejected was the right of the Buddhist community (and the extremist monks in particular) to dictate to non-Buddhists in matters of the common life of the country. In April 1962 the Revolutionary Council published a document called *The Burmese Way to Socialism* which could be described as a prospectus of its economic and political programme.

In 1969 it was considered time to 'put affairs of State on an enduring constitutional basis'. The Chairman of the Revolutionary Council, Brigadier San Yu, announcing this decision, offered some general suggestions concerning the new constitution: 'The greatest emphasis that I have laid is on the question of the states. All I want is to get the Burmese and the people of the frontier more intimate with one another.'[8] Who came to be included as the 'people of Burma's frontiers' was largely a matter of nineteenth-century historical chance for, as Peter Kundstadter has pointed out, the political boundaries of Burma are 'largely the result of British colonial efforts and British attempts to define a zone of influence as against those of France and China'.[9]

Broadly, the people of the frontier belonged to the following states; the figures show the number of people in each who had voting rights in 1973.

Kachin	329,517
Kayah	55,263
Karen	347,986
Chin	156,105
Mon	664,478

Arakan	844,019
Shan	1,491,639

It is in these states that most religious minorities are found in their largest numbers. In 1973 the Union of Burma comprised 14 states with a total number of 14,760,036 voters. The 'frontier states' contained 22 per cent of the total voters in Burma or 3,244,526 voters.

The highest proportion of votes in favour of the new Constitution occurred in a predominantly Burman area, the Magwe Division (97.44 per cent). Pegu and Rangoon Divisions also showed high rates in favour: 97.24 and 95.46 per cent respectively. In fourth place came the Chin State with 95.4 per cent. But apart from this one exception, all the other 'frontier' states cast the lowest votes in favour, and stand at the bottom of the table, in places 11-15, as follows (although there are 14 state divisions, another category in the list was 'embassies and consulates abroad':

11. Arakan State	86.09
12. Karen State	77.69
13. Kayah State	71.01
14. Kachin State	68.84
15. Shan State	66.40

Broadly, there appears to be some positive correlation between 'frontier' areas and a lower level of enthusiasm for the new Constitution which was being proposed in 1973. We now have to consider to what extent religious minorities played a part in producing this result. It has to be pointed out that the proposed Constitution made positive provision for freedom of religion within the bounds of the law. In view of these clear provisions for ensuring that there should be no discrimination or coercion of citizens on grounds of religion, it may be useful to consider that, with the one exception of Chin State, the 'frontier' states voted with much less enthusiasm than any other states for the new constitution.

The Case of the Chin and the Kachin

The high proportion of votes (95.4 per cent) cast by the Chin in the referendum on the proposed new Constitution suggests that relations between them and the Burmans were somewhat better than those between the Karen, Kachin or Shan with the Burmans. The Chin vote was, as we have noted, the fourth highest of all the state divisions of Burma, and distinguishes them from the other ethnic minorities of the Union.

Among the possible explanations for this difference from the Karen, Kachin and Shan in their attitude to Ne Win's government, there is, first, one of an historical and cultural nature. In his excellent study of the Chin, L.K. Lehman has emphasised the extent to which Chin society and culture is 'a response to Burman civilisation';[10] they 'are affected by Burman civilisation because they have always had close relations with it'.[11] This process began from about the middle of the eighth century 'with the development of Burman civilisation and of Chin interaction with it'.[12] Lehman demonstrates the considerable extent to which Chin legends about their origins 'purport to connect the development of the complex form of Chin sociopolitical organization to a former close connection with the plains civilization of Burma'.[13] If they had any grievance at all against Burman civilisation and society it was that they had been deprived of the share in it which was theirs by virtue of the fact that their own political order was 'in principle, of the same kind as that of Burma'.[14] This is in very clear contrast with the attitudes of the Karen, and with those of the Shan and Kachin. The nature of the relationship appears to be that the Chin must relate themselves to the Burmans as their reference level of advanced civilisation.

Yet it is important to them also to assert their own separate identity, especially through their association with Christianity. The actual number of converts among the Chins since the end of the nineteenth century has not been great: 'at most 25% of the Chin population at the beginning of the 1960s'.[15] But the importance of this to the Chins was of symbolical, political importance. Traditionally 'animists', the Chin, in order to 'appear to the Burmans as people with a literate and sophisticated cultural tradition' had two choices: either to become Buddhists of the Burman kind, or to identify themselves with some other international religion. 'The first course was unacceptable to most Chin, because it would have amounted to giving in to the Burmans; so the Chin took the second course, although this is obviously a vast oversimplification.'[16]

Nevertheless, 'Chin identification with a religious institutional link to the outside world carried little desire for political separation from the Burmans'.[17] Rather it was that they felt 'their age-old claim to be an integral part of the civilized economy of Burma proper' required the education and wider culture they gained from the Christian missions in order that they should appear to the Burmans as more than 'mere tribesmen'. The Chin have shown themselves ready to support the Burmese government in a military capacity. 'Rangoon was saved by Chin troops during the Karen attack on Insein in 1949, and the military itself called in Chin troops on several occasions to put down unrest in the capital.'[18]

A significant aspect of the Chins' adherence to Christianity makes clear that any political significance their conversion might have had (even where it was seen in that way) was limited to the Burmese political arena; that is to say, it did not necessarily extend to the world arena, or to identification with the United States, even though American Baptist missionaries had provided them with the occasion for adopting an international religion other than Buddhism. Chin Christianisation has to be seen within the Burmese arena, and in fact it expressed itself occasionally in criticism of American politics and culture.[19]

Such Chin 'foreign connection' as there might be thought to be, Lehman observes, 'has resulted in very little organized insurgency' against the central government.[20]

One of the greatest successes of Burma Communist Party insurgents in gaining the co-operation of other groups was (until 1981) with the Shan State Army, an insurgent force recruited from among Shan Buddhists, and with the insurgent Kachin Independence Organisation.[21] Among the Shans the proportion of Christians is negligible, and among the Kachins very slight, in spite of the work of Catholic and Protestant missionaries since the latter half of the nineteenth century.

The Karen: Buddhist, Christian and traditional

Of the various frontier peoples or ethnic minorities in Burma, the Karen have the largest number of Christians in absolute and percentage terms. Even so, from the figures available from the 1931 Census it is possible to calculate that out of a total of 1.228 million Karens only 188,000 (15.3 per cent) were actually returned as Christians. On the other hand, it is generally reckoned that about three quarters of the Karen population are Buddhists.[22] This leaves a minority of just under 10 per cent who follow traditional Karen religious practices. However, there is one important area in which Karen traditional ideas and beliefs have a strong affinity with certain

Protestant Christian ideas — a tradition about a book they are said to have possessed once and have now lost, but believe they will one day recover. When they find the book again, they will enter the new messianic era, the beginning of the golden age for them. Theodore Stern takes the view that the bitterness of the Karens' lot and their envy of the superior civilisation of their neighbours drove them to seek compensation in a religious form, especially when those neighbours became oppressors, as did both the Thai and the Burmese from time to time.[23]

Such religious compensation took the form of a movement of a millenarian kind. A major source of such millenarianism among the Karen may, in Stern's view, be found in the Buddhist mythology of 'the great cycles...which link the creation and destruction of the world...and the lesser cycles which relate to the advent of the Buddhas',[24] a mythology which possibly reached them through their contact with the Mon Buddhists, whose pupils in a cultural sense the Karen often were. The defeat of the Burmese by the British in 1852, together with the arrival of Baptist missionaries with their Bible, was interpreted by many of the Karen as the dawn of the new era: the White Brother had come with the lost Golden Book. It was thus a time of rising expectations; expectations which were not fulfilled, however, in spite of the incidental benefits some of the Karens who became Christians may have received. The fact that only a minority became Christians and that the majority of Karens are Buddhists suggests that it is a minority of Karens among whom such millenarian ideas were held with any vigour. Nevertheless, the friendly relations between some Karens and British colonial rulers and American missionaries were such that antipathy between Karens and Burmans was accentuated. The removal of the British rulers from the scene in 1947 and the departure of American missionaries from 1962 onwards left the Karen — or at least a militant minority of them — once again alone in their traditional attitude of confrontation with the Burmans and once again with their traditional millenarian belief that the day of the Karen will surely come.

Although 75 per cent of the Karen are reckoned to be Buddhists, their Buddhism will not necessarily dispose them favourably towards Burman Buddhism. Karen Buddhism exists in combination with a traditional Karen hostility towards Burmans. Thus, not only the minority among them who remain traditionally Karen in religion, but possibly also the Buddhist Karen, and most certainly the Christian Karen will be predisposed towards, at best, an uncooperative attitude towards the Burmans, and at worst open hostility.

Karen and Non-Karen Christians in Burma

The Christian Karen are, by and large, Baptist, nurtured in the tradition of American Baptists. Basically there are three types of Christian present in Burma: Catholic, Anglican (with some Methodists) and American Baptist. In 1931 (the last year a census which included figures on religion was taken) the position was as follows (to the nearest thousand):

Baptist	213,000
Roman Catholics	90,000
Anglicans	23,000
Methodists	2,000
Others	4,000

In Rangoon, where Catholics and Anglicans would be present in relatively greater numbers than in the remoter areas, the numerical differential would not be so great. For example, South Indians provided a large proportion of the Catholic community in Rangoon, but were not found outside Rangoon in the same proportionate strength. But out in the delta area of Bassein, and the Kayah and Karen areas in the eastern parts of Burma, Baptist Karens would be in a much greater majority.

The last two decades have seen a shift in Catholic attitudes towards non-Christian faiths, following the lead of the Vatican Council. There is no evidence from Burmese examples after 1962, but if the attitudes of Catholics in India since that time are any guide, there could have developed among the Burmese Catholics a new openness to Buddhist perspectives and practices. On the other hand, experience of the attitudes of most American Baptist personnel in Burma in the early 1960s suggests that Karens under their influence would have had their traditional antipathy to Burman Buddhists reinforced. It has to be remembered that it is among the Karen that most of the Christians in Burma are found. 'In 1970 an estimated 3 percent of the population of Burma was Christian, the majority belonging to the Karen (except the Pa-o Karen branch) ethnic group',[25] and 'official estimates for 1970 and 1971 placed the total population of Burma at about 28 million'.[26]

Karen insurgency and the Buddhist Karens

It is also from the Karen that a large and continuing share of the
armed insurgency against the successive governments of independent
Burma has come. The significant factor may be not so much the
Christian element as such among the Karens, but the educated
leadership; to a considerable extent this will have been received at the
hands of American Baptist and Karen Baptist teachers, but the link
with insurgency in such cases is not necessarily a strong one. The
tradition of hostility towards the Burmans could as easily have had its
roots in the Karen association with Mon Buddhists as in their
connection with American Baptists. And in any case, from the point
of view of the social analysis of conflict, these are likely to be
predisposing factors rather than immediate sources of tension and
conflict. What can be affirmed with certainty is the persistence of
Karen insurgency throughout the period from 1947 (when British
colonial rule ended) to the present time. It has certainly been violent
and seems likely to continue to be so until the Burmese Army succeeds
in crushing it. Recent reports suggest that the destruction by the Army
which the insurgent Karens are calling down upon their strongholds in
south-eastern Burma is likely to be total.[27] The Karen heartland in
Kawthoolei is now said to have been reduced to rubble.[28]

Kachin and Shan Buddhists

It was noted above that the four state divisions where the votes in favour
of the new (1973) Constitution of the Union of Burma were lowest
were Karen State; Kayah State, home of the Karenni, or 'red Karens';
Kachin State; and Shan State. When we enquire into the Buddhist
identities or affinities of each of these four, we find that a Buddhist
element is by no means remote from any of them. The Shan are
Buddhists although, as Edmund Leach points out, the 'majority...are
not very devout, and Shan Buddhism includes a number of decidedly
heretical sects, but being a Buddhist is symbolically important as an
index of Shan sophistication'.[29] In the Kachin state also, Buddhists
are prominent.

When 'religious minorities' are juxtaposed with the Buddhist majority
in Burma, it is easy to make the mistake of assuming that a plurality is
being contrasted with a unity. It is important to avoid this false view
of the 'majority' religion in which is seen a unified social or cultural

whole over against a disunited minority. This disunity which exists within the *demographically* defined Buddhist majority has its paradigm in the Shan, who exhibit in a particularly clear way the generally anarchic character which Burmese Buddhism has manifested, at least since the end of the monarchy and the destruction of Mandalay by the British in 1885. Michael Mendelson in particular has demonstrated the highly sectarian character of Burmese Buddhism in general.[30]

The Shan present a particularly good example in their local forms of this generally disunited Buddhist whole and they constitute a dissident and disaffected cluster of Buddhist minorities when seen in an all-Burma perspective. The Shan identify themselves as Buddhists, and are so identified by other communities in Burma. While their Buddhism is said to be more or less of the generally Burman type, the Shan have never, it seems, been incorporated into an all-Burmese sangha, and subjected to 'the jurisdiction of the Burmese Buddhist primate'.[31] During the period following the end of colonial rule, that is since 1947, 'the Shan had felt for some time that the central government was trying to impose Burman monks and Burman monastic traditions in the Shan State, and the State Religion policy [of 1961] only exacerbated this fear'.[32] The Shan have maintained a consciousness of their difference from Burman Buddhists (in much the same way as have the Thai), and their sense of the differences of history, tradition and culture which exist between them and the Burmans appears to have outweighed their common heritage of doctrinal Pali Buddhism. It might well be considered appropriate, therefore, to speak of the disunited Buddhist *majority* in Burma, in view of the disunity that exists between (some) Karen and Shan Buddhists, on the one hand, and Burman Buddhists on the other.

What makes the Shan a Buddhist minority in Burma is the combination of their cultural and political interests in a characteristically *Shan* stance, over against Burman Buddhists. Taken as Buddhists, Shans and Burmans together constitute a numerical or demographic religious majority, but since it is a *politically* divided religious majority its majority status is to that extent diminished. *Burman* Buddhists are not so clearly a majority as are the 'Buddhists of Burma'. This latter category is largely at present a theoretical abstraction, and it is an abstract unity that it indicates. 'Buddhists' are social actors like any other in that, collectively, they exhibit real and sometimes violent factional divisions.

The Muslims of Burma

In the public controversy aroused by U Nu's State Religion Bill, the voices of two minority religious groups were heard in addition to those which have already been mentioned. These were the Muslims and the Hindus of Burma. Among the former there were few voices in favour of the proposal. One of them was that of Moulvi U San Shar, President of the All Burma Moulvi Association. His support for it was based on the practical consideration that to do otherwise might attract the violent hostility of the more fanatical Buddhist monks towards the Muslim community. Generally, however, Muslim leaders and organisations opposed the Bill on the grounds that the Union of Burma had been constituted a secular state and should remain so. In the event, Moulvi U San Shar's forebodings proved to be well founded. The Hindu leaders, however, generally supported the proposal in order not to antagonise the more violent elements among the Buddhists.[33]

However, among the Muslims of Arakan peaceful loyalty to the Union of Burma was short-lived. Arakan, in north-west Burma, contained one of the major concentrations of Muslims in an area bordering what was then East Pakistan (now Bangladesh). Even before Burma had become an independent state, when British preparations were being made for the transfer of power in India and Burma, the North Arakan Muslim League had been demanding that the northern part of Arakan, where the majority of the inhabitants are Muslims, should be transferred to the adjoining state of Pakistan, which was then coming into existence. The moulvis of that region called for jihad against their Arakanese non-Muslim neighbours (who did not wish to become citizens of Pakistan) and what has come to be known as Burma's Mujahid rebellion began. The violence which this rebellion entailed caused the Buddhist population of northern Arakan to flee south, while Muslims who had been living in the south of Arakan fled northwards. In this way the concentration of Muslims in northern Arakan increased. Since Arakan was not incorporated into Pakistan it has remained the major concentration of Muslims within Burma. It is worth noting that, just as it was the Buddhists who *as a majority* in Rangoon violently attacked Muslims there, so also it was the Muslims *as a majority* who made violent attacks on Buddhists in Arakan.

Apart from this area, the other main constituents of the Muslim minority in Burma were Indian immigrants into Rangoon and lower Burma and some Malay Muslims in the coastal area of southern Burma (Mergui) adjoining northern Malaysia. The number of Indian

Muslims of the Rangoon area was reduced in the early years of the Revolutionary Government, that is, from about 1964 onwards, when Indians were leaving Burma at the rate of about 2,000 a week. On 12 July 1964, it was reported that ships were being specially chartered to aid victims of nationalisation, and that the number of Indians returned from Burma to India during the first six months of the year was said to be approaching 40,000, and was expected to rise to 100,000 before the stream died away.[34] It must be emphasised that this exodus of both Muslim and Hindu Indians was due primarily to the government's nationalisation measures which particularly affected Indian immigrants to Burma. By May 1964, it was being reported that the government of Pakistan had undertaken to facilitate the rehabilitation of immigrants from Burma.[35]

The Hindus of Burma since 1962

A recent study of Tin Maung Maung Than shows that there are about 100,000 Indians in Rangoon of whom approximately 30 per cent are Muslims and 20 per cent are Hindu. The other 50 per cent consists of Christians (10 per cent) and Buddhists (40 per cent). The Indians who are enumerated as Buddhists consist mostly of former Hindu Indians who have chosen to be counted as Buddhists. The relations between Buddhists and Hindus is generally good, as Tin Maung Maung Than shows, and this had made the transition from one religious identity to another relatively easy. The Indians in Rangoon who are enumerated as Christians are mostly Catholics, the majority of them of South Indian origin.

Hindu religious life in the Rangoon area is represented by a number of temples and by the Arya Samaj and the Sanatana Dharma Swayam Sevak Sangh. There is in addition an organisation called the All Burma Hindu Central Board (ABHCB) which coordinates Hindu religious affairs throughout the country. All these organisations are, of course, non-governmental, although the ABHCB is a body which would represent the Hindu community's interests to the government. It also engages in the publication of religious books in Burmese and Tamil, and religious pamphlets in Burmese and Hindi. Temples, and some Hindu religious study groups in Rangoon, are also affiliated to the ABHCB, as well as to the All Burma Hindu Students Society, which exists 'to foster religious and cultural awareness, unity and mutual understanding and to promote the welfare of the Hindu students'.[36] The

Ramakrishna Mission Society which was founded in Rangoon some seventy years ago was converted in 1977 into the Ramakrishna Temple Trust, and was divested of its links with its parent Mission in India. Compared with former days, and with the role of the Mission in India, it now exerts only a marginal influence on Hindu society in Rangoon. Tin Maung Maung Than comments that this reflects the changed composition of Hindu society in Rangoon; the previous activities of the Mission 'were on an intellectual plane remote and detached from the socio-economic sphere and daily activities'[37] of the Hindus of Rangoon in the early 1980s. But the ABHCB, in its Silver Jubilee Centenary Souvenir of 1978, takes the view that the 'fear that Hindu culture and religion would decline and disappear in this country does not seem to be so imminent as was thought' 25 years before, i.e. from 1953 onwards, in the days of Burma's AFPFL government and the euphoria of the approaching Burmese celebrations of *Buddha* Jayanti year.

Conclusion

In the space remaining only the briefest general observations and con-- clusions are possible. My remarks will be restricted therefore to the observation that the perception of religious minority or majority status is a somewhat local matter (whether by Buddhists, or Muslims, or Karens, or Shans, or others) and it is the perception of local *majority* status that influences the attitudes of the majority of Buddhists towards non-Buddhists, or of Muslims (in a majority) to non-Muslims (in a minority), and so on. At the risk of sounding banal (but only because it increasingly becomes evident), I suggest that in religious community relationships there is little to choose among the major religious traditions and their institutions in the matter of Lord Acton's famous dictum, that 'power corrupts, and absolute power corrupts absolutely'. And this in spite of the fact that more than one religious tradition, including what is now called Buddhist, had precisely this danger in view in its beginnings.

Notes

1. Having arrived in Burma less than two years before that date I was still very much on the outside of Burmese affairs, but even so I recall that in early 1962 it was being said in Rangoon that the Army would take over again before long. F.K. Lehman has recently recorded that, to his direct

knowledge, 'the troop movements in and about Rangoon that made possible such a bloodless coup were under way a couple of months at least before the coup itself'; see F.K. Lehman, ed., *Military Rule in Burma since 1962* (Singapore: Institute of South East Asian Studies, 1981), p.6.

2. D.E. Smith, *Religion and Politics in Burma* (Princeton, NJ: Princeton University Press, 1965); E. Michael Mendelson, *Sangha and State in Burma* (Ithaca, NY: Cornell University Press, 1975).
3. Smith, *Religion and Politics in Burma.*
4. Ibid., p.235.
5. Ibid., p.270.
6. Ibid., pp.277–9.
7. Ibid., pp.282f.
8. Albert D. Moscotti, *Burma's Constitution and Elections of 1974* (Singapore: Institute of South East Asian Studies, 1977), p.5. 'Burmese' is here used in the sense more usually indicated by 'Burman'.
9. Peter Kunstadter, ed., *Southeast Asian Tribes, Minorities and Nations*, Vol. 1 (Princeton, NJ: Princeton University Press, 1967), p.75.
10. F.K. Lehman, *The Structure of Chin Society* (Urbana, Ill: University of Illinois Press, 1963).
11. Ibid., p.5.
12. Ibid., p.22.
13. Ibid., p.34.
14. Ibid., p.171.
15. Lehman, *Military Rule in Burma since 1962*, p.5.
16. Ibid.
17. Lehman, F.K., 'Ethnic Categories in Burma and the Theory of Social Systems' Chapter 2 in Peter Kunstadter *South East Asian Tribes, Minorities and Nations*, 2 Vols., (Princeton, N.J.: Princeton University Press, 1963), Vol. 1.
18. Lim Joo-Jock and S. Vani, eds, *Armed Separatism in South East Asia* (Singapore: Institute of South East Asian Studies, 1984), p.65.
19. Lehman, *Military Rule in Burma since 1962*, p.6.
20. Ibid.
21. Charles B. Smith, *The Burmese Communist Party in the 1980's* (Singapore: Institute of South East Asian Studies, 1984), p.5.
22. They are said to have received their Buddhism originally from the Mon. See T. Stern, 'Ariya and the Golden Book', *Journal of Asian Studies, 27*, 1968, p.301; and Lehman, 'Ethnic Categories in Burma', p.97.
23. Stern, 'Ariya', p.29. Robert Taylor, 'Perceptions of Ethnicity in the Politics of Burma', *South East Asian Journal of Social Science, 10* (1), 1982, p. 18, takes a somewhat different view, namely that the depth of the conviction of their unique historical place in the region 'has made accommodation with the central state impossible'.
24. Stern, 'Ariya', p.30.
25. John W. Henderson, *et al.*, eds, *Area Handbook for Burma*, (Washington, DC: The American University, Foreign Area Studies), p.129.
26. Ibid., p.10.
27. *Far Eastern Economic Review*, 6 September 1984, pp.28f.
28. Ibid., 6 January 1985, p.32.

29. E.R. Leach, *Political Systems of Highland Burma*, (London and Boston: G. Bell & Co. and Beacon Press, 1954) p.30.
30. Mendelson, *Sangha and State in Burma*, and "Religion and Authority in Modern Burma" *The World Today*, 16, 1960.
31. Lehman, 'Ethnic Categories in Burma', p.96; Mendelson, 'Buddhists and the Burmese Establishment', *Archives de Sociologie des Religions, 17*, 1964, p.87.
32. Lehman, 'Ethnic Categories in Burma', p.96.
33. Smith, *Religion and Politics in Burma*, p.247.
34. *The Times*, 22 July 1964.
35. Ibid., 19 May 1964.
36. Tin Maung Maung Than, 'Some Aspects of Indians in Rangoon' (Singapore: mimeo, 1985), to appear in Kernial Sandhu, ed., *Indians in Southeast Asia*, forthcoming. Tin Maung Maung Than is a research fellow at the Institute of Southeast Asian Studies, Singapore, and the present writer acknowledges his indebtedness to him.
37. Ibid.

12 THE LOTUS AND THE CRESCENT: CLASHES OF RELIGIOUS SYMBOLISMS IN SOUTHERN THAILAND

Surin Pitsuwan

Introduction

The process of national integration differs from one nation to another. Some have been fortunate to be able to graduate from a fragmented feudal society to become one unified nation without much physical pain and psychological trauma. Others, however, have had to go through various national ordeals with much travail and, in some cases, bloody experiences. Some are still going through this process of what Clifford Geertz has called 'the integrative revolution'.[1] Many in the developing world are at present still involved in what Lucian Pye described as 'nation building'. Some may never reach their destiny as unified nation states. Many have failed and dropped out of the race to statehood.

Some may argue that this 'national integrative process' is an unending effort of modern nation states if they are to maintain their effective state structures and, through them, to proceed on their road to full development and a meaningful state of modernisation. Civic rituals, state and royal ceremonies, even 'impressive sacrifices', as Machiavelli would argue, all serve to create the sense of loyalty and instil the feeling of pride into the citizen so that they would feel as one people sharing a common heritage and inspired by the same ideals and institutions.[2]

The Thai nation state is no exception. From the very beginning, the state authorities have made certain that the various ethnic groups of different regions should have common civic values and feel motivated by the same set of symbols to reach the same vaguely described destiny. Indeed, the use of the word 'Thai' in the name of the state reflects, according to Professor Ben Anderson, a major conscious effort to bring the myriad of groupings into one organic whole.[3] Buddhism, the bureaucracy and the monarchy have been employed as integrative instruments to give a pattern, a frame or a theme to the mosaic of ethnicity within the realm of the Siamese kings ruling from the central plain. Or should we use the symbolic phrase: 'under the shadow of royal blessings' (*tai rom phra borom pothi somparn*)?

The three integrating institutions, Buddhism, the bureaucracy and the monarchy, have served the Thai state well in the past and did not encounter much resistance among ethnic groups in the far-flung regions of the realm. The only region where stiff resistance has been and still is widespread is the deep south where the people are not only of a different ethnic background, but speak an entirely different language, consider themselves to be a part of an entirely different cultural world and are inspired by an entirely different set of values of another civilisation.

Symbolically speaking, the Malay Muslims of southern Thailand, numbering approximately 1.5 million, find it difficult to consider themselves to be under the *phra borom pothi somparn* because the phrase reflects a deeper Buddhist cosmological belief than just 'royal blessings'. According to that cosmology, the state is the political manifestation of all Buddhist values and ideals. Its rulers are considered the very essence and best exponents of Buddhist teachings. The blessings that permeate the land flow from the charisma (*baramee*) of the highest ruling institutions which are the earthly images of the ideal Buddha himself. According to the phrase, all the people within the boundary of the Thai state are living under the Bo Tree, the symbol of Buddha's *baramee* and the blessings of his Enlightenment.

The only problem with that is the fact that Muslims are under an absolute oath to live under the commandments of One God alone. The cardinal principle of faith for Muslims is: 'There is no God but Allah, and Muhammad is His Messenger.' This is at the centre of the faith. It is the principle that gives it uniqueness. Islam demands absolute submission from its adherents to this principle. It tolerates no deviation from this short, simple but powerful concept. The Koran claims that all sins are forgivable in the eyes of God except inventing associates (*shirik*) with Him.[4] It also implies that Muslims must give Allah their absolute and total loyalty. No other power, charisma, influence, authority, blessing, or grace can stand in comparison to the majesty of His power. For Allah does not only provide daily subsistence to men , even their very existence depends on His Grace and remains entirely within His prerogative (*Hakk Allah*). Muslims must not and — theologically speaking — cannot live by the grace and blessings of other beings except those provided by Allah.

It is not an oversimplification to state that much of the problem, violent or otherwise, between the Thai state officials and the Malay Muslims of southern Thailand today has its deeper cosmological roots in this Islamic absolute demand for allegiance to Allah alone. It is a conflict of cosmic proportions and theological nature. Both sides are trying to present two different, complicated, and deep cosmological structures fundamental to their respective faiths. The Thai bureaucracy, with all its Buddhist trappings and rituals, is bound to get into clashes with the people who do not subscribe to the very fundamental assumptions upon which the Thai state structure is found. The Malay Muslims, for their part, do not consider their dealings with the state bureaucracy just as a secular power structure of a secular political entity. They feel that their very faith and spiritual purity are being compromised by their dealing with the Buddhist state officials.

The lotus and the crescent

It is the present author's assumption that what is considered 'political conflict' paralysing the Thai bureaucracy in the southern part of Thailand today can be understood as the Malay Muslims' resistance to the integrative and assimilative efforts of the Thai state.[5] The resistance is presented and organised through a series of actions inspired and given meaning by Islamic religious symbols. If religion is a well-integrated group of symbols created for human inspiration and guidance, then it is only natural that followers of a religion should articulate their own aspirations—political or otherwise—in terms of religious symbols prescribed. Social changes and political revolutions have occured and remain potent at present through the effective use of religious symbolisms or ideals. The Iranian Islamic revolution is only the most dramatic and latest example of the power of religious symbolisms. Max Weber's *The Protestant Ethic and the Spirit of Capitalism* is merely a scholarly description of the positive role of religious symbolisms and values within Western society. More recently, Abner Cohen, a Manchester anthropologist, presents an anthropological perspective of politics and calls it 'the analysis of the symbolism of power relations'. He describes political conflicts through careful scrutiny of a process of manipulation of religious or spiritual symbols that groups use to articulate their grievances, project their demands to the public authority and perpetuate their 'sacred cause' in the mind of their fellow religious or ethnic group members.[6]

In southern Thailand, obviously, the Malay Muslims are making selective use of Islamic religious symbols to express their grievances and articulate their demands to the state authority. As the state extends its reaches further and deeper into the many spheres of their lives, the influence of religion on their daily activities is receding, and dimensions hitherto belonging to the spiritual realm are being trans-formed into more secular ones. Language, dress, mannerisms, attitudes and perceptions are going through a process of change and transfor-mation. Deep in their psyche a sense of uncertainty, ambivalence and imbalance is replacing the certainty of faith and the assurance of dogma. Their 'ground of being', to use Martin Heidegger's phrase, is being shaken at its core. And state officials consider their acceptance of bureaucratic rituals and all state symbols, in whatever forms, as the litmus test for national integration and state security.

Since the time of Field Marshal Sarit Thanaarat in the late 1950s the central Thai government has aggressively projected its 'blessings' and control into the Malay Muslim community in southern Thailand. The constitutional concept that the Thai monarch must be the patron of all religion (*sasanupathampok*) has been translated into political reality. Central mosques have been built in the four southern most pro-vinces of Pattani, Yala, Narathivat and Stun. As the most apparent symbol of Muslim culture, the mosque summarises Muslim identity and evokes the deepest religious sentiments. Precisely because of these very qualities, it is also a most sensitive institution that requires most careful handling. The mosque is the seat of the community's religious rituals and the centre of all its social activities. In Arabic the word 'mosque' literally means 'the place where one prostrates to Allah'. Thus, it stands symbolically for the sacredness of Islamic rituals, prayer (*salat*).

Muslims have a phrase to describe hypocritical (*munafiq*) acts or political acts staged for public consumption to create a sense of loyalty or belonging among the people, or to make people identify with the state. The government mosques in the four provinces are referred to by some critical Malay Muslims as 'the mosques of Abdullah Ibni Ubaiya'. Abdullah Ibni Ubaiya built a mosque just to show off his faith while in reality possessing none. Muhammad ordered it to be destroyed because it was built as a symbol of hypocrisy rather than as a product of real faith. Thus many conservative Malay Muslims refuse to pray in the central mosque built for them by the government, preferring other small local mosques. The Pattani people congregate at the Chapangtika mosque, just a stone's throw away from the government-built mosque. The same situation exists in Narathivat and Yala. Only the mosque in Stun experiences no such problem of rejec-tion by the local residents.

Both central mosques in Pattani and Yala contain within their

structures even more blatant symbols of insensitivity on the part of
government architects. In the countryard of the Pattani mosque, the
message describing the noble intention and patronage of the central
government in building it was inscribed on a piece of marble resembling the
Sema Dharmmachark slab, the Buddhist Wheel of Dharma. Visitors
cannot miss it upon their entrance into the compound of the Grand
Mosque. It stands as a strong reminder to all worshippers and visitors
that their house of worship was built for them by people outside the
faith with ulterior motives. No wonder many Malay Muslims have
turned away and join other congregations for their Friday prayers.

The Yala mosque is only two years old. Compared to Pattani, Yala
is more penetrated and more heavily populated by central government
officials. Many of the government agencies especially established to
address the problems of alienation and irredentism in the south are
located in Yala. The Education Region II, charged with all educational matters for the four border provinces, has its headquarters
there. The Centre for the Administration of the Southern Border
Provinces, headed by the Deputy Permanent Secretary of State for
Special Affairs, Ministry of Interior, also maintains its head office
there. The Civilian, Police and Military Special Unit for the Southern
Border Affairs (also known as PTT 43) is located in the Sirithorn
military camp just outside the city of Yala. The province is, thus, the
hub of psychological and security operations by central government
officials.

The Yala municipality should have been one of the most integrated
or, indeed, assimilated areas of the south. But it is not. It is a centre of
conflict and the 'social distance' or communal gap between the two
communities remains wide. The central mosque can again illustrate
the phenomenon well. The main dome of the mosque was designed
rather ingeniously by government architects. It is in the form of a
lotus bud, a Buddhist symbol of the heart, thus the symbol of the faith
itself. On top of the lotus-shaped dome is a traditional Islamic
crescent. Some Malay Muslims say the dome represents a lotus bud
with a leaf from a Bo tree as the background, again a popular symbol
of the Buddhist faith. The design is very graceful and aesthetic. But it
is in the wrong place. It should not be on top of a mosque which, the
government claims, is a symbol of official respect and recognition of
the unique features of the Malay Muslim south. The crescent should
have been adequate in such a place.

Even some of the Muslim government officials at the Center for the
Administration of Southern Border Provinces refuse to go there for

their Friday prayers, let alone the common people. Many of them feel that the government is imposing Thai values on them and feel more alienated from the Thai bureaucracy. Some treat it as a joke and accept it as a *fait accompli*, just another place of worship. It is taken as a symbol of the government's heavy-handedness rather than that of respect for the Islamic religion. The construction of the Yala mosque has backfired. It has not served to create an atmosphere of mutual respect and friendship. It has generated communal tension and mutual suspicion in that province and beyond.

Language and ethnic identity

Another interesting phenomenon in southern Thailand at present is the resurgence of Islamic identity in the forms of a missionary movement, religious fundamentalism and exertion of political rights. Partly a reflection of Islamic revivalism in the wider Muslim world, the religious resurgence among the Malay Muslims has put government officials on alert for fear of political repercussions. The language used is 'we are watching it with an eye to security'. The rising tide of Islamic identity is testing the level of tolerance on the part of the government and raising many issues of religious freedom and cultural rights. Official ceremonies and bureaucratic rituals with Buddhist content are being examined to see whether Muslims can participate. Even the royal anthem has become an issue of high sensitivity with regard to its wording and the religious issue of Muslims singing it. This issue illustrates most vividly the nature and form of clashes between the two religious cosmologies on the plane of politics.

The first sentence of the royal anthem again relects one of the most fundamental principles of Theravada Buddhist statecraft: 'We the sevants of Thee, oh Lord Buddha'. The monarchies in the Buddhist states of South-east Asia have from the very beginning been identified with a mystical Buddhahood. Monarchs are buds (*noh*) of the Supreme Buddha who are on their way to becoming Buddhas themselves, i.e. attaining enlightenment and *nibbana*. Granted that it has now been accepted as an honorific title for the institutions of monarchy, it is rather disturbing for Malay Muslims who know the meaning and cosmological ideas behind these words and phrases. Singing the royal anthem with full realisation of what the words connote constitutes an act of blasphemy (*shirik*) — in what Islamic theology would call 'associating other beings with God Almighty'.[7]

The next sentence of the anthem is even more problematic: 'We put our hearts out and our heads down to *prostrate* before Thee, oh Master of the Realm'. In Buddhist practice prostration is considered the highest form of respect one can pay to anybody. In Islamic culture, it is the form of absolute submission that is reserved for Allah alone. Scholars have described it as 'a position in which one loses one's ego, the lowest physical position that an individual can [assume], a position in which one is defenseless'. Physically described, seven points of the human body touch the ground, the two fronts of the feet, two knees, two palms and the forehead. In the Malay Muslims' phraseology it is *tujoh ankata* or seven parts. In Arabic the position is called *sujud*. And it is the central feature of the Islamic formal ritual of worship or *salat*. The word *masjid* or mosque is a derivitive of *sujud* and thus designates the place of worship. It is at the core of Islamic theology. Muslims do not prostrate to any other being except Allah. Therefore, Muslims with full consciousness of its meaning and cosmological implications cannot sing the royal anthem.

Another dimension of this issue is the fact that it had never been a problem before the Thai language was pushed by the government among the Malay-speaking people of the south. The problem arose when the Malay Muslims learned the deeper meanings of the Thai words and they understood the concealed messages of the formulae, rituals and anthems. The very existence of the problem testifies to the success of the government's efforts to introduce the Thai language to the Malay-speaking Muslims. We can say that it is a side effect and an unintended result of 'development'.

Aware of the serious nature of this kind of problem, the government, via the Centre for Administration of the Southern Border Provinces, has sought the assistance of the *Shaikhu-al-Islam* Office in Bangkok. In Thai it is known as the Office of *Chularajamontri*. The Shaikhu-al-Islam is a respected Muslim religious scholar elected by 26 chairmen of provincial Islamic councils from around the country as spiritual head of the Muslim community in Thailand for life. Originally created in 1947 by Dr Pridi Bhanomyong, the civilian ideologue of the 1932 Constitutional Revolution, the Office was set up to provide counsel to the King. (Dr Pridi at that time was serving as an influential Regent for the young King Rama VIII.) Later on the Office was downgraded to counsellor on Muslim affairs to the Ministry of the Interior.

In spite of the fact that the overwhelming majority of the Muslims in Thailand live in the southern border provinces, all the *Chularajamontris* until now have been Muslims from Bangkok. But the Office is supposed to liaise between the entire Muslim community and the government. In 1982 the Office was asked to give an opinion on the question of Muslims singing the royal anthem. Government officials in the south had been quite disturbed by Malay Muslims, children and adults, refusing to join in the chorus at state ceremonies. The *Chulara-jamontri* Office, realising the sensitivity of the issue, aware of the anxiety on the part of Buddhist government officials and of its own position as mediator between officialdom and the Muslim community, was forced to find a delicate way out without offending either party. Its pronouncement (*fatwa*) was that the mere singing of the anthem was permissible as long as the singers were not conscious of the literal meanings of the words or phrases used. They are symbolic usages that need not be taken literally by singers. 'They are used symbolically as signs of respect for the monarchy. They are not to be taken literally', said Mr Vinai Sama-un, Deputy Secretary General of the *Chulara-jamontri* back in 1982.

But the Islamic legal opinion of the *Shaikhu-al-Islam* Office did not end the controversy. Even today the singing of the anthem remains a sensitive issue between the conservative, educated Malay Muslims in the southern border provinces and the Thai bureaucrats uninformed about the theological roots of the problem. Indeed, many other issues of the same nature have sprung up since then. Many of them are enlightening in many ways for students of national integration and nation-building.

Islamic legal opinions and Thai national integration efforts

On 16 July 1983, the Office of the *Chularajamontri* issued a series of *fatwa* on various issues pertaining to Muslims' participation in religious rituals and state ceremonies. The introduction of the 23 *fatwa* is very illuminating as far as the relationship between the Thai state and the Muslim community is concerned. It states:

The Chularajamontri Office has to use utmost care in considering these matters and wants to reassure all concerned that all answers to the questions posted have been based on Islamic principles with careful analysis. However, some of them may appear to be contradictory to the values of the mainstream of Thai society. The reason for this is the fact that these are religious matters and must be considered on the basis of religious teachings. The Office wishes to reiterate that some of the practices must remain in conflict with the values of the majority of the Thai people.

That cannot be avoided. We all must accept that fact, because the culture of the mainstream of the Thai society has been nurtured by Buddhism which is the religion of the majority of the Thai people. Muslims are a minority but have to practice their religious requirements strictly. Some things that the two religions teach differently will have to be tolerated by all Thais. They will remain different features of our society. If we try to synthesise them or try to compromise between them it will lead to more division within our nation. For example, the teachings of the two religions about expressing homage and respect are different even though the purposes are the same. Buddhism teaches that the highest form of respect is to prostrate oneself (*krab*). Islam, however, prescribes that prostration is reserved for Allah Almighty alone. If one should prostrate to other beings or things, one commits the unforgivable sin of blasphemy, of *shirik*, and falls outside of the Islamic faith. [Among Buddhists] paying respect to idols or images is encouraged as religious merit. Islam forbids paying homage to any idol or image in all circumstances.

This kind of religious conflict cannot be compromised and there is no way for the followers of the two faiths to participate in the same rituals or ceremonies of religious nature. The only way to preserve social security [political unity and social peace] is to accept the differences and allow the people to practise their religious teachings.

The fact that the state allows Muslims to practice their religion in all its aspects makes Muslims more aware of the sincerity of the state. As a result, everyone will feel proud of being Thai and be truly loyal to the nation. If government officials interfere in Muslims' religious practices, they will feel alienated from the nation. They will feel unjustly treated and will oppose state officials. This will lead to a deteriorating situation and serious political problems in the end.

The 23 questions posted by the southern Muslims involved rituals and ceremonies performed and organised by the state bureaucracy. They were real problems that occurred and needed to be addressed by the central Islamic authority. We shall consider only the most pertinent ones.

The first question was whether it was permissible for Muslims to stand up during the lighting of incense and candles by the presiding person at official functions. The Shaikhu-al-Islam's answer to that question was an unqualified 'no'. He suggested that Muslims should only stand up when the presiding officer entered the room to pay him, as a person in his capacity as presiding officer, their respect.

The next question was whether prostration to pay respect to Thai boxing teachers in a course on traditional Thai boxing was allowed for Muslim students. The answer for that was a decisive 'no' because prostration to anything or any being for whatever reason on whatever occasion is forbidden in Islam.

The third problem concerned the annual ceremony to pay respect to teachers organised by government schools. Could Muslim students present flowers, incense and candles to their teachers without prostrating to them? The issue is rather complicated and requires a long answer.

> Presenting flowers to teachers to be used in paying homage or respect by prostration is not permitted. Prostration to anyone or anything is forbidden for Muslims. As for the incense and the candles, it depends on the final usage of the objects presented. If they are used for paying homage and respect to images or idols, then it is permitted but not encouraged because in general incense and candles are used for religious ceremonies and rituals anyway.

It was pointed out further that

> paying homage to teachers is not an Islamic ritual and Muslim students must absolutely not take part except when the incense and candles of the Buddhist-Brahmanistic rituals are left out and an Islamic format is given. Only flowers are allowed for teachers as tokens of respect , incense and candles should be left out.

What should be done about social functions such as the Songkran, Loi Krathong and Lent Candle procession to which Muslims were invited? The answer given was that Muslims should not have been invited to such occasions, which are forbidden by Islam, in the first place.

Was presenting wreaths and paying homage to the equestrian statue of Rama V, Chulalongkorn the Great, on the day commemorating his death (23 October) permissible or not for Muslims? The answer was a decisive 'no' because paying homage or respect to any image, statue or idol is forbidden in Islam, no matter what kind of image.

Should the Muslims participate in Buddhist funeral ceremonies? The Office of the *Chularajamontri* gave a negative answer to that question, too, but suggested that Muslims could visit the relative of the dead to give them condolence and assistance.

Boy scouts paid their ritualistic homage to the statue of Rama V by kneeling on the ground. Could Muslim scouts do the same, even if it looked like sitting in Muslim prayers? The answer to this question was 'no' because it was an act of paying respect to an image.

Could Muslims dress in mourning as Buddhists do with black dresses?

The answer to that was 'no'. Islam prescribes 'mourning dress' for women only, and that is not to wear 'bright-coloured dresses and refrain from wearing jewellery and perfume'.

Could Muslims bend their heads to pay respect to the painted image of the King? Standing upright to pay respect to painted images is permitted. Bending one's head down, even if not as low as in Muslim prayer, is discouraged (*makruh*).

Should Buddhist officials be allowed to enter the mosques to meet with the Muslim congregations in order to explain official policies? The answer was that it would be up to the committees of the mosques in question. If they allow it, then that should be alright. If they rejected the request, then their decision should be respected.

The official statement of the *Chularajamontri's* Office ends with the following message:

> The phrase 'Thai culture' should not be confined to mean only the cultural practices of the Thai Buddhists. It should be extended to include practices of the Muslims as well. This is because the Muslims have been a part of the Thai society since the Sukhothai period. The phrase 'Thai people' as used in the Constitution is not defined by religions, languages or cultural practices and their Islamic culture does not mean that they are destroying the Thai culture. On the contrary, that will give it a unique feature and will convince foreigners that one dimension of the Thai culture is cultural and religious tolerance true to the principle of religious freedom enshrined in the Constitution.

A few interesting observations can be made about these Islamic legal opinions issued by the Office of the *Chularajamontri*. First, the mere fact that they had to be issued at all implies that real religious and communal tension and conflicts exist between the two communities in the deep south. The more effective the government bureaucracy becomes in its efforts to 'unify' the nation and integrate its Malay Muslim population into the national mainstream, the more resistance is bound to develop.

Second, the role of the Office of the *Chularajamontri* in the entire matter is a rather sensitive one. It has to tread carefully between two strongly firmly established bodies of religious and communal practices. While the central government recognises the *Chularajamontri* as the spiritual head of the Muslim community in Thailand as a whole, the Malay Muslims in the south may not yet accept him as their spiritual leader possessing the rights to decide on religious issues of such high sensitivity and cardinal importance. An interesting point to consider is the fact that a government agency (the Centre for Administration of the Southern Border Provinces) presented the questions for his consideration when he was invited to visit its headquarters in Yala. The submission of questions did not come directly from the Malay Muslims themselves.

Finally, the definitive answers to some of the questions provided by the *Chularajamontri* are certain to create further tension and conflict between officialdom and the Malay Muslim community. For example, if Muslims must remain seated while the presiding officer lights the incense and the candles as a part of their paying respect and homage to the Buddha image at official ceremonies, one can imagine an occasion when uninformed Buddhist officials interpret the Muslims' behaviour as disrespectful or even insulting to the whole ceremony.

Conclusion and reflection

The 'integrative revolution' or 'nation-building' in the Thai state is not yet over. While other ethnic groups in other regions of the country have been pretty well 'assimilated' and 'accommodated' into the national mainstream, the deep south is still going through a process of cultural adjustment and communal accommodation. The process is longer and more difficult among the Malay Muslims in the border provinces of the south because of their special communal characteristics. Their religion, language, history, culture and geography all conspire to keep them out of the national mainstream. While the central government is sensitive about their centrifugal tendency, moving away from the centre of gravity, which is Bangkok, the Malay Muslims themselves feel that they are being drawn by a centripetal force centring down in the Malay cultural world toward the south of the Thai–Malaysian border. They still feel that they do not fully belong to the Thai state and, therefore, are not trying to break away. They merely want to be left out by the Thai state bureaucracy.

The foundation of political conflict and armed violence between state security officials and Malay Muslim dissidents at present is the differences in the cosmological structures of their two distinct religions. More and more the conflict is being expressed in clashes of religious symbols displayed at state and official ceremonies and rituals. At one level, these conflicts appear to be superficial and unimportant. At another level, they are indications of deeper and more fundamental conflicts inherent within the two opposing communities. The problem could become explosive, threatening the security of the state itself. It cannot be ignored. At the same time, it should not be treated without utmost care and sensitivity. If the bureaucracy considers religious rituals and official ceremonies such important ingredients of state power, it should be aware of the fact that there are religious and spiritual dimensions to all rituals and ceremonies. These dimensions are often presented in the form of symbolism (physical, conceptual or linguistic) and are powerful in evoking sentiments and a sense of communal loyalty. The Malay Muslims feel that they, too, have religious symbols and rituals which have to be preserved and respected. Theirs, too, are powerful instruments for evoking communal sentiments and religious identity.

As the Office of the *Chularajamontri* had clearly and ably pointed out, some of the differences must remain just that, communal differences. Accommodation between them implies a certain degree of compromise or coercion. But the fundamentals of religion are not matters for compromise. Any form of coercion risks further trouble and more serious conflicts. Honesty, in this case as in all cases, is the best policy. Respect breeds respect. Social harmony and political stability can only come about when all elements of the society are given due respect and full freedom to fulfil their communal aspirations within the framework of the law. Social justice, equal economic opportunity and political freedom should be the binding forces of the society, not force alone. The bureaucrats and security officials should learn to admire the aesthetic values of religious and ethnic differences. They should appreciate the fact that a mosaic of multicoloured elements is more interesting to behold than a monotone canvas.

The 'integrative revolution' or 'nation-building' will never find a happy ending until each and every community within the state finds its own comfortable niche conducive to the fulfilment of its own aspirations. Until the crescent is left alone, and no effort made to replace it with the lotus, it is difficult to foresee harmony and security in the deep south.

Notes

1. Cliford Geertz, ed., *Old Societies and New States* (New York: The Free Press, 1963).
2. N. Machiavelli, *Discourses*, ed. B. Crick (London: Penguin Books, 1970), Vol. 1, p.25.
3. B. Anderson, 'Studies of the Thai State: the State of Thai Studies' in Elizer B. Ayal, ed., *The State of Thai Studies* (Athens, OH: Ohio University Center for International Studies, 1979).

4. *The Holy Koran*, transl. Yusuf Ali, V: 65.
5. S. Pitsuwan, *Islam and Malay Nationalism: A Case Study of the Malay-Muslims of Southern Thailand* (Bangkok: Thammasat University, Thai Khadi Research Institute, 1985); 'Elites, Conflicts and Violence: A Situation in the Southern Border Provinces', *Asian Review, 2* (1), 1980 (in Thai); C. Satha-Anand, *Islam and Violence: A Case Study of Violent Events in the Four Southern Provinces, Thailand, 1976–1981* (Bangkok: Thammasat University, Thai Khadi Research Institute, 1983).
6. A. Cohen, 'Political Symbolism', *Annual Review of Anthropology*, 1979; 'Political Anthropology: The Analysis of the Symbolism of Power Relations', *Man, 4*, 1978.
7. I.R. Faruqi, *Tawhid: Its Implications for Thought and Life* (Kuala Lumpur: International Institute of Islamic Thought, 1982); *Koran*, IV: 48.

References

Dulyakasem, 'Muslim-Malay Separatism in Southern Thailand: Factors Underlying the Political Revolt' in J.J. Lim and S. Vani, eds, *Armed Separatism in Southeast Asia* (Singapore: Institute of Southeast Asian Studies, 1984).

Omar Farouk, 'The Historical and Transnational dimensions of Malay-Muslim Separatism in Southern Thailand' in Lim and Vani, *Armed Separatism in Southeast Asia.*

C.F. Keyes, 'Buddhism and National Integration in Thailand', *Asian Studies, 30* (3), 1971.

C.F. Keyes, 'Millennialism, Theravada Buddhism, and Thai Society', *Asian Society, 36* (2), 1977.

C.F. Keyes, 'Structure and History in the Study of the Relationship between Theravada Buddhism and Political Order', no publication data available.

S. Tambiah, *World Conqueror and World Renouncer: A Study of Buddhism and Polity in Thailand against a Historical Background* (Cambridge: Cambridge University Press, 1976).

S. Suksamran, *Political Buddhism in Southeast Asia: The Role of the Sangha in Modernization of Thailand* (London: C. Hurst, 1977).

I.R. Faruqi, *Tawhid: Its Implications for Thought and Life* (Kuala Lumpur: International Institute of Islamic Thought, 1982). *Koran* IV: 48.

M. Walzer, E. Kantowicz, J. Higham and M. Harrigton, *The Politics of Ethnicity* (Cambridge, MA: Harvard University Press, 1982).

B. Anderson, *Imagined Communities: Reflections on the Origin and Spread of Nationalism* (London: Verso, 1983).

Thang Nam (bimonthly Thai magazine on Muslim Affairs), June 1985.

Sanyalak (weekly Thai magazine on Muslim Affairs), 20 June 1985.

Utusan Thai Salatan, (monthly newsletter on Muslim Affairs, in Malay and Thai), April 1984. (Special issue on 'Questions on Conflicts between the Islamic Practices and the Bureaucracy', with the answers from the *Chularajamontri*).

Suthasasna, Arong, *Pauha Kwam Kad Yaeng Nai Si Changwat Pak Tai* (Bangkok: Kring Siam Press, 1976).

13 SRI LANKA'S MUSLIM MINORITY

K.M. de Silva

Introduction

The recent (1984–7) outbreak of violence between Muslims and Tamils, especially in Sri Lanka's Eastern Province, drew national and international attention to the complexities of the island's ethnic problems. At the core of the problem lie two conflicting views of the Muslims' role in the Sri Lankan polity. Tamil politicians often speak of the Tamils and Muslims as one people divided by religion, but linked by language. This is at best a half-truth, and in any case it is passionately rejected by the Muslims for whom the language they share with the Tamils is much less important than the religion and culture that divides them.

Sri Lanka's Muslim minority has never made up more than 6–7 per cent of the island's population. They are geographically dispersed; unlike Sri Lanka's Tamils who form a clear majority in the Jaffna peninsula and most other parts of the Northern Province as well as in the Eastern Province's Batticaloa district. In no district do the Muslims constitute a majority; in all except the present Amparai district of the Eastern Province (until 1960 Amparai was part of the Batticaloa district), they are a small minority. There is a concentration of Muslims in the capital city, Colombo. This geographical dispersal of the Muslim community has presented difficulties in regard to securing adequate representation in the national legislature.

Then again their ethnicity is identified in terms of religion and culture, not language. Today most Muslims speak the language of the district in which they live, while a great many are bilingual, speaking both Sinhala and Tamil. During the pre-independence period, almost all Muslims spoke Tamil. Indeed, Tamil had long been the *lingua franca* of maritime trade in the Indian Ocean region; as a trading and seafaring community, Muslims had been exposed for centuries to the influence of that language. More importantly, the Koran had been translated into Tamil; thus even Sinhala-speaking Muslims had perforce to be proficient in Tamil up to now. (It is only recently that the Koran has been translated into Sinhala.) However, unlike Tamils — and Muslims in Tamilnadu — Muslims in Sri Lanka have no great emotional commitment to the Tamil language. They have demonstrated little reluctance to adopt Sinhala as a medium of instruction in schools and as the principal, if not sole, national language. But they have also found it exceedingly difficult to abandon Tamil altogether.

Sri Lankan Muslims consist of several distinct groups, among whom the common link is religion. In the 1930s, a significant controversy broke out among them over the use of the terms 'Moor' and 'Muslim'.[1] Which of the two was more appropriate for the community? Those who preferred and indeed took pride in calling themselves 'Moors' emphasised the historical origins of their community, stretching back to the ninth century AD, and its strong indigenous roots in Sri Lanka. They were clearly the majority group. Others felt this term was too exclusive, even elitist, and that the term 'Muslim' would help bring in a number of other Islamic groups who had come to the island in Dutch and British times. Most of these groups were small in number, but many of them — like the Borahs, Memons, Sindhis and others — were very powerful economically through their control of a great deal of the island's import and export trade. Also included were the Muslims of Indian origin who lived on the island as well as, of course, the small Malay community. The distinction between Moor and Muslim led to the formation in the 1930s of two separate political groups, the All Ceylon Muslim League and the All Ceylon Moors Association.

Ethnic stereotypes popular in the island portray the Muslims as largely a trading and business community. While this depiction tends to ignore the fact that most Muslims are cultivators (as in the Eastern Province) or part of the urban poor (as in Colombo), it would be true nevertheless to say that, to a larger extent than all the other ethnic groups on the island, the Muslims had — and continue to have — a penchant for trade at all levels. This explains why they played no part at all in the rivalry for places in the bureaucracy in the pre-independence period, and why Muslim representation in the professions was minuscule at that time and has not expanded substantially since.

The processes of religious revival among the island's Muslims were initiated during the last quarter of the nineteenth century and continued during the first quarter of the twentieth century; however, there was little or no political content in them in the sense of an opposition to British rule,[2] much less any anxiety to see it replaced by a national regime. The Muslims were generally well behind the Tamils and Sinhalese in the formulation of political demands and pressure for constitutional reforms.

Then came the Sinhalese Muslim riots of 1915,[3] by far the most

serious outbreak of communal violence on the island since the establishment of British rule. Although there was no evidence to suggest that
the riots were anything other than communal in nature, British
officials chose to see a sinister political motive in the riots. This belief
lay behind a series of panic measures of inexplicable harshness taken
against the alleged leaders of such an anti-British movement, namely
the Sinhalese Buddhists. In the island's Legislative Council, Ponnambalam
Ramanathan, a distinguished Tamil politician and elected representative
for the 'educated Ceylonese electorate',[4] rose to the defence of Sinhalese
leaders; he made a number of impassioned speeches, notable for a
fearless condemnation of the manner in which the disturbances were
suppressed and their cogently argued refutation of the conspiracy
theory. For two years or more Ramanathan combined his public
condemnation of the excesses committed under martial law with
persistent — though fruitless — appeals for the redress of grievances.

Sinhalese political leaders and their Tamil allies kept up their
agitation on these issues for a decade or more; as a result, Muslims
closed ranks and stood firmly in support of the British. One immediate
outcome of the riots was to strengthen the political conservatism of
the Sri Lanka Muslims at a time when their Indian counterparts
entered into a brief but lively alliance with the Indian National
Congress, under the leadership of Mohandas K. Gandhi. For a decade
or more after the 1915 riots, the mood of the Muslim community was
determined by a mixture of fear and suspicion of Sinhalese nationalism.
Thus there was very little support from the Muslims for the Sinhalese
and Tamil leadership's major constructive political achievement in
1917–19, the establishment of the Sri Lanka National Congress. The
Muslims stood aloof, somewhat apprehensive of this new political
organisation.

A Tamil–Muslim alliance

A prominent feature of Muslim political attitudes in the early 1920s
was an alliance between the Muslims and Tamils. While Muslims'
acceptance of Tamil leadership at this stage was a natural result of the
1915 riots, their acceptance of the leadership of Ramanathan (who
had turned against his erstwhile Sinhalese allies and supporters in the
early 1920s) is evidence as the depth of their disillusionment with the
Sinhalese. Ramanathan had been at the centre of a controversy in the
mid- and late 1880s over his publicly expressed views on the ethnicity

of Sri Lankan Muslims, or Moors as he preferred to call them. Ramanathan argued in 1885 that the Moors of Sri Lanka were Tamils in 'nationality' and 'Mohammedans' in religion, a contention which greatly offended the Muslims, and which was vigorously refuted by M.C. Siddi Lebbe, the main spokesman for Muslims at that time. Ramanathan made a more comprehensive restatement of these views in 1888 in a public lecture on 'The Ethnology of the "Moors" of Sri Lanka', delivered in Colombo.[5] As the representative of the Tamil community in the Legislative Council (1879–91), Ramanathan was often inclined to talk expansively on behalf of the 'Tamil-speaking peoples' of Sri Lanka, a categorisation which enabled him to place Muslims within the scope of his tutelage as a legislator. In this claim, as in so many other ways, Ramanathan was the precursor of views and attitudes of mainstream Tamil politics of the future. Then, as now, however, the Muslims rejected this claim and refused his tutelage. The persistence of this claim and its indignant rejection lie at the heart of the current crisis in Muslim–Tamil relations in Sri Lanka as well as the recent eruption of communal violence between them.

The Muslims' rejection of Ramanathan's views did not stop in the 1880s. Twenty years later, in 1907, the attack was renewed on a more systematic basis by I. L.M. Abdul Azeez[6] in a pamphlet which, significantly enough, was republished in 1957—at the height of the language conflict in Sri Lanka and when a similar attempt was made by Tamil leadership to speak once again on behalf of Muslims in a coalition entitled 'The Tamil-Speaking Peoples of Sri Lanka'. This, however, is to anticipate events. In the 1920s the Muslims' acceptance of Ramanathan's leadership—just a few years after his spirited defence of the Sinhalese leadership in the aftermath of the 1915 riots—was a triumph of hope over experience. On this occasion the hope was fulfilled in ample measure. The Muslims remained Ramanathan's allies until his death in 1930. Indeed, their acceptance of Tamil leadership on political issues lasted for some time after Ramanathan's death.

None of the Muslim representatives in the Legislative Council were major political figures. All were conservatives in political attitude; they were either somewhat diffident when they expressed their views or gave silent but unswerving support to the British administration and, later, Ramanathan. The impression one has of them is of men who were distinctly uncomfortable in the thrust and parry of debate in the national legislature.

The keynote of Muslim politics of the inter-war period was one of self-preservation: to safeguard, sustain and advance their distinctive cultural identity. They sought and obtained state support for this in two distinct fields: first, consolidation and recognition of the personal laws of Muslims. The Muslim Marriage and Divorce Registration Ordinances 27 of 1929, which became operative from 1937, set up a system of domestic relations courts presided over by Muslim judges (*quazis*). These courts explicitly recognised orthodox Muslim law pertaining to marriage and divorce; the same process was instituted for inheritance in the Muslim Intestate Succession and Waifs Ordinances of 1931. Second, there was the field of education. To the divisiveness of education — dividing Muslim from Tamil — we shall turn later on in this chapter.

A change of attitude — 1942 and after

The early-1940s marked the beginnings of a significant change in the Muslims' attitude to the nationalist movement as well as a reappraisal of their position on the impending transfer of power. The key figure in this change of attitude was a newcomer to the national legislature, A. R. A. Razik, whose father W. M. A. Rahiman had served in the Legislative Council during the years 1900–17. From this time onwards, the Muslims' response to political and constitutional changes can be viewed in terms of the attitudinal differences of T. B. Jayah, a Malay and senior Muslim member of the national legislature, on the one side, and Razik, on the other. These differences, subtle and muted at first, became more pronounced in time as Razik gained more confidence as a political leader and greater influence within the national legislature. Some of these differences were inherent in the controversy that broke out over the terms 'Moor' and 'Muslim', with Razik emerging as the advocate of the first and Jayah of the second. In 1942 a third Muslim, Dr M. C. M. Kaleel, entered the legislature; in time he became one of the most respected Muslim politicians, who still retains a prominent position in national politics. Equally important, Razik, who had until this time been a member of the Executive Committee of Local Administration,[7] switched over to the Education Committee on 10 March 1942, and that Committee thus had two Muslim members (the other being Jayah).

This concentration of attention on education, in a bid to give a boost to Muslim education, brought Razik into conflict with the Tamils. This was especially so with regard to the Eastern Province where Muslim schools had mostly Tamil schoolteachers or where

Muslims attended Tamil schools. Razik deplored this state of affairs. He used his influence, through the Education Committee, to build the resources of Muslim schools and secure the appointment of more Muslim teachers. The insensitivity of Tamils to these Muslim concerns brought home to men like Razik the need to emphasise a Muslim identity in the national education system.

The change of attitude was illustrated by the voting patterns in the State Council on J.R. Jayewardene's motion, debated in May 1944, to make Sinhala the national language of Sri Lanka. The difference in attitude between Razik and Jayah was clearly demonstrated on this issue. When Jayewardene first introduced his motion in 1943, there was much opposition to it on the grounds that it made no provision for Tamil. By the time the motion came up for debate in 1944, Jaye-wardene had agreed to amend it to include Tamil along with Sinhala as the national languages. With the mover's consent a Tamil member, V. Nalliah, moved an amendment 'that the words "and Tamil" be added after the word "Sinhalese" wherever the latter occurs'. The amendment was debated and put to a vote on 25 May 1944. It was carried by 29 votes to eight. Jayah voted for the amendment; Razik joined four Sinhalese in voting against it because they wanted Sinhala as the sole national language.

Razik's speech on this occasion [8] — a brief one — is worth quoting:

> I feel that in the best interest of Lanka, my mother country, I must stand up for the motion of the honourable member for Kelaniya [J.R. Jaye-wardene]; that is that Sinhalese should be the official language of the country. However, there is not the slightest doubt that this cannot be done in a hurry, in a year or two, or even in 10 years. I certainly feel that in the best interests of Lanka and her people one language will bring unity among our people. We are really divided at the present moment. Each community has its own language. But if we all take to one language, then we will not think in terms of Tamils, Moors, Sinhalese, Burghers, Malays, and so on.

The Tamils could no longer take Muslim support for granted in their political campaigns. By the early 1940s the political alliance between Tamils and Muslims came apart over conflicting attitudes to the transfer of power, with the Muslims supporting the Sinhalese leadership on this and the Tamils acquiescing in it with unconcealed reluctance. This contrast in political attitudes has persisted in the post-independence period.

Post-independence perspectives

In post-independence Sri Lanka, Muslims had two points in their favour in competitive politics, and both provided a strong contrast to Tamils. First, since 1956 mainstream Tamil leaders have regarded their community as a separate entity, that is, separate from the island's political community. Occupying as they did distinct blocs of territory, in some of which they constituted a majority of the population, their politics emphasised regional autonomy based on ethnic identity; this later took a separatist or secessionist form. Their politics was perceived as a threat both to the legitimacy of majority rule and the integrity of the nation. Muslim politics offered a complete contrast to this. Muslims deferred to the will of the majority on most occasions (such as their ready acceptance of Sinhala as the sole national language) and were shown deference in turn (on education, for instance). They were helped in this quite substantially by the volatility of the island's political system in which, from 1956 onward, the ruling party was defeated on six consecutive occasions (including 1956). The result was that Muslims were offered opportunities for political bargaining which they used to the great advantage of their community.

There is also the crucially important fact that the island's Muslims never faced the prospect, much less threat, of assimilationist policies. All governments respected the ethnic identity of the Muslims and have, in fact, helped to protect and foster this.

The Muslims have no 'ethnic' political parties of their own. Neither the All Sri Lanka Muslim League nor the All Sri Lanka Moors Association became Muslim political parties in the years after independence; by contrast their contemporary, the All Sri Lanka Tamil Congress, continued as a Tamil political party and was indeed the principal Tamil political organisation on the island until the mid-1950s. Muslims sought and obtained membership and achieved positions of influence in all major national political (except Tamil) parties, particularly the United National Party (UNP) and Sri Lanka Freedom Party (SLFP). Indeed the link with the UNP has given that party a majority of the Muslim vote at every election since 1947. The UNP has always had more Muslim Members of Parliament than the SLFP. Within the party, Colombo-based Muslims have been until very recently the dominant element.

The UNP's defeat in 1956 presented some difficulties for Muslims because of their strong commitment to the party. But soon the SLFP, as the party in power, began to attract substantial Muslim support, especially under the leadership of Badi-ud-din Mahmud. A man of considerable influence within the party who demonstrated the value of a place in the Cabinet as a political base for a national leadership role in the affairs of the Muslim community, Mahmud had two periods in Parliament, from 1960 to 1965 and from 1970 to 1977; on both occasions he was an appointed Member of Parliament, not an elected one. On both occasions he was a key figure in the SLFP, but during the second appointment he sought to expand the political base he had built by forming another political organization, the Islamic Socialist Front, which linked the SLFP with an articulate but numerically small group of Muslims to the left of the traditional SLFP supporters in that community. He was defeated soundly when he stood for election for the first time in 1977, and the Islamic Socialist Front did not survive his defeat.

Since 1947 every Cabinet has had a Muslim in it; the present one has three. This was not true of Tamils. The first Cabinet after independence had two Tamils; there was one between 1952 and 1956, but none at all from then until 1965. Even more remarkable is the ready acceptance of Muslims by Sinhalese voters in electorates where Muslims comprise less than a fifth and quite often less than a tenth or a twentieth of the total voting strength. Muslims are regarded as being so clearly integrated into the Sri Lankan political community that the Sinhalese will vote for them on party grounds against Sinhalese opponents.[9] In contrast, not a single Tamil candidate has won a seat in a predominantly Sinhalese area since independence, except for Indian Tamils who have won seats in the plantation districts or in the periphery of such districts.

The sagacity of the Muslims, in resisting the temptation to form a Muslim political party was noted as early as 1974.[10] Not all Muslims are happy with this state of affairs. Indeed, some have argued — especially those from the Eastern Province — the case for a Muslim political party, independent of existing national parties and pursuing the sectional interests of Muslims with single-minded commitment to Islamic principles.[11]

About 30 per cent of Sri Lanka's Muslims live in three districts of the Eastern Province; of these the largest concentration (nearly 15 per cent of Sri Lanka's Muslims) live in the Amparai district. This naturally encourages the hope in some that an ethnic political party would be a viable entity in the Eastern Province — at least as effective at protecting Muslim interests, if not potentially more so, than the prevailing system of Muslim representation through and within the main national political parties. There has also been a more recent demand (1986–7) for a Muslim province to be carved out of the Eastern Province. Neither of these two demands has any substantial support from the Muslims outside the Eastern Province.

The Eastern Province Muslims have their own style of politics: a mixture of regional loyalties, disregard for party ties and a continuing loyalty to a powerful family group overriding party ties. Thus Muslim political figures of national importance have frequently been rejected by Eastern Province constituencies in favour of local Muslims. A. R. A. Razik was defeated in Pottuvil in 1947, and B. Mahmud was much more comprehensively rejected in 1977 at Batticaloa. Then again, Eastern Province Members of Parliament have shown a disregard for political consistency measured in terms of party loyalty that the celebrated Vicar of Bray would have appreciated. The interested reader has only to turn to the political careers of M. E. H. Mohamed Ali and M. M. Mustapha for striking evidence of this. And finally, over the last 40 years the Kariapper family has enjoyed a remarkable, if somewhat unobtrusive, dominance in Eastern Province politics. Many, if not most, Eastern Province Members of Parliament of all political parties have kinship ties with this family. All this goes to show that Eastern Province Muslims have their own peculiar priorities.

In the mid-1950s some Muslims in the Eastern Province linked up with Tamils in the latter's attempt to build an organisation of Sri Lanka's 'Tamil-speaking peoples', on whose behalf the Tamil political leadership campaigned to preserve their language rights. Some Muslims stood on the Federal Party ticket in 1956 and won election to Parliament.[12] But their loyalty to the Federal Party did not survive the bitter conflicts over language that broke out from the very first months of the third Parliament. Soon the Muslims reconciled themselves to the new language policy introduced by the Bandaranaike government; the fragile alliance of Tamils and some Eastern Province Muslims as 'the Tamil-speaking peoples of the island' was shattered, never to be put together again.

As in the inter-war period, so now in the post-independence era Muslims have striven to sustain and advance their distinctive cultural identity. They have sought and obtained state support for this in two distinct fields: the consolidation and recognition of the personal laws of Muslims, and in education. The first of these areas was dealt with earlier in this chapter, and here we need do no more than state that this trend has continued after independence. The provisions of the Muslim Intestate Succession and Wakfs Ordinance of 1931, which relates to Muslim charitable trusts (wakfs), was superseded by the Muslim Mosques and Charitable Trusts or Wakfs Act of 1956; meanwhile the Muslim Marriage and Divorce Registration Ordinance 27 of 1929 was repealed by the Muslim Marriage and Divorce Act 13 of 1951 (operative from 1954), which enhanced the powers of the *quazis* who were given exclusive jurisdiction over marriages and divorces as well as the status and mutual rights and obligations of the parties concerned. The Wakfs Act of 1956 established a separate government department with an executive board comprising Muslims. The constitutions of the first and second republics preserved the personal law of Muslims.

The most substantial gains have been made in education, especially since 1956. The list of concessions won by the Muslims is quite substantial. Special government training colleges have been set up for them. In government schools Arabic is offered as an optional language to Muslim pupils, taught by *maulavis* appointed by the Ministry of Education and paid by the state. Until 1974, Muslim children had the right to pursue their studies in any one of the three language media — Sinhalese, Tamil or English — a privilege no other group in the country enjoyed. In recognition of Muslims' cultural individuality as distinct from Tamils, whose language is the home language of large numbers of Muslims, a new category of government schools was established. The usual practice had been to categorise schools on the basis of the language of instruction in them, and the Muslims formed part of the Tamil-speaking school population. In the new 'Muslim' schools, sessions and vacations are determined by the special requirements of the Muslim population. The establishment and expansion of these schools, it must be emphasised, vitiates the principle of nonsectarian state education which has been the declared policy of all governments since 1960.

This sensitivity to the special concerns of Muslims in education began with C. W. W. Kannangara as Minister of Education from 1931 to 1947, and was continued by W. Dahanayake in the same role from 1956 to 1959 in S. W. R. D. Bandaranaike's Cabinet. It received greater emphasis with Badi-ud-din Mahmud, who served as Minister of Education from 1960 to 1963 and again from 1970 to 1977. In the first period he piloted the landmark education legislation of Mrs Bandaranaike's first government; in the second his role was more controversial, especially with regard to a crucial change in university admissions policy, which adversely affected Tamils and, to a slightly lesser extent, Sinhalese in urban areas, especially Colombo. Muslims and Tamils have pursued diametrically opposed objectives on university admissions, with Muslims among the most persistent advocates of ethnic quotas and Tamils advocating open competition and academic merit as the main criteria for admission to universities. As in the 1940s, rivalry between Tamils and Muslims in education has been an important feature of the island's ethnic disharmony: apart from the Muslims' anxiety to break away from Tamil tutelage in schools of the Tamil medium, they have successfully lobbied for more Muslim schools and more Muslim schoolteachers. Mahmud's tenure of office as Minister of Education was an important landmark in the gains Muslims achieved both in literacy and a notable improvement in educational standards at the secondary level.

Equally significant has been the divergence of views on devolution of power. Muslims have been inveterate opponents of any attempt to tamper with Sri Lanka's existing unitary political structure. Two examples of this are: the opposition mounted by A. R. A. Razik, now Sir Razik Fareed, within the government parliamentary group to the District Councils scheme which Prime Minister Dudley Senanayake sought to introduce between 1966 and 1968. Similarly, two Muslim members of the Presidential Commission in District Development Councils wrote a lengthy note of dissent against the main recommendations of that commission in its report published in 1980.[13]

Neither the UNP nor the SLFP can take Muslim support for granted. While each has large reserves of Muslim support — the UNP's has traditionally been larger than the SLFP's — they are aware that Muslim voters can tilt the balance in not less than 15 electorates in all parts of the country, and often do precisely that. Muslims have seldom hesitated to vote against a governing party if it appeared to them to be inconsiderate to or negligent of their interests. Thus in 1965, the then government's failure to remedy the legal deficiencies which the Supreme Court pointed out concerning *quazi* courts was a significant enough factor to turn large numbers of Muslims against them in the general election that year. Then again, some of that support returned to the SLFP and its allies in 1970 as part of a national trend against the UNP, which was seen to have done more for Tamils than Muslims.[14]

Conclusion

Briefly, then, while Muslims have not been reluctant to consider themselves as a counterweight to Tamils in communal rivalries that have been so prominent in political developments in post-independence Sri Lanka, they have seldom hesitated to express their displeasure at signs of neglect of their interests, or hostility to them, by a government. And Sri Lanka's electoral system has provided them with all the opportunities they need to make this displeasure felt. Governments have changed with remarkable frequency in Sri Lanka, and the Muslim community, small though it is, has contributed mightily to these swings of the electoral pendulum.

It would be too naive to assume that these concessions were won because of Sinhalese altruism. On the contrary, one has the feeling that quite often Sinhalese politicians have used state resources to build Muslims as a counterweight to the Tamil community in a game of checks and balances, which is an intrinsic element in the process of government in a plural society. As we have seen, Muslims—in striking contrast to Tamils—have no distinct ethnic or religious political parties of their own to contest seats to Parliament in competition with, if not in opposition to, the main national political parties. Instead, their political organisations work in association with and as adjuncts of the latter. The result is that the Muslim community, although numerically much smaller than the Tamils, has far greater bargaining powers electorally than their numbers seem to warrant.

Notes

1. Very little research has been done on this interesting theme. Some of the issues are outlined in the pamphlets issued on behalf of the main participants in the controversy: see, for instance, S. L. Mohamed, *Who are the Ceylon Moors?* Colombo: The Moors' Direct Action Committee, 1950.
2. Vijaya Samaraweera, 'Orabi Pasha in Ceylon, 1883-1901', *Islamic Culture, 49*, October 1976, pp.219–27.
3. For a discussion of these riots and their historical significance, see 'The 1915 Riots in Ceylon: a Symposium', *Journal of Asian Studies, 29*(2), 1970, pp.219–66; A. P. Kannangara, 'The Riots of 1915 in Sri Lanka: A Study', *Past and Present, 102*, 1984, pp.130–65.
4. This electorate had just over 3,000 voters. Its importance lay in the fact that it covered the whole island. Ramanathan defeated Sinhalese candidates on two occasions, in 1911 and 1917.
5. P. Ramanathan, 'The Ethnology of the 'Moors' of Ceylon', *The Journal of the Royal Asiatic Society, Ceylon Branch, 10*(36), 1888, pp.234–62.
6. I. L. M. Abdul Azeez, *A Criticism of Mr. Ramanathan's Ethnology of the 'Moors' of Ceylon* (Colombo: Moors' Union, 1907; repr. Colombo: Moors' Islamic Home, 1957).

214   *K.M. de Silva*

The unicameral legislature of this period had seven executive committees whose chairmen, elected by the members, became the minister of the subject under the purview of the executive committee. The committees had a powerful influence on policy-making, and even on the implementation of policy.
8. Hansard (State Council) 1944, Vol. I, p.812.
9. For discussion of this, see K. M. de Silva, *Managing Ethnic Tensions in Multi-Ethnic Societies: Sri Lanka 1880–1985* (Lanham, MD: University Press of America, 1986), pp.229–31 for details.
10. K. M. de Silva, 'Hinduism and Islam in Post-Independence Sri Lanka', *Ceylon Journal of Historical and Social Studies*, 4(1–2), pp.98–103.
11. M.A.M. Hussain, 'Muslims in Sri Lanka Polity', The Muslim World League Journal, September 1982, pp.46–50; October 1982, pp.53–7; November 1982, pp.45–7; December 1982, pp.44–8.
12. M. S. Kariapper, Kalmunai, and M. P. M. Mustapha, Pottuvil.
13. *Sessional Paper* V of 1980, *Report of the Presidential Commission on Development Councils*, pp.83–102.
14. One of the points made was that although the Muslims had voted in larger numbers for the UNP than for the SLFP, Muslim members of UNP Cabinets generally held rather unimportant portfolios such as labour, whereas Muslim Cabinet ministers of the SLFP were entrusted with more important areas of responsibility such as health and education.

INDEX